The Risk Mitigation Handbook

T0362215

Disruption, over-regulation and cyber threats are typical of the major risks that management has to cope with. But until now there hasn't been a formula to contain them.

In *The Risk Mitigation Handbook*, Kit Sadgrove provides practical and actionable steps you can take to minimise the threats to your business. With over 160 checklists and a wealth of revealing case studies, this is the first book to recommend detailed action plans. After reviewing each risk, the author provides a list of measurable tactics necessary to neutralise the threat. The book lists a comprehensive range of risks that organisations face today, with a special emphasis on business strategy, security and people management. Sadgrove also takes a sharp look at how to reduce the risk of operational failure, supply chain weakness and regulatory compliance.

Unlike previous books on enterprise risk, *The Risk Mitigation Handbook* sets out detailed solutions rather than generic risk management theories. The book has been carefully edited to provide fast information for the busy senior manager. Stripped back to the bare essentials, *The Risk Mitigation Handbook* gives the reader bullet points and strategies that give you the information you need to mitigate hundreds of risks.

Kit Sadgrove is the author of several best-selling books on risk management. He is chief executive of the Cortant risk consultancy and the Blackford Centre. His Sure™ model helps businesses create strategic plans that take account of future risks, including competitor behaviour and disruption.

The Risk Mitigation Handbook

Practical steps for reducing your
business risks

Kit Sadgrove

Routledge
Taylor & Francis Group

LONDON AND NEW YORK

First published 2017
by Routledge

2 Park Square, Milton Park, Abingdon, Oxfordshire OX14 4RN
52 Vanderbilt Avenue, New York, NY 10017

Routledge is an imprint of the Taylor & Francis Group, an informa business

First issued in paperback 2020

British Library Cataloguing in Publication Data
A catalogue record for this book is available from the British Library

Library of Congress Cataloging in Publication Data
Names: Sadgrove, Kit, author.
Title: The risk mitigation handbook : practical steps for reducing your business risks /
    Kit Sadgrove.
Description: Abingdon, Oxon ; New York, NY : Routledge, 2017. | Includes
    bibliographical references and index.
Identifiers: LCCN 2016030362| ISBN 9781472462770 (hardback) |
    ISBN 9781315599014 (ebook)
Subjects: LCSH: Risk management.
Classification: LCC HD61 .S223 2017 | DDC 658.15/5—dc23
LC record available at https://lccn.loc.gov/2016030362

ISBN: 978-1-4724-6277-0 (hbk)
ISBN: 978-0-367-60597-1 (pbk)

Typeset in Bembo Std
by Swales & Willis Ltd, Exeter, Devon, UK

To my partner Jayne, with love

Contents

4 All risks are people risks   **55**

Illustrations

Figures

Tables

Preface

It's time to come down from the watchtower.

Previous books on business risk have focused on how to identify and categorise risk, but in a generic sort of way. They're light on practical solutions. It's the 'watchtower' attitude. Authors, like managers, are good at identifying risks, but less smart at suggesting ways to overcome them.

This book is different. It recommends actions that will overcome the most prevalent and threatening business risks. We look at each risk in turn, and examine how to pre-empt or mitigate it.

The Risk Mitigation Handbook covers not only the most common risks but also some you may be less familiar with. It discusses standard topics such as health and safety, but also considers how to mitigate security and marketing risks.

There are hundreds of 'Mitigating Measures' in the book, some of which you will already have implemented. A few may seem obvious, but only to those who have adopted them. Not all Mitigating Measures will apply to every reader, but everyone will hopefully find some of the points relevant. You can check the index to identify risks that matter to you, and go to the relevant section when the need arises.

Some threats are highly specific to just one industry and would be irrelevant to most readers; and so I have omitted them. I've also excluded risks that are insufficiently severe or not very likely.

Many risks could be categorised under more than one heading. So if you don't find a topic where you expect to see it, check the index at the back of the book. It might be somewhere else.

The wide scope of the book means that each topic gets only a quick overview, but that has advantages. It forces me to focus on what's important, which means more value per page for you, the reader.

If you think I've omitted an important risk or some Mitigating Measure, get in touch and I may be able to add it in a future edition. I welcome your feedback. You can reach me at Cortant.com or by email at Kit@Cortant.com

Kit Sadgrove

Acknowledgements

I have drawn on information from many sources. They include *The Academy of Management Journal,* ACAS, Agency for Toxic Substances and Disease Registry, Airmic, Allianz, Anti-fraud Collaboration, Asis Foundation, Auditingresearchsummaries.org, Baker & McKenzie, BBC, Becker's Hospital Review, Bizshifts.com, Bloomberg, Booz and Company, Boston Consulting Group, Bright Hub Project Management, Bureau Van Dijk, Business Continuity Institute, Business Insider, Career Partners International, Center for Information Systems Research at MIT, Centre for the Study of Regulated Industries, Centre on Intelligence Research (France), CFA Institute, Chainalytics, Chartered Institute of Purchasing and Supply, Chatham House, Cifas, Circadian, CNBC, Computer World, The Conference Board, Continuity Forum, Control Risks, Corker Binning, COSO, Covalence, Credit Suisse, Crunch, CSO online, *Daily Record, The Daily Telegraph,* Deloitte, Dun & Bradstreet, Distilnfo, Eaton Corporation, *EE Times, EHS Today,* EIPA, Environment Agency, Ethical Consumer, Eurasia Group, Euromonitor International, European Agency for Safety and Health at Work, EY, FEMA, *Financial Times, FTI Journal,* Gallup Inc, Global Healing Center, Glyn Holton, Goodguide.com, Greenbiz. com, Groceries Code Adjudicator, *The Guardian,* Harris Poll, *Harvard Business Review, Hawkamah Journal,* Health & Safety Executive, *Health Forum Journal,* HM Inspectorate of Constabulary, HM Revenue and Customs, *The Independent,* IIA, IFC Review, *Inc Magazine, Industry Week, Insurance Journal,* International Institute for Counterterrorism, IT Process Institute, Kellogg School of Management, Kingdom Security, Know your Flood Risk, KPMG, Leadership IQ, London Fire Brigade, London School of Economics, Macmillan Cancer Support, McKinsey & Company, MIND, National Counterterrorism Security Office, National Fire Protection Association, National Institute for Health and Care Excellence, Newsweek, Nielsen, OMTCO, *Phoenix Business Journal,* Police Scotland, Poole College of Management at North Carolina State University, PwC, Questia, R3, Raise Hope for Congo, Real Clear World, Regeneration, *The Register,* Reputation Institute, ResearchGate, Sadex, Sans Institute, School of Law at New York University, Simmons & Co, Small Business Research Centre at Kingston University, Society for Human Resource Management, *South China Morning Post, The Star* (Canada), Standard & Poors, Stratechery, *The Sunday Mirror,* Taxpayersalliance.com, The Turnaround Society, TMF Group, Trendwatching, UKCampaign4Change, Unite the Union, United States Postal Inspection Service, Universiti Malaysia Perlis, University of California Berkley, University of Sussex, University of Tennessee at Chattanooga, US Department of Commerce, US Department of Energy, US Department of Justice, US Department of Labor, US Federal Financial Institutions Examinations Council, US Insurance Research Council, USA River Network, Victoria Public Sector Commission,

Waitbutwhy, *The Wall Street Journal,* Wikipedia, Wilmer Hale, Wired, Wired Magazine, XpertHR, Zendesk, Zurich Insurance.

I am also grateful to people who have commented on selected chapters, including Russell Price and Valerie Spillman, as well as all the individuals and organisations who have helped to create this book; any errors and omissions are my responsibility alone.

1   Terminal impact

How to deal with strategic risks

When we think about business risk, most of us have a mental image of a polluted river or a company scandal. But while these are important, they're rarely fatal. Poor strategy is responsible for most business failures. A survey by the Turnaround Society showed that the biggest cause of failure is management continuing with a strategy that's no longer working (cited by 55% of experts).

Losing touch with the market and their customers was cited by 52% of respondents. Thirty per cent said that management underestimated changes in the market and did not adapt to them appropriately.

Being successful is a risk in itself. 'When a company becomes dominant, its dominance precludes it from dominating the next thing,' says Ben Thompson of Stratechery. 'It's almost like a natural law of business,' he says.

So while we need to manage everyday business risks, the strategic ones are more important. They can cause the organisation to run out of money, get closed down or be taken over. As shown in Figure 1.1, strategic risks come from four sources: politics and the economy, customers, competitors and internal failure.

1   *Macroeconomic (political and economic) threats* are the first strategic risk. A slow down by China could harm the automotive industry. A government intent on cutting costs could stifle consumer spending. Protectionist tariffs on steel or a commodity could choke off a flourishing export market.

  Political and economic risk is one of those big external events that you can't avoid, but how you respond to it will determine the organisation's future. These risks can usually be spotted some time in advance, and businesses can do much to protect themselves.

2   *Changes in customer behaviour.* As we argue later in this chapter, it's rarely that customers' needs change. They usually just respond to a competitor giving them a better product. Being able to see customers' evolving options especially at a time of changing technology, will allow the business to innovate and stay ahead.

  That's not to say we can ignore changing customer needs. Far from it. In the Strategic Uncertainty Risk Exercise (SURE) later in this chapter, we emphasise the need for continual experimentation to provide the customer with new opportunities that will provide competitive advantage.

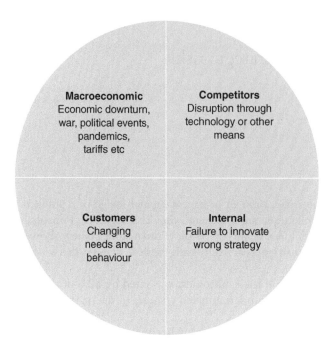

Figure 1.1 The four categories of strategic risk.

3   *Competitor activity* is the third strategic risk. Business models that once seemed permanent have melted in the face of quite simple technology that has made life easier for consumers. Uber's impact on taxi companies is one example, while Amazon's effect on book shops is another.

4   *Internal failure* comes from failure to adapt or choosing the wrong strategic path. In turn, these stem from lethargy and exuberance respectively. Many organisations are the source of their own failure. Chapter 2 is devoted to stopping that from happening.

In this chapter we look at the kind of political and economic events that can capsize the business, followed by a review of technological and competitor threats.

Macroeconomic change: hostile political events

There are many political uncertainties. Will China remain stable? Could war break out in the Middle East? Will the EU break up? Will a military takeover occur in Africa?

Businesses often continue amid strife, not least because people always need to buy things. But sometimes politics can have major impacts. Governments can place politics above the economy. Russia's income declined 34% between 2014 and 2015, but this had no effect on Russia's decision to support Ukrainian separatists or its bombing of Syria in support of President Assad.

You need to be able to forecast the political stability of any country where you do business or are planning to. As Ian Bremen of Eurasia Group has pointed out in *Harvard*

Business Review, a country's economic facts – its income, growth and inflation – often obscure the political threats. A country can be wealthy, but be at risk of serious political upheaval. Analysing a country's political stability and its potential exposure to shocks can provide a more accurate forecast than the economic data.

Jordan has a liberal state and is economically developed, but it lies in an unstable region, suffers massive immigration, is vulnerable to extremists and could be capsized by unrest.

With nations being interconnected, an upheaval in one country can cascade into another. A coup in Venezuela could cause problems in Colombia, which could affect Ecuador in turn.

Political problems are caused by irrational leaders, new laws, popular uprisings and military takeovers. These are especially found in emerging economies, many of whose leaders view politics as being just as important as economics. And the fact that emerging economies are attractive for their low labour costs should remind us that poverty and aspiration can be a cause of political instability.

Rigid political systems also give rise to instability. Because its ruling communist party can't be voted out, China has no mechanism for change. Its people have economic freedom but not the right to express dissent. With a growing Chinese middle class getting more exposure to the internet, it remains to be seen how long the country's political system can survive. Under pressure, its leaders may decide, as rulers so often do, on aggressive acts towards its neighbours.

Some countries are more capable of withstanding major shocks, while others aren't. The United States is a prosperous and open society (albeit with great inequalities) which permits debate and is constantly changing. A fragile and impoverished state like Somalia is less able to withstand economic shocks.

A few countries such as North Korea have the ability to cause major upheavals, due to their military might. By contrast an implosion in South Sudan will have little impact on the world. On the other hand, a business with major investment in that country could lose it all.

Below is the first of our Mitigating Measures. Each of these checklists has actions you can take to mitigate the threat. Not every risk will be immediately applicable to every organisation. But each threat will affect some businesses, some of the time.

Mitigating Measures: responding to political events

Gain expertise in understanding your political risks, whether in-house or through outside experts.

Seek to measure the political stability and likelihood of shock in countries where you operate, especially emerging nations. Measures such as corruption, inequality and unemployment may be useful.

Get insurance against losses caused by political action.

Spread the risk by investing in more than one risky country. If in Latin America, you may choose to be in both Chile and Argentina, rather than deciding on one or the other.

Use public affairs consultants to keep abreast of the potential policy and regulatory implications of political events nearer to home.

Restrictive legislation

There are many kinds of restrictive legislation. The USA or Europe could introduce anti-dumping legislation, which could increase the cost of supplies. Local or national government could reduce the development of building land by restricting what can be built, or by imposing additional requirements for planning approval.

Safe within limits – but it's got a bad name

Parabens, a family of chemicals, are widely used as preservatives in personal care, cosmetics and pharmaceuticals.

Following a review by the European Union's Scientific Committee on Consumer Safety, several countries have considered restricting their use. This would have a negative effect on companies that manufactured them or used them as an ingredient. Among some consumers parabens is a dirty word, even though the EU has declared them safe as long as their concentration is kept within specific limits. But those who make 'natural' alternatives to parabens are not slow to raise alarms about the product.

It's an example of how legislation can have a detrimental or even terminal effect on a business.

Protectionism

Protectionism makes life complicated for an individual business, increases costs, and runs the risk of retaliation, leading to a downturn in trade.

Germany has required foreign international hauliers to notify them of any movement within their territory, even when they are merely in transit, in order to check whether the drivers are complying with German law on minimum wages. Foreign haulage firms are obliged to complete a form on the planned route, time of entry into and exit from Germany, employees' personal data and other information. They have to complete the form in German and send it by fax. This kind of activity complicates the life of businesses sending goods through Germany and massively increases the paperwork.

Mitigating Measures: restrictive legislation

Stay alert to the possibility of protectionist legislation, and seek to counter its introduction. Undertake measured lobbying and gain the support of legislators. Once legislation has been passed, review the steps you can take to limit its impact, such as lobbying for its repeal or reducing the scale of investment in that territory.

Get staff on to legislative working parties, or make representations to them.

Ensure that you have stocks of vital materials or components to tide you over in the short to medium term, giving you space to plan for longer-term action.

Killer legislation

When the UK government announced a plan to end the right to cash compensation for minor whiplash injuries, the stock market value of Australian law firm Slater & Gordon, which specialises in personal injury claims, fell 51%.

Any business model that could be wrecked by government legislation, and whose revenue costs the government money, rests on shaky grounds.

When the UK government cut its subsidies to renewable energy, the Mark Group failed, putting 1,000 employees out of work. Later two other companies called in the receivers. The worst case scenario by the government's Department for Energy and Climate Change estimates that 18,700 jobs could ultimately go.

The same applies to US for-profit universities that relied on federal funds paying their tuition fees. As the costs mounted, the US government put a process in place to restrict the cash outflow. One of the largest universities, Corinthian Colleges, which had 107 campuses, went bust, its closure affecting more than 16,000 students and employees.

The UK motor repair and car hire industry relies on arcane referral fees. Garages, car hire firms, lawyers and insurers all boost the final cost of the job. Many will be out of work if this racket is outlawed.

Mitigating Measures: legislation

Assess the premise on which your model is based. Identify whether it benefits from a point of law that might be changed. To what extent is it based on protectionism or some third party having to pay your clients? If it is, your business model is at risk.

Consider adopting an alternative, less vulnerable model.

Will the Eurozone break up?

The Eurozone could conceivably break up, with various countries, notably those in southern Europe, leaving and reinstating their own currency. This would allow them to default on euro debts, which might precipitate a downturn throughout Europe. The breakaway countries might impose capital controls, as Greece did, preventing businesses from taking money out of the country; and they might appropriate company assets.

This scenario might seem extreme, but Greece came close to exiting the euro, while the UK voted to leave the EU.

Any business that trades in Europe could be adversely affected by currency devaluations in the countries that had left, which would reduce imports. Trade customers might not be able to pay for goods supplied, or might not be able to pay in an agreed currency. Raw materials might become difficult to obtain or overly expensive. Any ensuing downturn could reduce company sales and profits.

Mitigating Measures: Eurozone break-up

Stay alert to the possibility of a Eurozone break-up.

Assess what would happen to your revenues in affected countries.

Make plans to reduce activity in those countries if the scenario becomes a possibility. Repatriate cash, and prepare for a downturn by determining what measures you could take to reduce costs and exposure.

Hedge the cost of geographically vulnerable raw materials.

Maintain strict credit control and active debt collection procedures.

Facing an economic downturn or crisis

The risk of a downturn or a financial crisis is never far away. Images of Greek citizens queuing at ATMs to take out the maximum €60 they were allowed during the country's debt crisis should remind us that economic problems may be only just around the corner.

With medium to large businesses operating in many countries, even when one market is doing well, another is likely to have a problem. Most businesses have one or two really important markets, typically their home market, which generate the majority of the organisation's cash. And if that suffers a downturn, it has repercussions for the company as a whole.

If the banks restrict mortgages during a downturn, house builders' sales decline. Organisations that sell to government departments are always at risk of a spending cutback. They include government-funded products and services, such as schools, colleges and universities, as well as social welfare departments, the military and research-based organisations. In such cases, a reduction in government spending poses a real threat.

Many businesses see the developing world as an opportunity for growth, but these economies are more susceptible to economic crises.

Surviving a downturn is of paramount importance. But you also need enough cash or lines of credit at the bottom of the cycle to meet the opportunities that become available as the economy picks up. You need to see around the bend and beyond the horizon, which isn't easy.

Mitigating Measures: facing a downturn

Have efficient intelligence on the economy of each country you operate in. This information should be supported by forecasts. You need a plan, with trigger points that require you to take action. Track leading indicators that will warn of an impending downturn.

Each country unit should be ready to act in the event of a deteriorating economy. Typically this means reducing head count, closing plants and rationalising operations.

Take into account the country risk when it comes to investment. You can invest more in stable countries and less in risky ones. Or require a higher risk-reward ratio in the

---

less stable economies. You can also reduce the risk by taking local partners (though that increases other risks).

Ensure that your voice is heard by policy makers and politicians, so that economic decisions are soundly based. Being seen to be meddling in politics can result in a backlash, so lobbying must be done prudently, possibly through a trade association or through the medium of white papers and conferences.

Have a strong budgeting process that allows the business to reduce spending when necessary.

Be prepared to cut costs, reduce investment and cut the dividend.

Match output to the economic health of your market. Reduce the supply of your product or service by closing offices or mothballing production facilities.

Maintain a flexible overhead, making more of your costs variable. This can include outsourcing some production or operations. This will allow you to manage the downturn.

The threat of overcapacity

Overcapacity happens when a market doesn't grow as anticipated, and/or when several businesses in an industry have invested in additional production capacity. This is especially prone to happen in industries where plants are large, such as automotive, energy and steel, but most markets are prone to overcapacity at one time or another.

Overcapacity occurs after a period of increased demand has pushed firms into adding capacity. When this is followed by a downturn in demand, businesses find themselves with too much capacity. It can also happen in markets that have low barriers to entry, produce low tech products and where health and safety is not well protected.

Overcapacity eventually resolves itself as the weak players leave the market or mothball their plant, or demand grows.

Mitigating Measures: dealing with overcapacity

Determine whether you have the appetite and cash to last out a debilitating period of losses, and on what scale. This will determine whether you continue to offer those products.

Identify whether you can reduce costs by closing some capacity. Can you retire some products, especially those low profit ones?

Seek to reduce costs in order to achieve break even at a lower price point.

Innovate by providing new products, upgrading your technology, and offering higher value goods that are superior to your competitors'.

Beating the business cycle

From boom to bust and back again, the business cycle is utterly predictable but it usually catches businesses by surprise. The peak or tipping point is almost impossible to predict, although obvious in retrospect. Some industries, such as construction, are especially vulnerable to the cycle, while others such as food tend to be more consistent.

We tend to assume the good times will continue for years; and the pessimists are forever claiming that assets are overpriced, so people ignore them. The risk lies in holding overpriced assets and too much overhead at the top of the cycle. There isn't enough revenue to pay for the overheads, the assets have been bought with debt and the company can't sell them except at a loss. That's when businesses go bust.

Mitigating Measures: beating the business cycle

Be aware of where you are in the business cycle. Be alert to signs of the economy overheating. This includes overvalued property, high share prices and rising interest rates.

Don't get caught with overpriced assets, such as commercial property, at the top of the market.

Don't follow the herd. Be prepared to liquidate assets before the market turns.

Don't let cheap lending dictate your investment plans. Unless you get a fixed rate, assume that rates will rise during the lifetime of the project.

Be cautious about head count. Estate agents always end up with too many staff after the boom. Fixed-term contracts, sub-contract labour, agency staff and staying lean may provide some solutions.

Be alert to the risk of having too many fixed assets, such as expanding into more marginal locations or having too many stores. Avoid long-term leases in uncertain times.

Move into markets that suffer smaller fluctuations in the business cycle. These include food and pharmaceuticals but there are many others.

Broaden the portfolio into products or markets that may have a different response to the cycle. For example, rich consumers are less affected in a downturn.

Be ready to seize the opportunities that the downturn brings. This may include acquiring distressed businesses. Banks are less willing to lend in the downturn and your cash may be limited, so this is not always possible.

Retain sufficient cash to get you through the bad times.

Avoid betting the farm in boom times. Investments should never risk capsizing the business.

Convert fixed costs to variable ones. Outsourcing logistics or even manufacturing will allow you to operate profitably at lower volumes.

We have spent some time looking at political and economic risks, the first of the three great strategic risks. It's time to examine the second strategic risk, the threat of competitor disruption.

Dealing with disruption

Technology is the great disrupter of existing business models. Uber broke into the taxi monopoly by a combination of cheap assets – the self-employed drivers – and software that connects customer and driver. Reviews then give added consumer confidence. Many of today's disruptive businesses have had the same characteristics:

1   They give more power or information to the customer, or put the customer in control.
2   They involve the use of the customer's mobile phone, a tool that is always with them.
3   They simplify previously complicated processes.
4   They save time.
5   They let the consumer buy directly from the provider rather than an intermediary.
6   They provide a feedback loop.
7   They provide convenience.
8   They transfer costs to a contractor, usually a self-employed individual.
9   They replace human-based systems with technology.

Corporations need to assess how difficult their transactions are for customers. Dawson, Hirt and Scanlan of Mckinsey say companies are vulnerable if:

- the supplier has much more information than the customer
- search costs are high
- there are fees from intermediaries. Well-entrenched physical distribution or retail networks;
- transactions take a long time to complete.

They say organisations are also at risk if:

- information or social media could greatly enrich your product or service;
- the physical product is not connected to the internet but could be;
- there is a significant lag time between customers purchasing your product or service and then receiving it;
- the customer has to go and get the product, for instance rental cars and groceries;
- there is too long a chain of activities, such as a high number of handovers or repetitive manual work;
- the existing business model charges customers for information.

Businesses must ask themselves: 'How do I know what disruption I might face?' One answer comes from forecaster Trendwatching.com, which says its insights are simply based on innovations that businesses *have already created*. These innovations change consumers' expectations. 'That's why any customer today riding in a car expects the entertainment system to be as intuitive as an iPhone,' they say. 'It's why customers, primed by streaming content (Napster became iTunes became Spotify), now expect instant access to a whole range of *physical* goods, from cars to clothes.'

They imply there's little point in looking at consumer trends, or even doing market research, because consumers will only want a faster horse, not a Model T Ford. So a tiny business innovation in, say, Puerto Rico, could lead to a major change in global customer behaviour in ten years' time.

And disruption need not be complex. Uber is really nothing more than a piece of straightforward software that drivers and customers can sign up to. But let's examine what these disruptive technologies are.

Disruptive technologies

Mobile internet: This gives internet access to those who have never had it, such as sub-Saharan Africa. It's invaluable to people in emerging economies who can use it for weather forecasting, online banking and access to commodity prices. It has also led to the increased use of the internet for local services.

The automation of knowledge work: Machines that have the ability to learn, and can deal with uncertainty, are increasingly taking over from humans. Electronic assistants will become more knowledgeable. As voice recognition becomes more common, humans will be able to ask machines to undertake tasks that specialists once did. Computers are now doing discovery in legal work. They're also better at making investments. They can diagnose better than doctors – because they can be programmed with the knowledge of thousands of doctors, and learn from each new patient. Technology can also teach students, recognising where the learner is weak, and not just in simple tests.

Robotics will also play a much bigger role, displacing attendants in manufacturing, petrol stations, care homes, shops and restaurants.

The internet of things: Through embedded and interconnected sensors in lamp posts, clothing, stores and fridges, the internet of things will monitor, support, warn and inform people in ways tailored to the individual.

Autonomous vehicles: Self-driving cars, taxis, buses and lorries will displace hundreds of thousands of commercial drivers, as well as reducing the need for consumer-oriented petrol stations, car washes, traffic police officers and traffic wardens. Armed with sensors, drones will provide a wide range of automated services, displacing security staff, spraying fields and monitoring farm animals. Battery storage systems will allow more power to be preserved, making renewable energy more easily stored and allowing electric vehicles to be more practical.

3D printing: With consumers, hospitals and local garages able to print their own products, both in metal and plastic, many manufacturers will simply not be needed. Printed body parts that incorporate the recipient's cells will permit new types of surgery.

Payments: The ability to pay for low-value items with a mobile phone or contactless debit card is already with us. This could resolve some of the problems around news media giving away free information via Google, and the high costs associated with processing debit and credit card payments. This is especially relevant for emerging economies, while mobile phones allow for peer-to-peer payments.

Industries liable to disruption

Medicine will change, following ever more advanced and cheaper self-assessment tools. This will be matched by advances in treatment and surgery, using stem cells to rejuvenate and replace body parts.

Mining may be done on asteroids in the not so distant future, leading to changes in the choice of minerals we use and their prices.

Agriculture will change beyond recognition, with meat developed in labs rather than animals, and plants grown under factory conditions.

Finance will no longer be the preserve of a small number of big institutions. Banks already have got rid of their armies of bank managers, and are reducing the number of city centre buildings and vaults. Big data provides instant information about the applicant's credit worthiness, while financial startups can raise millions overnight, This is too big an opportunity for the new tech businesses such as Google to ignore. Meanwhile pooled self-insurance of healthy people, driven by data from wearable sensors, could seriously affect the profitability of the insurance industry, while peer-to-peer lending could harness the wealth of the population.

Education will be affected by the rise in machines that can assess each learner's knowledge, by the rise of streaming video and by the rejection of the notion that education must follow termly schedules, forcing all students to learn at the same pace. Cohorts of student may still work together, though dispersed in space. Lecturers will become curators, reviewers and coaches, rather than repeating the same lecture every year. The high and rising costs of tertiary education will hasten these changes.

Defence: Drones, robot fighters and pilotless planes will take over the battlefield, allowing politicians to take more risks, knowing that there will be no casualties on the home team.

Water: A growing world population, increased extraction and a warming climate is leading to an urgent need for more water. Water shortages will lead to new solutions in this field.

Elder care: The huge increase in old people needing care, along with rising wage bills, will lead to the introduction of robots, in-home care and a growing acceptance of assisted suicide.

Construction hasn't changed much since mankind first started building houses. The tradition of workmen up ladders in muddy construction sites is unlikely to last long.

Transportation will be affected hugely by the driverless car, taxi, van, lorry and plane.

Energy: The move away from carbon-based energy, such as coal and oil, and the development of solar- and wind-based energies, allied to better storage systems, will allow individuals to create their own energy. Other innovative forms of energy will emerge.

Traditional industries and professions: Big risks lie ahead for the large traditional centralised industries. New entrants will provide new cheap ways of doing things. The legal profession still operates as it did hundreds of years ago.

In decentralised industries with many players, their owners and senior managers will benefit by taking advantage of the new systems they will be offered. A haulage company merely has to lease driverless trucks and fire its workers. A very different outcome awaits the millions of laid-off drivers.

Mitigating Measures: dealing with disruption

Start innovating before you must. By the time you have to change your business model, you will have less opportunity to do so. Then it may be too late.

Regularly scan your market and unrelated ones for new business models.

Set up a test system or production unit to learn more.

Seek your customers' view of alternative business models.

Become your own competitor. Set up a competing business, using a skunk works – an independent unit that won't be hampered by your own corporate rules.

Ask yourself: 'How could a competitor with a different business model put us out of business?' If the answer is clear, you need to implement the new model before another business does.

Place multiple bets, rather than replying on one big one. You never know which new product will succeed. Create a portfolio of different growth strategies and see which ones take off.

Team up with partners. Don't innovate on your own. Find other businesses with complementary markets or skills. Identify those on the outskirts of your market. They will have a different perspective. Set up joint ventures.

Treat disruption as an opportunity. It is a way to ensure the continuation of your business.

Spot disruption while it is still at the edges. Disruptive products initially look small, are expensive and are adopted only by geeks. They are often ignored by the traditional big operators until it is too late.

Set up an Emerging Risks committee, as outlined in the EU's Solvency II framework. The latter is aimed at the insurance industry but could be applied to other markets.

The threat of technology

Not since the arrival of the internal combustion engine has technology developed so quickly and disrupted so many markets. A combination of smartphones, embedded chips, Wi-Fi and the internet has suddenly made everyone and everything connected in a way that was unthinkable a few years ago.

As a result, every business fears that a competitor, usually an unknown new one, could emerge from nowhere with an attractive technology and make the existing business model obsolete.

Some things will always stay the same, at least outwardly. There will still be restaurants and retail shops, though new categories will have arrived and others will have declined. Cars will still run on four wheels, because that's an efficient mode of transport, but their ownership and what lies under the bonnet will be different. Governments will still need police officers and nurses, though many won't be human and the tools they will use will make ours look primitive. The 'connectedness' of things will change what we do, and hence most businesses that are offline now will be connected in the future. The scale of that connectedness will vary from category to another.

When technology disrupts a market, it provides advantages to the user, whether that's a farmer in Peru, an Alzheimer's sufferer in a care home, or a large retail business. It offers convenience, knowledge, experience, independence, cost saving, simplicity, choice, speed, free time or power.

It can elevate the emotions, making the user feel satisfied, in control, excited, fashionable, healthy, aware, involved or part of a community. It may be enabling, allowing the user to do things they couldn't do before, whether faster, more accurately or more easily. The previous product or method is usually the opposite of that: inconvenient, limited, hard to use and time consuming.

Employers stand to gain the most, acquiring more information, lower costs and better control over their staff, while employees may find they lose a measure of freedom and independence.

Some businesses take technological change seriously, while others pay lip service to it. Every organisation needs a commitment to staying ahead of technological change.

Simply embracing technology is not enough. Some businesses have major investment programmes, but little seems to come of it. Technology is a branch of creativity, which means you need a freewheeling environment where people are free to think, to challenge the status quo and to make mistakes without fear of reprimand. At the same time there has to be a disciplined process to ensure customer-focused outcomes.

When it comes to choosing a technology, there is a risk of choosing the wrong one. It is easy to buy into a supplier's system that promises much but ends up being less flexible and more costly than expected. Or worse, it doesn't deliver the solutions you wanted. At that point you have to decide whether to dump the investment and start again. Stephen Carver of the Cranfield School of Management suggests that up to 68% of technology projects fail. Google has successively launched four social networking sites to rival Facebook and Twitter – Buzz, Friend Connect, Orkut and then Google+, with none of them gaining traction. Google+ has 2.5 billion users, but 90% of these accounts have never been used.

There are also risks in choosing which standard or platform to adopt. From the failure of Thomas Edison's electric car to Betamax, the minidisc, the Beenz internet currency, the OS/2 operating system and Google Glass, some products should have worked but failed. Sometimes the idea returns in a new form decades later.

Mitigating Measures: managing the threat of technology

Become familiar with technologies that could support or threaten your markets. Keep abreast of technology trends.

Engage in thinking 'outside the box' as to what the future might look like.

Beware of hanging on to old technology systems. They are often a sign that the organisation is falling behind or lacks market awareness. That's not to say we should be a slave to the latest fashion, but falling behind carries risks.

Identify where you could replace manual processes with automated ones, both inside the business and by customers.

(continued)

(continued)

Use agile development methods and extensive user testing at all stages, to ensure the technology is right.

Determine whether you need external help in developing or implementing the right technology.

Ensure that IT management understands the needs of the business and the customer.

Develop a close relationship with suppliers and customers, to identify technological improvements to your product or service.

When buying new systems, get reviews from existing customers to avoid being locked into badly designed systems.

Identify how your existing products and services could be re-purposed or adapted to new technological platforms.

Everything's going digital

Digitisation – converting physical products into digital ones – is a risk for those who fail to adapt. Digitisation has been developing for two hundred years, with computers or their predecessors replacing manual systems. In 1801 the Frenchman Jacquard introduced punched cards into the weaving industry. These allowed a machine to make intricately designed cloth and to repeat the job at will. It displaced thousands of skilled hand weavers. The punched cards eventually became IBM's first computers.

Retail banks once relied on their network of physical branches and their monopoly in payment clearing systems to lock out competitors. But the internet, online banking and e-commerce has allowed new online banks, online payment systems and peer-to-peer lenders such as Zopa to threaten those traditional players.

Fast internet connections enabled businesses to operate in ever more flexible ways, such as remote working and the use of distant suppliers. This was followed by the internet of everything whereby sensors send and receive information to the outside world. This ultimately leads to planes without pilots, driverless cars and mini bars that know you've drunk the whisky.

The music industry has had to face the challenge of streaming, with artists reaching a hugely increased audience but at a massively reduced cost per play. Appointment-based television is on the way out. Content has become largely 'free', and newspapers have been closing.

Classroom teaching is under threat from online learning, while a doctor's medical diagnosis is set to be transformed by machine knowledge, while home-based 3D printing could make many small products redundant. The biggest threats are as follows:

- believing that the company's current service level is *the* way to do it, as in 'We've always done it this way';
- failing to recognise the disadvantages of the current product or service;
- not understanding IT. Failing to realise what improvements digitisation could bring.

Traditional taxi services are a prime example of these three weaknesses. In retrospect, it seems obvious that a service like Uber's was waiting to happen. It gives three advantages over a traditional taxi:

1 *Convenience.* The customer can quickly call a taxi to their location. The customer doesn't have to find a taxi rank or scour the streets.
2 *Accountability.* The customer can rate the ride, and Uber gets rid of drivers with low ratings. This motivates the driver to be courteous. The traditional taxi driver is almost anonymous and therefore has no such incentive.
3 *Knowledge.* The customer knows which taxi is coming, where it is, how long it will take to arrive, and roughly what the cost will be. This contrasts with traditional taxis which provide none of this information.

The traditional taxi customer was at a disadvantage, kept there by a monopoly that benefited city councils and taxi drivers.

This isn't to say that Uber is perfect, for there are many flaws: Uber transfers its costs to the driver; the driver's existence is precarious; there is a lack of insurance; Uber faces hostile legislation and at time of writing it had massive losses.

But Uber has four advantages that make it a logical service to introduce:

1 It's a platform-based business that brings buyers and sellers together, with minimal intervention by Uber, the platform owner.
2 It's self-regulating. The feedback mechanism continuously raises quality.
3 The costs are largely borne by the driver at present. Known as digital sharecropping, the contractor is self-employed and has no tenure. They work only with the tolerance of the owner. Pizza delivery drivers operate the same way.
4 It costs almost nothing to scale: Uber doesn't pay for cars, dispatchers, radios, licences or insurance, though legislation may change that.

Mitigating Measures: digitisation

Stay aware of digital trends in your market. Be ready to change your strategy.

Consider how user feedback or input could improve your product. Allow the consumer to personalise your product with their own data.

Determine how your real-world products and services could be augmented by digital enhancements.

Assess how a new competitor could launch a competing digital version of your product or service.

Be aware of the many ways that digital technology could enhance or threaten your business, including your relationship with suppliers, customers and employees, and your products.

Ensure your product or service combines real-world and digital-world experience.

Understand where your manual processes could be replaced by digital ones.

Facilitate online reviews, which are increasingly a discriminator in the purchase decision. 80% of consumers believe peer recommendations, but only 14% trust advertisements.

The SURE way to beat strategic risk

The lists of Mitigating Measures are extensive but the quantity of detail can make it hard to know where to start.

It helps to have a methodology to identify and manage your strategic risks. One such exercise is the author's Strategic Uncertainty Risk Exercise™ (SURE). There are four elements, as shown in Figure 1.2. They're simple to describe, but less easy to achieve.

1   *Scan.* The business must be on the lookout for threats to its survival and the potential for disruption. This is 'healthy paranoia'. If the organisation doesn't have that fear, it may be lulled into a false state of security. Scanning involves systematic search and research into: raw materials; technologies; customer behaviours and needs; processes, channels, markets and products.

2   *Understand.* You need to make sense of all the information. Not every threat is of a strategic level, and not every threat will come to pass. Some risks will affect one business but not another. When you're operationally engaged it isn't easy to stand back and see which risks are the important ones. You need to evaluate possible responses to the risks and opportunities that you have identified.

   Will traditional universities be overtaken by online colleges? Will the high street lose its retailers? Will energy companies lose out to home-generated power? Will paper suppliers be affected by electronic paper? The difficulty is to determine which risks will actually happen, and how they will affect your business.

3   *Respond.* When threats have been identified, the senior team must be able to take rapid action. Leaving things a year or more may seal its fate. How fast can the business create change? As we see in Chapter Two, many businesses are weighed down by corporate systems. The procedures and controls that help an organisation avoid its mundane risks may impede its ability to create change. Decisiveness leads to future survival.

4   *Experiment.* The organisation needs to test a range of new ideas. Not all will work. But failing to innovate is a guaranteed route to failure. You need to invest in those areas that could be the future of your industry. Failure to carry the exercise through to live practical experiments is a sign of future failure.

Figure 1.2 The SURE route to survival. From www.Cortant.com.

2 We should have done it differently

Internal corporate errors

In Chapter 1 we looked at the first two areas of strategic risk: political/economic threats and competitor disruption. In this chapter we look at how the business can be the cause of its own downfall. Internal failure includes the following:

1 Lack of vision
2 The wrong business strategy
3 Lack of innovation
4 Mishandling change programmes
5 Retaining an outdated business model
6 Stagnation
7 Excessive bureaucracy
8 Weak execution
9 Lack of strategic capabilities
10 Errors in diversification
11 Failed acquisitions.

In the sections that follow, we look at each in turn.

A lack of vision

A lack of vision is a major cause of business failure, cited by 51% of turnaround experts in the research by the Turnaround Society we saw earlier.

Leaders need vision to drive a company forward in order to maintain a competitive edge and to beat the competition. A management team without vision will cling to the status quo; it won't invest in new ideas and will have no clear direction.

Few organisations can maintain their market share and profitability over the long term without changing. This option is available only to companies that operate in markets with very high barriers to entry or that have a state monopoly.

Mitigating Measures: building a vision

Identify the organisation's strengths, weaknesses, threats and opportunities. Speak to stakeholders and other sources.

Decide where the business should be some years hence. What will be its ideal position in the market? What markets will it have entered? What problems will it have overcome? How will it have changed? Focus on ideal outcomes. Don't take into account any problems that might prevent these achievements: they may become a self-fulfilling prophecy.

Place these accomplishments into broad categories, such as product development, staff training or acquisition.

Write a plan that will achieve these accomplishments. Include roles and responsibilities, budgets and timings.

Review progress regularly. Hold people to account. Facilitate change.

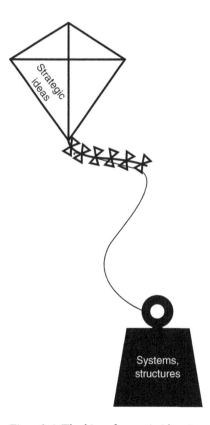

Figure 2.1 The kite of strategic ideas is anchored by effective systems.

The wrong business strategy

It's great to have a visionary leader, but can you be sure that the vision is the right one? The amount of activity or 'busy-ness' is not a useful measure, because it could be misdirected.

Successful strategy is a combination of free-flowing ideas, anchored by effective systems (Figure 2.1). Neither on its own will produce effective new developments.

Organisations need a plan, for without it employees can't see the direction of travel. Yet strategic planning often fails. Companies dedicate huge amounts of time and effort to it, while producing little of value. Henry Mintzberg of McGill University said that real strategies are 'rarely made in panelled conference rooms but are more likely to be cooked up informally and in real time – in hallway conversations, casual working groups or quiet moments of reflection on long airplane flights'.

'Creative thinking can't be forced,' says Mihaly Csikszentmihalyi, the academic who developed the concept of 'flow', a highly focused mental state.

McKinsey consultants Beinhocker and Kaplan said that annual strategy reviews are frequently 'little more than a stage on which business unit leaders present warmed over updates of last year's presentations, take few risks in broaching new ideas, and strive above all to avoid embarrassment'. They argue that the role of strategic planning should be two-fold:

1   To build 'prepared minds'. This should give decision makers a solid understanding of the business and its strategy, which allows them to respond to challenges and opportunities as they occur.
2   To increase the organisation's innovation. While it can't guarantee creative insight, it can increase the odds that it will occur.

Mitigating Measures: strategic planning

Facilitate chance meetings. Recognise that strategic planning comes largely from insights gained from ad hoc discussions.

Allow the strategic planning process to provide information and ideas, rather than expecting it to provide answers.

Ensure strategic planning events are followed up, with meeting notes and a plan of action to bring ideas to fruition.

Avoid treating strategic plan presentations as an inquisition. Use these sessions to create collaborative team work that will encourage creative thinking.

Create innovation systems that will foster new ideas.

As shown in Figure 2.2, strategic planning stems from an understanding of the internal and external forces. These include on the one hand the organisation's capabilities and

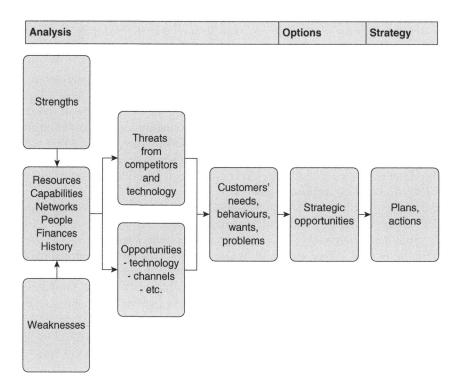

Figure 2.2 Strategy is arrived at through an understanding of internal and external opportunities and threats.

resources, and on the other the opportunities presented by new channels, technologies products, services, raw materials and processes.

Mitigating Measures: business strategy

Understand trends. Recognise the changing needs and preferences of customers, and know the difference between fads and long-term trends. Identify the business's weaknesses and vulnerabilities, and find ways to avoid those dangers. Monitor leading indicators, such as the sales pipeline, requests for tender or debt collection times.

Do existing things better. Respond faster, with better customer service and improved value for money. It can mean hiring better people, and using technology to better effect.

Differentiate the business from its competitors, by providing better branding or personality, a commitment to employees, and an overarching concern for the customer whereby you have meaningful solutions to their current and unmet needs. In publicly quoted businesses this sometimes conflicts with the short-term needs of shareholders.

Digitise or augment with technology. Provide online customer access to your products, digitising your products and services. This overlaps with the point about using technology to meet customer needs. Businesses are at risk if they simply provide online access and believe they have done all that is necessary. The internet of things will lead to old brands being replaced by brash new businesses which benefit from being ignorant of the limitations imposed by history and custom, or 'the way we do things round here'.

Pursue growth markets: find those opportunities, often close to your existing products, where you can leverage your knowledge and gain added revenue. This can include offering your products in overseas markets. It can also mean the acquisition of growing brands.

Have strong, independent non-executive directors (NEDs). After insurance giant AIG had to be bailed out by the US government with an injection of $85bn, its non-execs were found to be politicians, friends of the chairman and officials not known for their knowledge of insurance.

Align risk and remuneration. Some board members and financial traders have made fortunes when profits were high, but haven't suffered losses when the risks they took went sour.

Don't leave bad people in place. Some leaders lack vision, leadership and the will to create change. They're content with the status quo, and are good managers – until the point at which change is needed. People who are loss averse are unsuited to leading a business at times of change.

Lack of innovation

With innovation cycles getting faster, the life of any product is shorter. One that might have lasted 10 years may now be superseded in two.

These days it's cheap and easy to set up a business, get products made and shipped, using outsourced factories, suppliers and logistics companies. You can hire an expert on anything overnight. Even major companies like Apple, Samsung or Siemens are at risk from a company whose founder is still at university. This means that management must be more aware of changes in its market and be ready to change when necessary.

Although it varies by industry, observers reckon that 50% of current revenue should come from products launched in the last five years. Markets are always in flux, and competitors are always thinking of ways to steal customers, aided by new technology and consumer trends.

Businesses can get complacent, especially those with the biggest market share, which tend to become defensive. Few want to change a profitable business model, or launch products that could cannibalise their existing brands. But a competitor will have no such reservation.

Some businesses don't take innovation seriously enough. One corporation, talking about the risk of being overtaken by competitors, says it responds by 'producing relative market share information and timely trading performance data and is monitored by the executive teams and the Board'. This business is not looking at the future, it's merely benchmarking its current performance.

No market remains still. Top-selling products often decline over time – though not always: the Mars Bar has been going strong since 1932. As new consumer products become established, they move from novelty to routine, so the consumer gets bored and looks for something new.

Some B2B markets have a slower pace of change. Construction techniques are much the same as they were a century ago. But as we see later in this chapter, it is dangerous to assume things won't change, and there are indicators that identify which markets are ripe for upheaval. Failure to find successful new products or sticking with a declining business model or channel may lead to decline.

Mitigating Measures: innovation

Set up an innovation system. This requires mechanisms to foster ideas, capture them, evaluate them and drive them through to commercialisation. It requires a long-term commitment and board-level attention. The system will also require metrics to judge its progress and success.

Identify what types of innovation you're seeking. Are they incremental improvements in existing products, new products that will sit comfortably alongside existing ones or radical innovation that will disrupt the market? Each needs a different process.

Encourage employees to provide critiques of the business and suggest improvements. Organisations that succeed in innovation are those that listen hardest and implement suggestions. Create cross-departmental thinking.

Set employees challenges and contests to solve problems.

Reward employee innovation, especially with recognition.

Award employees time and budget to develop promising ideas. At Eaton Corporation, employees pitch proposals for money in competitions set up like Dragons Den or Shark Tank.

Identify and foster creative and critical thinkers in the workforce: they are more likely to come up with ideas if allowed to. Few organisations value the role of creativity; mostly this is thought to be limited to a design or R&D department. IT innovation is critical, yet most IT staff are viewed as mere technicians. Andrew Polanski at Avery Dennison seeks people who have 3Cs: they're creative, curious and collaborative.

Develop meaningful relationships with suppliers and business partners to come up with better solutions. Suppliers will have greater knowledge of raw materials, components and packaging, while downstream partners may be closer to the end user, and see problems more clearly.

Use crowdsourcing systems and techniques to gather good ideas.

Work with universities on new projects.

Discover innovative customers. While most loyalists will blindly accept what the organisation does, there is a minority with strong critical faculties.

Ask yourself what you would do if starting from scratch. What would the service look like? This is a zero-based analysis that deliberately ignores all your current operating and delivery methods.

Activity has two extremes, as shown in Figure 2.3. *Sloth* – too little activity – will cause the business to slide. Excessive activity in areas that the business knows little about (*Overreaction*) are also likely to lead to failure.

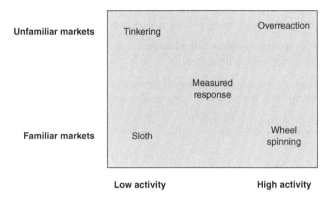

Unfamiliar markets — Tinkering — Overreaction

Measured response

Familiar markets — Sloth — Wheel spinning

Low activity — High activity

Figure 2.3 Is there enough activity, and is it the right sort?

Wheel spinning happens when the organisation spends too much time on small, safe projects, while *Tinkering* is where insufficient effort and money are spent on high risk projects, and produce little to show for it.

Mishandling change programmes

Change is a dangerous thing. Businesses that don't adapt end up being stranded and irrelevant, with customers defecting to competitors. But when organisations try to adapt, they sometimes get it wrong. Forecasting the wrong future, pursuing the wrong solution, or implementing it badly can mean the decline and failure of the business.

Transformational projects tend to be large ones, which makes them vulnerable to poor project management, especially as the outcomes are unknown, unlike, say, constructing a new building where the variables are well established.

Sometimes the organisation provides inadequate resources for the change programme. This can include allocating staff with insufficient experience or authority, or being unwilling to pay the costs of new systems.

Mitigating Measures: creating change

Consider appointing a chief transformation officer to create and implement a significant change programme.

Provide change workshops for senior managers.

Ensure support for those tasked with implementing change.

Give added support to staff moving to new roles.

Make the case. Get the CEO to communicate the purpose and need for change, and disseminate that widely through cascading meetings, newsletters, video and the intranet.

(continued)

(continued)

Choose your timing to prevent change from affecting key sales periods.

Ensure that the company's structures allow for change. This can mean challenging baronial power bases, and if necessary dismantling them.

Be ready for the unexpected. As the programme moves forward, there will be surprises, in the form of unexpected events and outcomes. Be prepared to modify the programme, while sticking to the vision.

The out-of-date business model

According to Scott Anthony's 'Innovator's Paradox', the best time to innovate is when you don't need to. But when you don't have to innovate, you won't. And when you must innovate, you have less freedom to change.

An example of this is Microsoft whose revenues have continued to flow, despite its not having launched innovative products for years, while the decline of PCs, the growth of smartphones and the rise of competitors like Google continue to challenge it.

Clark Gilbert of Harvard said 'Absent a sense of threat, response to disruptive opportunities is inadequate. But with threat the . . . response is too rigid.' He was referring to how newspapers responded to the internet, where those who didn't embrace the internet tended to put their print editions online rather than see the broader picture.

'The core business, no matter how great it seems today, has a finite limit,' says Scott Anthony in *Harvard Business Review*. 'No great growth business was built from a defensive crouch.'

Mitigating Measures: the business model

Identify whether the business model is still fit for purpose. Are there signs of change that will make it redundant?

Map other models, even those far removed from the existing one, on to the existing product and services. Could any of them work?

Set up a competing model as a small experiment.

Conduct research in other territories and industries to see how their models compare.

Evaluate new and emerging models to see whether they pose a threat.

When the organisation stagnates

Business stagnation can be hard to spot until you look back at the past. At the time, the organisation will have looked stable and well managed. It may have ascribed periodic falls in revenue to weak market conditions, rather than recognising more fundamental problems.

Stagnation is characterised by an excessive focus on managing the status quo, a lack of enthusiasm for new projects and a cautious approach to borrowing and development.

Senior management will believe that the business is orderly, that good procedures are in place and that customers will continue to place orders.

The head of the organisation may have lost their zeal. They may feel the need to consolidate hard-won gains, rather than seeking new challenges. Sometimes the business has failed to respond to changes. Costs may be rising as a percentage of revenue.

The CEO may be someone with a long and distinguished history of honourable service. They usually look the part of a senior statesman, someone with considered opinions and an unruffled manner. It is only after a period of contained stagnation that a new CEO is brought in.

Mitigating Measures: avoiding stagnation

Review key performance indicators (KPIs) such as sales over a long period to establish whether the organisation is becalmed.

Agree trigger points or dates which will require action to be taken.

Seek the view of a consultancy, bearing in mind that most will assert that their services are definitely needed.

Consider whether the organisation needs a new CEO.

Take soundings from the world around you. Has the market suffered, or is the business losing share?

Excessive bureaucracy

There was a time when businesses were run with armies of clerks, secretaries and administrators. But the IT revolution, followed by the internet, has rendered much of that bureaucracy unnecessary, even dangerous. Bureaucracy can be a killer in today's organisation, stifling initiative and new ideas, and demotivating employees.

But for those with an orderly mind, the neatness of bureaucracy is an attractive proposition. It seems to tie up loose ends, and it gives a clear reporting structure to everyone.

For some organisations, a traditional bureaucracy is necessary. Every welfare applicant should be treated according to the rules, with no deviation. In the radiology department, protocols must be adhered to. Prisons must be rules-bound. Anything less is either favouritism or bias.

And as businesses become vast, they need rules that ensure consistency. But above the clerical level where the procedures must be followed, management needs to avoid bureaucracy. Research by Gallup found that sensible plans can develop into bureaucracy when beset by what it calls 'missteps'. They comprise:

- Parochialism: The elevating of a *department's* role rather than that of the *organisation*.
- Territorialism: This is an extension of parochialism. But while parochialism is driven by a focus on the department, territorialism is an attempt to corral resources inside the department. It shows up as hostility to outsiders, including employees outside the department.
- Empire-building: The manager seeks wider responsibilities, not necessarily in the interests of the business.

It can be difficult to know where to draw the line between anarchy and bureaucracy. With insufficient controls comes a lack of good governance, lack of management information and an increased risk of financial or ethical failure.

On the other hand, bureaucracies are characterised by excessive red tape, with requests having to be sent to higher managers; slow decision making, an out-of-touch senior management, a hierarchy with departmental silos and formal operating procedures.

At times of rapid change, most organisations need to err on the side of anarchy rather than bureaucracy, excepting situations where safety is paramount. It's a question of balancing the need for systems versus the opportunities that empowerment brings.

Mitigating Measures: beating bureaucracy

Remove the rules that unduly limit freedom of action, unless they are necessary, essential or common sense.

Imbue staff with the primacy of the organisation's overarching goals, in contrast to parochialism.

Determine which parts of the business are most likely to be harmed by bureaucracy. Give research and design more freedom from the bureaucracy than other departments.

Establish feedback mechanisms such as surveys, to determine where the bureaucracy is hampering success or demotivating staff.

Consider taking out a layer of management. This will remove a level of bureaucracy and force staff to be more innovative and decisive.

Weak execution

Execution is how businesses translate strategy into action. Yet most companies are poor at doing this according to Booz and Company, which questioned 125,000 individuals representing more than 1,000 companies, government agencies and not-for-profits in over 50 countries.

'Employees at three out of every five companies rated their organization weak at execution,' say the consultants, quoted in *Harvard Business Review*. 'That is, when asked if they agreed with the statement "Important strategic and operational decisions are quickly translated into action," the majority answered "no".'

So while a brilliant new product, an advance in technology or a new strategy can be the launch pad for success, it requires execution to make it work. It follows that being weak at execution is a risk. Strategy and execution go hand in hand. Organisations need both to succeed.

Booz and Company say that the most important elements of execution relate to 'decision rights', that is, knowing who has the right to make a decision. The second most important element is information, namely that information should flow up and down the line freely, and that people have access to information that tells them the financial impact of their day-to-day choices. Motivational tools and getting the organisation's structure right were found to be less important.

Mitigating Measures: faster, better execution

Ensure everyone knows what actions and decisions they are responsible for. Blurring of decision rights leads to delays and poor outputs.

Create procedures and a culture that sends information to and from the centre, and across departments and business units.

Provide metrics at all points of the organisation: allow staff to see the financial implications of their work.

Ensure that appraisals distinguish between high, medium and low performers. Without this, the organisation cannot put performance improvement programmes in place, nor reward and promote the high flyers that it needs. Performance must determine career advancement and promotion.

Lack of strategic capabilities

Poor execution can be caused by a lack of capabilities. Every organisation needs a set of capabilities, assets that are either essential for survival or else necessary to gain a competitive advantage. Capabilities are whatever produces meaningful business results. They are the organisation's equivalent of an individual's competencies. Without these capabilities, the business will go into decline.

Examples of capabilities include lean operations, effective project management or the fostering of talent. Yet according to a McKinsey survey, only a third of companies focus their training programmes on building the capability that adds the most value to their companies' business performance. In addition, three-quarters of respondents don't think their companies are good at building relevant capability.

In short, companies provide the wrong kinds of training. To put it another way, training is misaligned. Nor do companies focus on activities that could improve their strategic capability – that which contributes the most to their business performance. This might include financial awareness, tendering skills, product development or knowledge management.

Mitigating Measures: building capabilities

Identify the capabilities that are most needed and are in shortest supply.

Align training with those necessary capabilities.

Know that changing mindsets and behaviour is harder and more important than providing information or knowledge. But since capabilities are made up of behaviours, that is what training must achieve.

Errors in diversification

Diversification is a big attraction, for three types of business in particular:

1   Those in a mature or declining market where there is little prospect of growth.
2   Businesses that have cash in the bank and are keen to spend it.
3   Companies that worry about the risk of being overly reliant on their existing market.

A business that is in all three categories is very likely to seek diversification.

Compared with the dull routine of existing markets, where there are limitations to action, and sometimes little to do other than manage the status quo, diversification holds the excitement of future growth.

And many CEOs assume that because they have succeeded in one market, they have the skills to operate in any other. After all, they argue, operations, marketing and sales are broadly the same, irrespective of the market you're in. But when the rubber meets the road, they can find it isn't so easy. Diversification, like acquisition, is risky and fails more often than it succeeds. It adds complexity to the business, and makes it harder to manage.

Known for disposable lighters and pens, Bic tried to launch throw-away products in other markets, but its disposable knickers didn't sell. Consumers didn't like ready meals from the Colgate toothpaste company. And Virgin closed its wedding dress business saying, somewhat tongue in cheek, there was no such thing as virgin brides.

Yet diversification is logical. Having different income streams reduces the organisation's dependence on any one of them, and hence makes survival more likely. It gives the business access to a wider range of skills and capabilities, and broadens the organisation's horizons.

Some businesses succeed at diversification while others find it is a way to lose lots of money. There are two ways to diversify:

- *Related*: moving into adjoining markets. Microsoft moved into hardware such as the Surface (and the ill-fated Zune media player). Similarly, selling existing products in a new territory is a relatively low risk, especially if you use a local partner.
- *Unrelated*: going into a totally new market. This carries higher risks. When a B2B business moves into a consumer goods market, the chances of failure are bigger.

Research generally suggests that diversification much beyond the core business will fail, though some succeed very well. On the flip side, retrenching increases profitability. Diversified businesses include both high and low performers, as do non-diversified ones. So neither strategy is a guarantee of success or failure.

But businesses will always seek diversification, because the urge to survive, the need for excitement and experiment, and the motivation for increased profit are prime drivers in humans. The challenge is to do so in a way that balances the risks against the reward.

Mitigating Measures: how to diversify

Before diversifying, assess whether there is the possibility of growth in your existing market, this having a higher chance of success and less risk.

Quantify the costs of diversification. Failure can drag down the main business.

Identify the competitive advantages you will bring to the new market. If there aren't any, re-think the plan.

Determine the trigger points that will require you to exit from the diversification because it has failed.

Failed acquisitions

Some markets provide many low-risk opportunities to acquire new products. In the food industry there's no shortage of new brands that have grown from kitchen table to medium-sized businesses and are ripe for acquisition. They often look fresh and contemporary, making them an ideal stable companion for more established, cash-rich businesses. In turn the bigger business can offer them capital investment and better access to markets, including international ones, as well as paying off the founders.

In the world of digital apps, there are regular meetings where startups seek finance from business angels and hold out the promise of being the next eBay or PayPal.

Declining businesses sometimes try to buy their way out of trouble. An example is Yahoo which has consistently acquired and then closed would-be growth businesses. These have included del.icio.us, Astrid task management software and Geocities.

The big problem is that 70% to 90% of acquisitions fail. And because acquisitions are expensive, these failures become a drain on the company.

When BMW bought Land Rover everyone imagined the German company would make a success of it. But that wasn't the case. By the time BMW decided to sell it, the Rover group was losing £2m a day. Insiders say that BMW did insufficient due diligence, deliberating for only ten days before buying the company. They didn't know that sales figures were false, and there were problems with staff attitude. The Land Rover board was split, and many directors resigned. The BMW board wasn't fully behind the purchase, and subsequently deprived Land Rover of investment.

By contrast, its more recent owner Tata made a successful acquisition. It turned losses of £42m in 2008 into a profit of £2.6bn by 2014. In this they had been aided by Ford, Jaguar Land Rover's interim owner, which had started to turn the company around before running out of money in the recession.

There are many reasons why acquisitions fail:

Failure to do adequate due diligence: This can result in unexpected weaknesses and liabilities being discovered once the business has been acquired, leading to the conclusion that the business wasn't all it was thought to be.

Acquisitions in emerging economies: Acquisitions of businesses in developing nations carry further risks, because the financial information may be less clear.

The original owner leaves: When a business loses its entrepreneur before it has became fully established, it can lose its impetus and suffer a declines in sales.

Loss of the purchased business's distinctive culture: This happens when the purchaser imposes its 'big company' values and systems.

Lack of integration: Companies often fail to integrate the acquisition into the business. This means the purchaser fails to achieve the hoped-for economies. It is especially hard to integrate overseas businesses, and this is even more problematic when acquiring a business whose culture, language and systems are difficult to penetrate, and where local business conditions may be opaque.

All of that having been said, acquisitions can produce strategic opportunities such as extra market share, buying competitors, reaching new markets and acquiring new technology.

Mitigating Measures: acquisitions

Create an acquisitions policy and procedures. Targets should have products that fulfil a real need, rather than being a fad. If the business is a startup, it should have a solid management team. It should be capable of scaling up. It should be the main business in the market, not an also-ran, because the me-toos are more likely to fail. Ideally, there should be barriers to entry, to prevent others copying the business model.

Review whether your organisation can add value to the target business. Are there weaknesses you can overcome in its reach, marketing, product range or human capital? If there aren't, you're reliant on it giving you benefits, which may or may not materialise.

Conduct thorough due diligence. Identify the financial effect of any guarantees or indemnities acquired at the time of purchase.

Don't rush to purchase. Another opportunity will always come along.

Create a plan for integrating and supporting the new business. Too many small tech businesses have failed after being bought by a large organisation.

Allow the acquired business to retain its culture, if it has one. Sometimes that culture is crucial to its future success. At the same time, ensure that controls are in place.

Buy insurance. With the complexity involved in buying or selling a business, there are those who will go to court if they think they have been misled, or if the outcome is less favourable than they anticipated. Mergers and Acquisitions insurance provides protection against claims, and can avoid litigation between buyer and seller after the deal has been completed. Having M&A insurance can also help to push the deal through, since it will reassure both parties.

Tie the price to future performance. This will ensure that the price you pay fairly reflects the potential of the organisation, and will encourage the seller to be supportive.

Don't rely on future cost savings as the way to make the numbers work. There may be unknown extra costs, such as necessary investments, which will offset the savings.

Divest the business of failed acquisitions or those that no longer fit. In such cases, be cautious about giving warranties. They could affect the business many years hence. Buy warranty and indemnity insurance, which means you won't have to leave money in escrow or add reserves to the balance sheet.

Mitigating Measures: overseas acquisitions

Reduce the risk by having local knowledge. You might start by selling into a country through agents.

Allow local management to run the business on a day-to-day basis. But hold them to account with targets, and by engaging with them.

Ensure full due diligence is carried out. Involve local experts.

Weigh up the risk of political and economic instability as a factor in the investment decision.

3   The ever changing market

Mitigating customer risks

The chances are that your organisation's most popular products and services are different from what they were only a few years ago.

Domestic coffee drinking has moved from powder to instant granules to filter to pod (or even bean-to-cup). Vacuum cleaners are multi coloured and robotic, while electric vehicles are too common a sight to attract notice. Even these changes look tame against the markets where technology has been a force. CDs, DVDs and appointment TV have given way to streaming.

Houses are listed online, and commodity trading floors are closing, with their work now done by algorithms. But even tech giants have suffered: MySpace yielded to Facebook. But the future is never predictable: the much heralded BRICS economies have faltered.

In this chapter we consider the main marketing risks that affect consumer and business markets. We review the following troublesome issues:

- genericisation of brands
- customer concentration
- unprofitable customers
- intermediation
- comparison sites
- stagnant and low-growth markets
- extreme competition
- low-cost competitors
- the threat of low prices
- overreliance on a few products
- dated sales process
- the risks of social media
- weak product design and performance
- reputational failure
- overseas marketing
- joint ventures
- counterfeiting.

As we saw in Chapter 1, not all of these risks apply to every market; but all apply to some markets.

Brands at risk

Brands offer the customer evidence of reliability; and a good brand will pay dividends for years. Jockey underwear has been selling since 1935, Rice Krispies since 1928 and Twinings Tea has been delivering profits since 1706.

But brands are continuously at risk from own label products, with private label taking a 41% share in the UK, 34% in Germany and a much smaller 18% in the USA. Shoppers are much more brand loyal in developing economies. In China, Brazil and India, own label takes 5% or less, according to Nielsen.

Own label takes most of its share from weaker brands, while the category leader is often unscathed. Share is highest in undifferentiated or commodity categories, where the customer sees little difference in performance between brands.

Brands can win if they pursue innovation, provide marketing support and differentiate themselves. Those in categories that are bought less frequently (such as shoe polish or toilet tissue) have an advantage. Meanwhile stores can win share among staples that provide little differentiation and low innovation, and which are bought in volume and frequently, so the consumer is aware of the price.

Once a customer believes that a cheap generic product works as well as the brand, there is no reason for them to continue buying the original. This can happen in the case of pharmaceuticals, food products and household goods such as cleaning fluids. In the USA, the Food and Drug Administration (FDA) authorised two generic versions of Suboxone, a drug used to wean drug addicts off heroin. Once that happens the maker is faced with either reducing the price of its product, or building additional benefits that the generics don't have. In the case of Suboxone, the company innovated – converting it into a film that the user places under their tongue and slowly dissolves. It also removed the original tablets from the market, citing risk to children. Others saw this as a ploy by the manufacturer, Reckitt Benckiser, to maintain its sales.

Private label reaches a maximum of around 45% to 50%, which means there is room for brands to succeed. Equally, the ready availability of suppliers with design and formulating skills will allow stores to extend the reach of their own labels.

Mitigating Measures: brands

Brand owners must innovate, promote their brands and differentiate them.

Stores need to add value and boost perceived quality. Provide both standard and premium tiers to extend the sales opportunity.

Customer concentration

Customer concentration happens when consolidation takes place in the market, and the number of buyers reduces, known as oligopsony. If more than half of the company's income comes from fewer than ten customers, the corporation is the victim of customer concentration.

Around half of GKN's revenue comes from ten customers. At Land Securities, by contrast, no single customer represents more than 4.8% of income. Looking at it another way, 71% of Land Securities' revenue comes from customers who contribute less than 1% of total rents. In other words, the company is not dependent on any major customers.

Like GKN, businesses that sell consumer goods via retailers face the same problem of customer concentration. The ability to increase sales through relationship selling has declined in favour of fact- and data-based selling. Moreover, store buyers get regularly moved around, to reduce the possibility of capture by suppliers.

A strong brand, regularly refreshed, is the strongest determinant of survival. Many grocery manufacturers continue to sell their products successfully to supermarkets and live with the constant threat of being de-listed.

Some service businesses have the same problem. Advertising agencies are prone to losing a valuable account when a new CEO or advertising director is appointed. Sometimes, the new executive appoints a favourite agency from their past. Losing a major client will cause a huge loss of income.

When you have few customers, you risk losing money if one of them goes bust. This can lead to the loss of future revenue and the possibility of not getting paid for goods or services already delivered.

Mitigating Measures: customer concentration

Review your exposure to customer concentration.

Maintain intelligence about your customers' financial status.

Set a limit to the maximum you are willing any one client to represent (for example no more than 10% of revenue). In some markets this may not be possible.

Build close relationships with your main customers.

Ensure that top management act as salespeople, and have regular dialogue with the major customers. Ensure that the business continues to align with customers' needs.

Enhance your brand identity so that you're seen as the right organisation to do business with. Depending on the market this could mean integrity, technological advances or high fashion.

Seek other, less oligopolistic markets that don't suffer from customer consolidation.

Review your credit risk regularly. **Set limits** on both scale and payment time.

Consumer industries

Maintain a visible profile among trade buyers, for example in the trade media.

Address the end user; build brand loyalty. Don't reply on the loyalty of the retail buyer.

Business-to-business industries

Keep track of the movement of key executives as they move to other businesses, and stay in touch with them. Go for the long-term win: don't expect instant business.

(continued)

(continued)

Be ready to respond rapidly to major gains and losses, in terms of taking on and removing staff.

Maintain continuous, possibly low-level marketing activity directed at the small number of buyers, to ensure you are on their radar.

Search for non-traditional buyers and new entrants who might become customers.

Unprofitable customers

An accountancy practice recently found that for every hour it had billed a client for the last three years it had lost 45 pence ($0.63) in direct costs. This compares with a charge-out rate that should have been double the salaries involved. So the losses were substantial. It goes to show that many customers are unprofitable, and that even accountants can get it wrong sometimes.

Keeping unprofitable customers represents a threat to the business. They drag down the company's profits and put it at risk.

This can happen because the business has failed to properly analyse its per-customer profitability, or because its cost structure has changed. It may have occurred because you were desperate to win or retain a major client. In some cases the revenues keep some employees busy or a plant running. In other cases the company has failed to increase prices in line with inflation.

Customer profitability partly depends on your attitude to contribution – that is, how much each sale is expected to contribute to overheads. After variable costs have been paid for, every dollar thereafter contributes to fixed costs. If you get rid of a low-paying customer, you lose the contribution they were making to overheads. And it is to be expected that major clients will provide a slimmer margin but a bigger dollar amount.

The customer's behaviour is another factor to consider. If they constantly complain, take up customer service time and are rude to staff, these will be added reasons to disinvest.

Overall you need to be in possession of the facts on which you can make decisions.

Mitigating Measures: unprofitable customers

Assess the total revenues and costs attributable to each major customer. This can reveal major variations.

Determine what the lowest acceptable contribution is to be.

Decide how to recoup the margin from unprofitable customers. It may be that the product or service could be unbundled, requiring customers to pay for certain services such as printed invoices or paper statements, or adding a premium phone line for support. Alternatively, a programme of annual price rises could be inaugurated.

Forecast what proportion of the customers would leave if you put the prices up, and how many would stay. This in turn depends on the availability of suitable alternative suppliers, how cheap your products are in comparison with the competitors, how price-sensitive the customer is and how keen they are to retain you.

Educate the customer on the true costs of providing the product or service. Negotiate higher prices, unbundling of services or reduced servicing.

Consider reducing the amount of service provided to a certain set of customers, for example domestic as opposed to commercial clients. This may encourage them to leave of their own accord.

If necessary, fire unprofitable customers. Where the customer provides small revenues ands requires a high cost of servicing, disinvestment is an easy solution. An alternative would be to change the terms on which business is based. For example, you might require them to pay for services or pay an annual fee. But withdrawing from major clients isn't always an option.

From disintermediation to intermediation

Disintermediation is the process whereby suppliers deal directly with end users, rather than having to go through retailers or agents (intermediation).

Car insurance is a good example. It was traditionally sold by high street agents who would recommend a provider to their customer. Directline, a subsidiary of the Royal Bank of Scotland, broke the mould in 1985 by advertising directly to consumers, and selling to them using a telephone call centre. Its first TV commercials with its distinctive red telephone appeared in 1990.

Other insurance companies started doing the same thing: set up similar call centres and started advertising directly to consumers – bypassing their agents – in an effort to keep margin and build loyalty.

This innovation was swept aside with the arrival of the internet; when online aggregators such as GoCompare and CompareTheMarket stepped in to provide a price comparison service. In essence, the market had gone back to an agency model, albeit one that was driven by algorithms. Not to be outdone, however, Admiral launched its own price comparison site, Confused.com.

The same has happened in other markets, with eBay, Amazon, Alibaba and Google's various shopping services acting as intermediaries.

A different group of intermediaries arrived to exploit the huge amount of information on the net by scraping information off others' sites. Examples of these consolidation websites are Money Supermarket, Expedia and USwitch. Sites like TripAdvisor, which originally focused on curating information, have become more aggressive in promoting their own booking services.

Intermediation is more prone to happen where services can be digitised, as we have seen with insurance. Digital products have no cost of delivery.

Markets that have been greatly affected by intermediation include bookshops, travel agents, insurance, recruitment, taxis, music, hotel booking and investments.

A newer form of disintermediation is peer-to-peer activity. This includes peer-to-peer loans which are mediated through computer algorithms without the need for banks or bank managers. Airbnb and Uber are similar such businesses.

At another non-commercial level disintermediation is people's new-found ability to network and share. This ranges from tool sharing to ride sharing and car pooling, which has been classified by Paul Mason as post capitalism. In this scenario, citizens have less need of businesses, since information tends towards free, and machines such as 3D printers can produce much of what is needed. Squats, free kindergartens and communal food production are examples of community-based enterprise.

But leading service companies and manufacturers will continue to seek top-of-mind awareness among consumers, though branding and advertising.

The threat of the comparison sites

Price comparison websites lead to a focus on price, to the detriment of almost everything else. This can damage companies' margins and create an ever declining price spiral. Businesses reduce the quality of their services, and seek to recoup their lost profit by stealthily increasing their prices to existing customers each year.

Price comparison sites also reduce companies' visibility in the market, leading to commodification. If you've booked a hotel or a restaurant recently or bought a house you probably went through one of these intermediaries. The advantage for the restaurant or hotel is that it can reach more people. But there are disadvantages. The hotel may have to pay the site for referrals, and often pay more for prominent rankings. As sites become fewer in number and better known, they can exert a stranglehold on the market, with a constantly rising price per click.

It also encourages consumers to buy the cheapest brand. Where there is no human to advise the customer on the quality of an insurance product, cheaper but inferior providers can gain more customers simply by paying more per click, even though in the longer term they may go out of business.

In the insurance world, it's common to offer a low price to new customers, and then increase the price when the service is renewed. Some companies go further and keep increasing the price, relying on customer inertia to avoid defection. This can affect the company's reputation if the consumer finds that the company has been fleecing them, or that the second-year price is much higher. Whether this method of selling is right must vary from one market to another and depend on the scale of the annual increases. Each business must set a balance between losing the initial sale (and the renewals) against upsetting loyal customers.

Some industries have tried to set up their own consolidation sites. To combat the consolidators, travel agents launched RoomKey.com, while estate agents set up OnTheMarket.com to beat RightMove and Zoopla. These are sometimes less efficient than the competitors, because the trade lacks the investment, commitment or know-how to provide a quality experience.

Mitigating Measures: intermediation

Ensure that your website provides advantages that can't be found elsewhere. Hilton Hotels provide free Wi-Fi to guests who book direct.

Create a competitive edge that distinguishes you from the competition.

Seek solutions that increase customer loyalty.

Seek ways to take cost out of your product.

Provide innovative solutions that make it more convenient for the customer to buy through you.

Provide tiered products that meet the needs of different price points in the market.

Living in a stagnant pool

Many Western markets show no signs of major growth. Companies are usually advised to milk the business, which is a strategy for abandonment. Ultimately the company may have to shutter the business if there are no buyers for it.

If your prime market is stagnant, this type of advice isn't very helpful. It condemns the business to a slow and lingering death. And treating the unit as a 'dog' will be demotivating for those who manage it.

Low growth or declining markets also suffer from high levels of competition because, like snakes in a bag, the businesses can't escape and can only compete with each other. They can only do this by taking share from the others, and when sales are declining there will be overproduction.

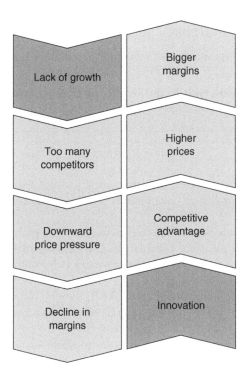

Figure 3.1 If no action is taken, businesses in stagnant markets will decline. Innovation is one of the solutions.

But there are ways out of this problem. Hammermesh and Silk point out in *Harvard Business Review* that, when faced with a declining motorcycle market in the 1950s, as people increasingly drove cars, the Japanese manufacturers invested in improved models, with smaller, cheaper bikes, and created the recreational motorbike market. Rather than disinvesting, they created a new segment of the market and prospered as a result.

Mitigating Measures: escape from a stagnant market

Innovate. There are always ways to distinguish one business from another, though this isn't always obvious, especially after years of fruitless searching. You may need to seek outside experts.

Avoid excessive advertising and line extensions. They are a quick and easy solution but rarely bring the additional revenues that they would in a growth market.

Identify growth areas within the market. These may be demographic or psychographic segments, regional or overseas sectors, or new price points. They may be upstream or downstream possibilities, added services or additional technology.

Conduct research, possibly in ways different than before. Analysing customers' needs and problems may provide answers, as will competitor strengths and weaknesses.

Commit funds to R&D, once opportunities have been identified.

Pay attention to cost reduction. It will help the business survive.

Consolidate operations or manufacturing into fewer facilities. This will bring costs down and increase efficiency.

Allocate ambitious, high-quality managers with fresh ideas to such units. Avoid treating such businesses as a place to retire average managers to.

Severe competition

Few businesses don't operate in a competitive market. And even where a company has a monopoly, such as Google in the online search field, competitors are always plotting to overthrow it.

Competition is evident in high-growth markets where businesses strive to grab territory and establish themselves in a leading position. But mature, low-growth markets face even greater competition because the only way to gain revenue is by taking it from others.

The stronger the competition, the more likely that prices will fall, thereby reducing profits. Any business that fails to innovate, or whose new product development is weaker than its competitors, will lose market share and potentially go into decline.

No business can afford to ignore its competition. It is a mistake to think that your competitors are second rate. Some may be; but other, smarter companies will be waiting to grab your market. New competition can come from many sources:

Low-priced competitor: The long-standing supermarkets were badly affected by the arrival of discounters such as Lidl. When a competitor pares away all the add-ons, and reduces the product to its bare elements, the consumer may or may not decide that's all they need. Discount supermarkets stock fewer varieties of each product, which allows for smaller stores, a reduced cost of stock and fewer staff, leading to lower prices.

Larger scale: Small high street retailers have given way to large out-of-town stores. While smaller local food stores have made a return, the little pet stores and toy shops won't.

Technologically better: The driverless car simply didn't exist as an idea until we learnt that Google was testing one. The car companies were caught napping, lulled into a false sense of security by their view of what a car looked like.

Convenience: Why fight the crowds when a supermarket employee will pack and deliver them for you? On-demand services, one-stop shopping and online payments have trained the customer to expect 'done-for-you' services. Supermarkets that failed to recognise the value of delivery have lost a chunk of the market. Amazon benefits from instant gratification plus effortless shopping.

Advertising-based model: Online businesses may provide free information or services and earn revenue from advertising, rather than a subscription or the sale of content.

Freemium: Like advertising-based models, some online organisations will provide a basic service for free, and encourage customers to pay extra for additional services. RecruiterBox allows companies to manage one vacancy for free, a service that lets recruiters trial the product. Indeed.com lets companies advertise their vacancies and provides massive exposure free of charge, with an upsell for a more tailored service. This undercuts the traditional agency model which charges for each vacancy it promotes.

Going direct: Traditionally most markets were structured into supplier-wholesaler-retailer-customer. Everyone knew their place, and this applied to industries as diverse as insurance and book publishing. But with the internet and crowdfunding, most businesses can reach their end users directly.

Low-cost competitors

Technology isn't the only way that disruption happens. Low-cost competitors are another risk. Take spectacles. In the old days, you went to a high street optician, got a prescription, and then bought a pair of £100 glasses. But an increasing number of people are buying £2 glasses off the shelf at pharmacies and discount stores. After being told they must have their eyesight checked by a qualified ophthalmologist, they shrugged their shoulders, tested various strengths and chose the one that seemed best.

Mitigating Measures: competition

Regularly assess the market and its needs.

Invest deeply in new opportunities.

Create close relationships with customers.

Build brands in related markets to prevent competitors from getting a toe hold.

Establish a portfolio of businesses in other fields or in other countries, to reduce your reliance on one area.

Consider making a bid to buy your competitors.

Low, low prices

There's room in most markets for no-frills products that feature low prices as their unique selling proposition (USP). We have discussed the discount food stores such as Aldi and Lidl. There are also no-frills airlines including Ryanair. Car manufacturers provide basic cars with small engines and little sound proofing for cost-conscious motorists. And there are budget gyms, hotels and mobile phones.

For other businesses, cheap is a threat because it reduces profit or produces losses. Falling prices happen when:

- There are too many suppliers in the market, and often only a few major customers (for example, when farmers sell to supermarkets).
- The demand for the product keeps falling.
- The product has become a commodity. Buyers seek the cheapest supplier. There is a rush to the bottom.
- There is oversupply.
- A business is making a 'land grab' – seeking to secure customers for the long run.
- The business has failed to identify its full costs.
- The business wants to keep its staff or machinery employed and is pricing work so that it will contribute to the overheads rather than paying all its costs. In other words it is paying for the variable costs plus a bit.

Not every customer buys the cheapest product. The cheapest wine on the restaurant menu is never the biggest seller. Customers have needs other than buying the cheapest, such as prestige, the confidence that a brand name brings or even the promise that a higher price provides a better product.

Why Asda held out against Black Friday discounts

Faced with competition from discounters such as Aldi and Lidl, traditional UK supermarkets such as Tesco and Morrisons opted to offer loss leaders – products on which little or no profit is made, in an attempt to lure shoppers into the store.

For Black Friday 2015 Asda chose not to run one day of major price cuts but to spread the discounts over a longer period. Loss leaders, said Andy Clarke, Asda's CEO, 'kept people away from the core shopping mission': they buy the cheap televisions but not the food. This resulted in Asda's lowest market share for nine years, but profits remained at around 5% while its rivals' profits dived.

Talking to the *The Guardian*, Clarke said he wouldn't give away profit to boost top-line sales. 'It's very easy to buy short-term sales with promotional activity, but I believe that's not the way to long-term sustainable success.'

Keeping profits steady, he said, would give him the cash and flexibility to ride out the following year and he would be able to ramp up price cuts as other struggle. However, the loss of sales is not something that can be ignored for long.

Mitigating Measures: low prices

Have a clear understanding of your costs. Make that information central in all pricing decisions.

Subject pricing to proper analysis. Sales staff should not be allowed to offer below-cost deals.

Differentiate your product from low-cost suppliers. Emphasise your difference.

Ensure customers know *why* you are more expensive than low-cost suppliers. Provide information on your website, with a comparison chart or a features and benefits table.

Provide products at different price points. Instigate a no-frills 'fighting brand' that will compete at the bottom of the market, with other higher-priced, value-added products.

Be prepared to wait it out. If low-price competitors have the same costs as you, they cannot continue to sell below cost or at very low prices for long. Ultimately, their customer service or product quality will flag, they will withdraw from the market, or go bust. Sometimes it's a matter of who has the deepest pockets.

Relying on a few big products

Most companies have product stars, those that contribute the biggest revenue. But businesses that are reliant on one market or one product are at risk from the market changing.

Apple, for example, derives over 60% of its revenue from a single product, the iPhone. It is scrambling for revenue from other products, including music subscriptions, its watch, TV set-top box, and self-driving cars. In the faddy phone market it would only take another company to design a more fashionable phone for the company to be in trouble.

Google gets 90% of its revenue from advertising. It would only take one business to provide a better search algorithm for Google's sales to decline. But Google has the advantage of huge experience in, and resources devoted to, its search engine, and its search function links to its powerful maps application, which in turn is linked to Google

Local search, and so on. Companies that buy its ad space come from every industry, and its users – those who type queries into the search engine – come from every stratum of society, in almost every country in the world. That makes it less vulnerable. It also gained an extraordinary grip on the smartphone market, with its launch of Android. But like Apple, Google has been desperate to find new markets, from cars to space exploration.

GoPro was the darling of extreme sports enthusiasts, who could show off their skiing or diving skills. But it's at risk from smartphones and cheap lookalikes. FitBit is known for its activity tracking devices. It too is at risk, from cheap lookalikes, and from encroachment from smartphone makers including Apple.

Dropbox only has one product, cloud storage. Although every major tech business and many small ones have tried to emulate it, it has held off the competition by the effectiveness of its service. It also fulfils a lasting need – the ability to collaborate with others, and to transfer and store files without fuss. It has achieved a critical mass in medium-sized organisations, but needs to succeed in enterprise computing to survive and prosper.

Beyer Peacock exported steam locomotives all over the world. In the 1850s, the Manchester-based company was turning out a massive loco every six days. It was sending them everwhere, especially to the British colonies. But with the turn of the new century, electric trams began to appear. London County Council Tramways sold 3.3m tickets in its third year of business.

According to the Manchester Museum of Science and Industry, Beyer Peacock experimented with electric trains and steam road vehicles. But steam locomotives were what its customers wanted. In 1955 British Rail moved from steam to diesel. Beyer Peacock was by now offering diesels – but not the kind that the railways wanted, and the company ceased all production in 1966.

Surviving for over 100 years is an achievement, but its last 50 years were a continued decline. When you've been so successful in one market, it's hard to succeed in another one. But it can be done. Nike extended its reach from sports shoes to golf balls and clothing, always staying within a reasonable distance of its original market.

Figure 3.2 Beyer Peacock locomotive on the Madras Railway, 1860.
Source: Wikipedia.

Mitigating Measures: product concentration

Continue to invest in the flagship product, to make it more effective and more necessary, without adding unnecessary functionality and bloat.

Lessen your dependence on the flagship product, by creating other products, whether in complementary markets or new ones.

Watch for signs that the market is moving away from your core product. Develop products in areas that could be the future.

Dated sales process

The sales process is a vital part of business-to-business markets, and especially where high-value contracts are at stake. Failing to win business puts the business at risk. When a shipyard loses an order, it can tip the company into bankruptcy if there are no more orders, as happened with Ferguson Shipbuilders in Glasgow.

In recent years, companies have put major effort into systematising their sales process into a formidable machine, using customer relationship management (CRM) software and sequential steps that were intended to qualify leads and create a sale.

But in many cases sales cycles have lengthened, conversion rates have fallen and margins have got narrower. This has been partly due to customers becoming more knowledgeable, armed with more information, and becoming more questioning.

Some experts now believe that B2B companies need to be less rigid in their approach to selling. They should focus on solving customers' problems, embed themselves into the customer's operation and build engagement. It also means being more aware of the role that the internet and social media can play.

The sales department needs creativity and expertise in social media, and an understanding that it must advise customers rather than sell to them.

Mitigating Measures: updating the sales model

Examine whether your sales model is still suited to the twenty-first century.

Align your efforts with the clients' buying funnel which may be different from your own.

Adapt your products and services to clients' changing needs.

Identify segments in the market that might need different solutions.

Be aware that customers may not regard your sales team as the sole experts. They're more sophisticated now, and have access to other influences, not least your competitors.

Equip the sales team with facts that help the customer. Facts should not be limited to those that support your own case. Partnership and evidence-based selling are needed.

Are your products commodities?

Commodification is the process whereby your products become seen as commodities, indistinguishable from other companies' offerings, and the customer buys whatever is cheapest.

These are products where the customer expresses no brand preference, and where each product has no USP.

In the past this happened to nails and screws, but has more recently happened to some packaged goods through the power of grocery stores and price comparison websites who 'own the customer'. Own label foods and white label pet insurance mean that the real suppliers of these products and services are invisible to the consumer. Energy companies and car dealers can quickly become commodified when consumers can use comparison websites to identify whose prices are cheapest.

Mitigating Measures: avoiding commodification

Innovate to prevent commodification. Look for new ways to differentiate your product. Add new benefits.

Augment products with an element of service. Personalise the service or tailor it to the consumer. NikeID allows the consumer to choose individual elements in its trainers. Xerox provides a managed print service, rather than just photocopiers. Many software companies have moved to a subscription service.

Bundle products. Add services into the product to provide different price points.

Provide asymmetrical information which makes direct comparison harder.

Ensure that sales force compensation does not prioritise volume over profit.

If there is no hope of escaping from the commodity trap, you must cut cost, so as to be competitive and thereby win sales.

Consider buying out your competitors, which will allow you to raise prices.

Fire unprofitable customers, those who seek to constantly reduce your selling price.

Exit the market if, ultimately, you can't avoid commoditisation.

Weak design and poor product performance

In this age of Trustpilot, Amazon reviews, TripAdvisor and Angie's List, almost every product and service gets reviewed somewhere.

While some sites are known for sock puppets (a fake identity used for deception), consumers value others' opinions highly. Ninety per cent of consumers read reviews before visiting a business, according to Invesp. Hence weak product performance can no longer be hidden. Failings will be pointed out by reviewers, and sales will suffer. While this applies mainly to consumer products, service businesses and B2B organisations will increasingly be reviewed in the future, not least because web entrepreneurs can make money from review sites.

A reduction in students' satisfaction with their UK university now affects the university's ranking. A lower ranking will reduce the quality of students applying to the university the following year, and therefore the quality of other rankings in future years. The same applies in reverse. In other words, product performance is more visible, has a bigger impact and affects more markets than ever before.

Design, too, has an effect on performance. Most managers recognise that design is more than just packaging or labelling. It's about making everything work as it should. Customers recognise clunky systems. The price of good design, including the cost of talented coders, is cheap compared with the penalties of living with awkward systems. It usually starts with a clear understanding of the customer's needs.

Mitigating Measures: boosting product performance

Conduct user reviews. Evaluate users' experience. Determine what users value most, and assess your product on those dimensions. Use this information to improve the product or service. Seek to identify and gain a competitive advantage.

Analyse your competitors' products. This will tell you about their strengths and weaknesses. Adopt the things they do well, to narrow or overcome their lead.

Use Google Alerts to identify new events among your competitors.

In B2B markets, seek to sample your competitors' offerings. There are many ways to do this, including examining their sales materials and website, and talking to the trade.

Use a market research firm or an industry analyst to provide a more objective analysis.

Use a 2×2 grid to position your business and competitors. Then decide which area of the grid you should be moving towards, and identify how to achieve that. Alternatively use the 'Strategy Canvas' method outlined in the book *Blue Ocean Strategy* by Kim and Mauborgne.

Ensure good design is built into every part of the customer experience.

Danger: social media

Social media is both an opportunity and a threat. Twitter has the ability to create a storm of protest, sometimes justified and sometimes not. This is often picked up and magnified by mainstream media.

When two children were killed by carbon monoxide poisoning in a Corfu hotel, the tour operator's CEO refused to apologise ('There's no need to apologise because there was no wrongdoing by Thomas Cook.'). This response caused an outcry in social media. Commentators felt the failure to apologise stemmed from the CEO taking instruction from corporate lawyers. An inquest found that the firm had not carried out a sufficient health and safety audit, and had breached its duty of care to the family.

Later, Thomas Cook gained ten times more financial compensation than the family received, which caused still further anger. And nine years after the event the company made half an apology, which sounded insincere.

By contrast, after a high-profile roller coaster accident at Alton Towers theme park, Nick Varney, the company's CEO, fronted the media response, and issued an apology. He said he was 'totally devastated' by the incident and said his 'heart goes out' to those affected. He also visited a student who had lost her leg in the accident, and apologised again. Social media response was muted.

These two cases demonstrate that no business can hide from social media. But smart businesses know how to respond to its sudden storms. Authenticity, humanity and even showmanship can turn a bad situation into one that wins reluctant approval.

Customers also expect a fast response from social media, which requires dedicated and knowledgeable staff to handle their queries and comments.

According to Zendesk, 88% of consumers have been influenced by an online customer service review when deciding what to buy. Reviews on Amazon and Yelp can have an impact on sales and reputation, and a bad review can push you down in the rankings, making you less visible or less attractive to customers. Yet some organisations ignore criticisms. O2's UK community site (community.o2.co.uk) publishes streams of user-generated criticism about its unwanted marketing activities, to which the company never replies.

Mitigating Measures: the dangers of social media

Constantly monitor what is being said on social media.

Build a brand identity online. Communicate your core values on social media..

Use an online reputation monitoring tool like Social Mention, Reputology, Ninety per cent or Review Trackers. Set up Google Alerts for your business name or use a site like Talkwalker, both of which send email alerts. Use a social media software such as Hootsuite or Sprout Social to monitor your own Twitter or Facebook feeds.

Respond promptly. There is nothing worse than a criticism that goes unanswered. It looks as though the criticism was justified, and that the company doesn't care about its customers. This means you need to have people dedicated to answering criticisms on social media, and software to alert them to new comments.

Be polite, no matter how unjustified the complaint. Say, 'Thank you for your valuable feedback. I am sorry you were not happy about your stay with us. I would welcome the opportunity to speak with you about your experience. Please contact me at your earliest convenience.'

Encourage the complainant to discuss the matter offline, by saying; 'Please get in touch with us on telephone number . . .' This allows you to deal with the problem in a less public arena.

Ask the review organisation to remove defamatory reviews.

Actively seek reviews. Recent reviews serve to reassure potential customers that your organisation is providing good service.

Accept that some reviews will be less than perfect. This can be a good thing. Consumers are suspicious of businesses that only get 5 stars.

Treat criticism as a way to improve. One online course got regularly criticised for the quality of its videos. When the videos improved, the reviews got better.

Share reviews with employees. It will encourage them to be more aware of the need to satisfy customers.

Identify loyal fans, and harness their motivation and enthusiasm. They will be your ambassadors. 'Prosumers' are consumers who produce content, such as videos and blogs. Encourage them to talk about your product.

Mitigating Measures: after a disaster

Don't stay silent: Respond in a way that sounds human and genuine. Saying nothing makes the business look callous.

Have the CEO front your response to major incidents. This is what the boss is paid for. CEOs are the face of the business.

Emphasise the good things you do. This might include a good safety record and support for the victims.

Have an incident response plan in place.

Reputational damage

Reputational damage is one of those curious risks that are downstream of the actual event. It's the outcome of some other failing. Almost all the risks in this book cause reputational damage. So reputational failure isn't something to be guarded against. Taking care of all the other risks prevents reputational damage.

That said, it is the organisation's response to a bad event that determines whether or not it ends up suffering reputational damage.

Companies build a good reputation over years of behaving in a consistently ethical manner. This can then be damaged by a scandal, such as corruption, working against the public interest, or a product disaster.

A Harris Poll showed that Volkswagen Group fell steeply in light of its emissions scandal, dropping from a 'very good' (75) score in 2015 to a 'very poor' (55) rating in 2016. It fell more than 25 points on Emotional Appeal (on attributes of trust, admiration and respect) and 20 points on Social Responsibility (attributes of environmental and community responsibility).

In Chapter 9 we look at the continued failings of the energy firm npower, and the damage that was caused to its reputation and hence its sales. The company suffered a £9m loss, and had to cut 2,400 jobs in the UK.

A survey by the Reputation Institute showed that 83% of consumers say they would definitely buy the products of companies with excellent reputations, whereas only 9% would do the same for companies with a weak reputation. Examples of expected behaviour and transgressions are shown in Table 3.1.

Table 3.1 Expected behaviour and transgressions that cause reputational damage

Expected behaviour	Events that can cause reputational damage
Fair treatment of employees	Pays low wages
	Bad working conditions
	Abusive terms and conditions
	Uses suppliers who treat their workforce badly
Environmentally responsible	Causes pollution
	Damaging wildlife
	Uses up limited natural resources
Provides value for money products	Product or service failings
	Product catastrophe or recall
	Poor response to customer complaints
Behaves ethically to suppliers	Abuses its power over suppliers
Good governance	Undeserved pay awards for senior staff
	Scandals at board level
	Fraud
	Punitive action by the regulator
Well managed	IT failure
	Products fail to keep up with changing tastes and technology

In addition, there are some reputational issues that concern bankers, shareholders, suppliers, regulators, business partners and business customers, rather than consumers and the general public.

Although they are less visible, often being reported only in the business media, they are no less significant to public companies and business-to-business organisations. Some of these issues are listed below as Table 3.2.

Another influential group are what the Harris Poll organisation calls Opinion Elites, those members of the public who are better informed on public issues, and who are likely to be opinion formers.

United Services Automobile Association (USA), The Walt Disney Company, Publix Super Markets, Samsung and Johnson & Johnson, all companies on the general public's top ten list, did not appear on the 2016 Opinion Elites' top ten.

Individual failings do not necessarily lead to reputation failure. Organisations that are quick to respond often end up unharmed. When faced with a possible reputation problem, such as a product failure or a labour dispute, it is important for company spokespeople to communicate the organisation's position clearly and openly. Failure to do so can adversely affect its reputation, even though it may have right on its side.

Table 3.2 Reputational issues that can affect an organisation's financial standing

Expected performance	Events that can cause reputational damage
Profitable	Loss making
Good governance	Board disagreements and departures
	Criticisms at shareholders' meetings
	Pay for failure

Mitigating Measures: avoiding reputational failure

Assess the probability and severity of the organisation's major risks, in terms of the reputational damage they would cause. Prioritise them.

Implement solutions that will prevent their occurrence. This will involve policies, procedures, audits and reviews.

Have continuity plans in place to deal swiftly and effectively with the biggest risks.

Monitor the organisation's reputation among stakeholders. Identify areas for improvement, and put plans in place to achieve that.

Have an active social media presence that is capable of responding fast to trending issues.

Take out cover against insurable risks, such as Directors and Officers liability insurance (D&O), environmental impairment liability (EIL) and product liability cover.

Marketing abroad

Taking your product to other countries often seems a logical solution for gaining new revenue. But it's harder than it looks. Tesco failed with Fresh & Easy in the USA because West Coast consumers prefer to do a weekly or fortnightly shop, buy in bulk and expect assistants to pack their purchases.

Travelling the other way, BestBuy didn't realise that Europeans preferred smaller stores. And Starbucks closed all its 84 Australian coffee shops, having opened in low-traffic areas and charging more than other coffee outlets.

In a study of Brazilian companies, the University of Sussex found that the majority of new products introduced by exporters do not survive beyond the first year. The problems include the following:

1   *Cultural issues.* Even nearby countries are more foreign than we imagine. And a country like the USA is not one big market but a set of separate ones.
2   *Technical issues.* Other countries use different standards. The product or service may need to be adapted.
3   *Logistics and support.* There will be a lack of backup and infrastructure. The business will need to provide support to those on the ground.
4   *Economic and political problems.* Some emerging countries have a higher risk of social unrest and economic instability, and undergo wide swings in political control.
5   *Security dangers.* The organisation may encounter the threat of terrorism, civil war and lawlessness, as well as the risk of kidnap and ransom.
6   *Bribery and corruption* is common in some international markets.

Emerging markets

Emerging markets can offer higher returns, especially those countries that have high growth rates and underserved markets. Their youthful populations and growing middle classes may offer big opportunities. A country like South Sudan is starting everything from scratch and so for some businesses it holds the promise of rich rewards. The size of France, it has only 60 miles (100km) of paved roads, according to Reuters, and hardly any hospitals and schools, and is the ultimate frontier territory. But the rule of law there is uncertain, government officials are inexperienced and corruption is widespread.

In countries like South Sudan, the markets are underserved, and governments are buying. Western businesses often have the scale and global experience that local businesses may not have.

Equally, prices in consumer markets may be lower, reflecting consumers' smaller disposable income. Business-to-business markets can be fraught with ethical risk such as bribery and corruption. The judiciary may not be wholly independent, the laws can be applied inconsistently or lack clarity and companies may not get fair access to justice. Those in opposition to the state may find it hard to get redress. Intellectual property rights can be flouted.

According to the TMF Group, getting electricity for a business is a laborious task in Russia, with firms having to wait between four months and a year to get switched on, depending on the city.

Quoted on CNBC, Sergei Pugachev, a Russian billionaire, said the Soviet state had expropriated his $15bn business empire spanning shipbuilding, coal and real estate. At the time of writing he was suing Russia for $12bn. Russia, meanwhile, was seeking Pugachev's arrest for embezzlement and misappropriation of assets, charges Pugachev denied. Given the secrecy of Putin's Kremlin, it was impossible to confirm Pugachev's account. But a Russian spokesman said 'We see them as the words of a citizen who is on a wanted list.'

The problem lies in identifying which countries offer the best opportunity for growth. It is hard to know which will remain economically and politically stable. But the danger spots are as follows:

The Middle East: Conservative, oligarchic families own entire states and democracy is limited. Expect continual risks where people's aspirations are not being met. Meanwhile the fight for supremacy between Shia and Sunni will continue in local proxy wars. Palestine and Israel will continue to boil over unless an accommodation is made.

China: The contradictions between a controlling one-party state run by old men will come up against a youthful, internet-savvy population. Meanwhile China's growing military and economic power could lead to conflicts with other states, especially in the South China Sea.

Africa: East Africa may continue to suffer with failed states, poverty, depopulation and low investment. Other parts of Africa, especially West Africa, may grow and succeed. The pace throughout will be uneven and subject to unexpected events.

South America: Low commodity prices and a slow down in the world economy will harm some developing nations' economies. Political volatility will continue in some states, but overall the outlook overall is positive.

Mitigating Measures: more effective international marketing

Acquire detailed knowledge. You need a detailed understanding of the territory before taking action. Assess the political, economic and social risks, as well as the level of competition.

Avoid the most corrupt and violent countries unless there are overriding reasons not to (such as being in the extractive industries).

Work with a local partner or buy an established organisation. They should be able to adapt your methods into ones that satisfy the local culture.

Go for markets that more closely resemble your own. There will be fewer differences, which increases the chances of success. Safer markets are those that are reasonably established, are stable and have good prospects for growth.

Serve more territories. This will dilute the risk of relying on any one market.

Invest in local talent. Ensure you have managers who speak the local language and understand the environment.

Ensure strong financial control and auditing.

Joint ventures

Joint ventures and consortia are good tools for helping a business bid for large contracts, use others' expertise and share risk. But they also provide added risk.

The partner business may have a different culture, management style or objectives. Tensions can build, communication can be weak and this can lead to disagreement. With a joint venture you aren't in full control, and you may be unable to direct the project as you would like. This is particularly difficult if you have to get approval from a joint venture partner for strategic decisions. And as time goes by, the gap between partners may widen (though equally, it may reduce).

If problems occur, and they are not managed, the project can fail. Costs will have to be written off, and the business may suffer reputational damage.

Technology is one of the prime reasons why companies want to partner, as Table 3.3 shows. CEOs also use collaborations to find new markets and become more innovative.

Mitigating Measures: successful joint ventures

Establish pre-venture due diligence on potential partners to ensure they can perform their required duties.

Participate only in joint ventures in which your interests match those of your partners.

Have formal systems in place to monitor the performance of the joint venture. Have clear documented procedures for resolving differences.

(continued)

(continued)

Consider collaborating with partners from different spheres. These can include unexpected allies, such as NGOs and startups, as Table 3.4 shows.

Create a separate legal entity if the joint venture creates extra risks, for example because the outcome is hard to forecast, the potential for losses could be high or you could face legal threats. This will prevent the loss of your assets. Setting up a limited liability company costs little. And although the extra accounting adds complexity, it provides a major safeguard.

Stopping the counterfeiters

The counterfeit goods market is worth $1.77tn, according to the OECD. It is not just luxury goods and trainers that get copied, but medications, movies, software, perfumes, watches, jeans and toys, among others. The internet has greatly facilitated the sale of pirated goods.

Counterfeit goods are often produced in factories with poor working conditions including the use of child labour. The profits from these goods sometimes support drug cartels, gangs and terrorist groups.

Table 3.3 Why CEOs want to partner. 'What are your reasons for collaborating in joint ventures, strategic alliances or informal collaborations?'

Reasons why CEOs want to partner	% who ranked each option 1st, 2nd or 3rd most important
Access to new emerging technologies	47
Access to new customers	47
Access to new geographic markets	42
Ability to strengthen our innovation capabilities	40

Source: PwC.

Table 3.4 Partners from different spheres. 'Are you currently engaged or considering engaging with any of the following types of partners, through joint ventures, strategic alliances or informal collaboration?'

Type of collaborator	%
Suppliers	69
Customers	66
Business networks, clusters or trade organisations	53
Academia	52
Firms from other industries	52
Competitors	50
Startups	44
Government	37
NGOs	36

Source: PwC.

For many consumers the allure of buying a luxury brand at a low price is irresistible, even though they know it's a fake. But although the impoverished individual may not have been able to afford the real suitcase, scarf or shoes, other consumers can be hoodwinked into buying a fake, believing it to be the real thing.

This is especially a problem for luxury goods companies, where the manufacturing cost of the product is only a small part of the final price. This allows counterfeiters to create rip-off versions.

The brand's reputation may also be tarnished once purchasers see the poor quality of the item, believing it to be an original. However, many replicas are almost indistinguishable from the real thing.

Tiffany tried suing eBay in a US District Court, but its case was rejected on the grounds that eBay could not be held accountable because it did not intentionally induce anyone to infringe Tiffany's trademark and because it lacked specific knowledge of infringement by any seller.

Research has shown that piracy correlates with national GNP, income inequality and the individual's need for conformity. In other words people in poor countries with big wealth divides are more prone to buying pirated goods, and these products are attractive to young, low-income, less confident purchasers.

Other research suggests that stressing the low quality of fakes and the harm that purchasing them does to jobs and the national economy can reduce people's propensity to buy.

However, the cost of surveillance against counterfeit goods, if done thoroughly, will be considerable.

Mitigating Measures: counterfeiting

Build an anti-counterfeit team. You will need expertise in security, legal matters and communications. And you will need sources of local knowledge.

Identify your most important markets, the ones that must be protected from counterfeit goods.

Focus on the most common places of manufacture. Are goods made locally or in China? New York has a thriving counterfeit manufacturing economy.

Understand the points of sale. Is it the internet, eBay, Amazon or street markets?

Decide your strategy for clamping down on pirated goods. Taking down a street trader is easier but less effective than removing the entrepreneur who commissions and transports the goods.

Alert the police in cases where street vendors are selling counterfeit goods that purport to be yours. But be aware that vendors will continue to pop up.

Use third party agencies or individuals if necessary to identify counterfeit goods on the street, and discover their source.

Use Cease and Desist letters against the infringement of your trademarks, followed up by legal action.

(continued)

(continued)

Be aware that to take legal action in China, you must first have registered your trademark there, which is not a straightforward task.

Work with Customs to identify imports of counterfeit goods.

Demonstrate authenticity on labels and packaging by means of technologies such as authentication seals, high-quality security printing, taggant markers that uniquely identify the product, encrypted micro-particles, hologram graphics and 'track and trace systems' that use codes linking the product to your database.

4 All risks are people risks

All risk stems from people. Machines can go wrong, due to faulty programming or poor maintenance, but these problems are usually predictable. Humans, by contrast, have an infinite capacity for failure. They make mistakes and do foolish things. They forget to do tasks. They sulk and plot. From alcohol addiction to disengagement, and from bullying to a skills shortage, there is never any shortage of problems for the HR department and the chief risk officer to worry about. Left unattended, HR risks turn into client defection, sabotage or law suits.

In the sections that follow we examine how to recognise and then manage the many risks that people bring as they walk through the company's doors each day.

Bad leadership

A lack of leadership will slow the business and then see it overtaken by competitors. But leadership requires more than decisiveness. At a time of rapid technological and cultural change, the requirements for a leader are changing.

An understanding of technology is essential, just as it was in the first and second waves of change, from agriculture to the printed press, the arrival of steam, followed by the age of cars and then microcomputers, leading to the internet and artificial intelligence.

The coming years will synthesise chemical, biological and communications technologies. But it is not just the hard technical skills that are essential; leaders need an understanding of the opportunities and threats this brings to specific industries.

Leadership also requires emotional intelligence. Command and control are less relevant in an era of decentralised activity. Employees are no longer corralled into a factory. They are dispersed, up poles, on the road and working from home, with no immediate management oversight. Hierarchies therefore have less to contribute. The leader must empower and motivate the workforce, and help them network with their colleagues. The richer the network and inter-communication, the stronger the business will be.

Leaders who are self-aware, self-critical and open to questioning will help their business to flourish, as long as they also have the ability to be brave, decisive and creative at the same time. It's a big job, but not dissimilar from the one that allowed military leaders to succeed – an understanding of the terrain, how to motivate the soldiers and how to innovate on the battlefield. From Nelson who broke the line at Trafalgar to Montgomery who misled the Nazis with fake airfields, the great military leaders have never been conventional.

Getting the key decisions wrong will lead to the organisation's failure. In 1938 the average lifespan of an S&P 500 company was 60 years; it has now slumped to a mere 15, such is the speed of change and the difficulty of foreseeing the future.

Mitigating Measures: leadership

Be prepared to consider the unthinkable. It may stop you being outmanoeuvred by the competition.

Don't assume you have the exclusive ownership of good ideas. Listen to what others are saying. Encourage debate and what-if scenarios.

Be alert to trends, and assess how they might impact on the business. Stay curious about what is going on in the world. Assume the future will be different from the present.

Focus on the few important matters, not the many unimportant ones.

Ensure the leadership team gets adequate and regular training. 360 degree reviews are a way of teaching painful truths but should be allied with coaching to support improvement.

The troublesome CEO

As with politicians, so it takes a certain type of personality to become a CEO. It requires self-belief, determination and a certain ruthlessness. As a result most CEOs are **sociopaths**, but that goes with the job and doesn't necessarily make them a risk, providing their tendencies are restrained by good governance.

Good CEOs are simply **suitable**. They have a vision, they create sensible change to achieve that, they're good with people and they have sufficient sense of detail to identify problems.

The four other types are the risky ones. There are the **spenders** (who in extreme cases end up as **swindlers**), the **sleepers** and the **startups**.

The **spenders** often take over a slightly ailing, mature business that is past its best but has lots of cash. They start buying companies or creating new ventures, seeking to find new markets. Sometimes they get lucky and the acquisitions turn out well. But often they don't. Acquisitions appeal to CEOs because they're more interesting than the dull business of growing organically. Acquisition adds instant revenue, and that is especially attractive if the CEO's remuneration is tied to sales or profit.

The extreme version of the spender is the **swindler**. They don't usually set out to commit fraud, but become a fraudster when seeking to hide losses. In doing so they create products from smoke and mirrors, and engage in accounting fraud, while for a time appearing to be highly successful. Ken Lay was one such example. He took Enron, a dull gas pipeline business, on a buying spree, purchasing utilities companies that made losses, and set up the biggest utilities trading business in the USA. Enron hid its losses in businesses that didn't appear on the balance sheet, and included revenues from the future outcome of new deals. Enron eventually went into bankruptcy, and its executives were indicted for conspiracy, fraud and insider trading.

A third type is the **startup guy**. They need not delay us long, because most founders are pushed out from their business when it grows to any size. A survey by *Harvard Business Review* of 212 American startups revealed that most founders had given up management control long before their companies went public. By the time the ventures were three years old, 50% of founders were no longer the CEO; in year four, only 40% were still in the corner office and fewer than 25% led their companies' initial public offerings (IPOs).

Founders are great at starting the business but are often unable to delegate because they're used to being in charge of everything, and don't want to let go. Often the roguish qualities required for a startup are ill suited to running a major business.

Occasionally former founders turn **screwy**. In 2014 and 2015 American Apparel spent $40m in lawsuits against claims of sexual harassment from female employees and counter-claims from its maverick founder Dov Charney. Charney took to waiting outside the main entrance to harass the new CEO Paula Schneider. From selling colourful USA-made T-shirts in his parents' basement in 1989, Charney had built a major apparel business which ran divisive ads showing under-age girls in provocative poses. He also reputedly held meetings wearing just a strategically placed sock, and walked through the office in his underwear. His hand-picked board of directors sacked him following allegations of misconduct, and the company went into Chapter 11 bankruptcy protection.

The **sleeper** CEO is a manager who as a No. 2 appeared statesman-like, but once in power is found to lack leadership qualities. Sleepers have no charisma and no sense of direction. Under their leadership, the business will take no risks, enter no new markets and gradually go into decline. The person who looked so thoughtful and wise when second in command is found to be overly safe when given control. The sleeper CEO fails to make decisions, and so staff stop trying new things, knowing they won't get the go-ahead. Good staff leave. Poisonous baronial rivalries and feuds break out and are allowed to continue.

As we have seen, many CEOs are **sociopaths**, people who care little about other people, and whose main role in life is to get what they want, by whatever means possible. It is hard to reach such seniority without being able to take difficult decisions about others, and a certain lack of empathy is possibly even desirable. The question, though, is about the scale of the pathology. Most CEOs can be restrained, if not totally reined in, by their board. But where their ego is rampant, they refuse to listen to advice. This usually happens where the CEO is also the chair and where the board is weak.

Mitigating Measures: the CEO

If the CEO has sociopathic tendencies, seek to restrain them with supportive but strong-willed C-level executives and good governance.

Be ready to terminate the sleeper CEO. While there are few major faults that can be attributed to this boss, it's the lack of activity that will bring the organisation down.

Identify whether the CEO is more suited to running a startup than a large business. Coaching may help, but sacking may be the easier answer. If the CEO is the former founder, assess the individual's skills in leadership, delegation and finance. If these are in short supply, the CEO may have to go.

Does the boss deserve it?

Executive pay has been controversial for many years. Some executives have been criticised for receiving large bonuses when their business achieved poor results. The media and pressure groups have been loudly disapproving. The average UK CEO earned £4.96m in 2014 or 183 times what the average full time worker earned. Shareholders have mostly accepted high pay as long as it was accompanied by good returns.

Tesco's finance director, Laurie McIlwee, received a £1m payoff, even though the retailer was embroiled in an accounting scandal. Following his departure, Tesco discovered that profits were overstated by £250m. This news wiped £2bn off the company's market value on the day it was announced. There was no suggestion that McIlwee played any role in the scandal, and his payout was purely as set out in the terms of his contract. But it is easy to see how onlookers would be irate.

According to Alexander Pepper, professor of management practice at the London School of Economics, studies have either failed to demonstrate a link between executive pay and corporate performance, or have detected a weak correlation at best.

A different problem occurs when pay is made variable, and set against targets which, for whatever reason, do not materialise. In such cases, senior executives may consider leaving the business, which in turn could be a setback for the business.

The remuneration package offered to senior management needs to be sufficiently attractive to draw high-calibre people, but it must also influence them to focus on the company's long-term goals.

Executive compensation is often based on performance measures such as share price or earnings per share. This can encourage directors to put their own interests before those of the organisation. Senior managers can manipulate these figures by the way revenue and costs are shown in the accounts, and by share buybacks.

The reward structure should discourage senior management from making decisions that improve short-term results but may harm the business in the longer term.

Even where rewards are tied to non-financial achievements, the results can be controversial. Fifty-nine per cent of shareholders voted against the £14m pay awarded to BP's CEO Bob Dudley in a year when the company lost a record $6.5bn and the share price fell 13%. The company argued that he'd met his targets for safety, cash flow and other measures, and the loss was largely due to the low price of oil and the Deepwater Horizon reparations. But the scale of the pay offended the shareholders in a year when the company had imposed a pay freeze on staff and cut 7,000 jobs. Ann Dowling, chair of the remuneration committee, said that Dudley's 20% pay rise 'appropriately recognised' the company's excellent performance.

Matteo Tonello, managing director of the Conference Board, suggests boards should design executive compensation in a way that reflects the company's goals. This might include cash or stock option plans that only come into force when specific long-term performance goals, not related to the stock price, are met.

However, plans should be kept simple. Quoted in the *Financial Times*, Colin Melvin, chief executive of Hermes EOS, which represents institutional investors worldwide, says:

> The way executives are paid has become overly complex, with too many cash and share-based awards, long and short-term targets and a profusion of measures of success. Many chief executives struggle to understand what is in their pay packages or how to hit their targets.

> **Mitigating Measures: executive pay**
>
> **Give shareholders binding votes, not merely advisory ones, on pay awards**.
>
> **Set clawback provisions in the contract that allow the business to recover bonuses** if financial results are restated downwards.
>
> **Adopt non-financial criteria**, like improvements to product quality, customer satisfaction or attracting higher quality institutional investors. Insurance companies, pension funds and investment banks invest in safer, more established businesses, and their investment indicates that the business is well managed.
>
> **Require top executives not to sell a percentage of the shares** they're awarded until a period of years has elapsed after they leave the business or until their retirement.
>
> **Grant restricted stock that has to be earned out over a period of employment**.

Succession planning

According to Ernst and Young, only 45% of high-performing businesses and 36% of the low performers agree that their organisation has addressed the question of succession planning. That is, they haven't got a plan for replacing people in critical roles.

Hence, says EY, there is a real lack of confidence about the next generation of leaders.

Only 54% of companies say they have a strong pipeline of future leadership talent. Companies are even less optimistic that they will find leaders with sufficiently diverse experience and backgrounds. Just 45% of the high-performing businesses and 36% of the low performers agree that their organisation has addressed these aspects of leadership development.

Without succession planning, the business may unexpectedly lose institutional knowledge, and be rushed into making errors. Even the best new hires can take 12 months to become fully effective, and are a drain on the business during that time. See Figure 4.1 for a structure.

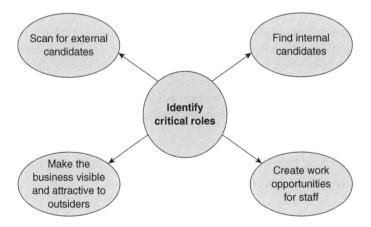

Figure 4.1 Finding suitable internal and external candidates is part of the challenge.

Mitigating Measures: succession planning

Identify critical roles, the ones that are crucial to meeting the organisation's objectives. Apart from senior management, they can include project management, IT, operations or technical roles.

Identify staff who could fulfil those roles in time.

Create opportunities for a range of potential candidates to gain wider experience, and give them scope to be judged on their work.

Scan for external candidates. The business should be aware of where external candidates might be found, for example in a competitor or comparison business.

Ensure the organisation is sufficiently visible and attractive to outside candidates. This is more important than ever in a world where public perception and corporate social responsibility is influential.

Treat succession planning as a continuous process. People are forever considering whether to move on. You never know when you need someone to step up to a major role.

Skills shortage

Some 5,000 UK jobs are left vacant because the automotive industry can't find enough designers and engineers. Similarly, garages can't get trained mechanics to service customers' cars. These skills shortages restrict company growth. Companies are having to hire temporary contractors and recruit from abroad, as well as taking on more apprentices. Meanwhile, costs are rising because qualified technicians are commanding an ever higher salary in a market suffering a shortage of expertise

In 2013, some 15% of employers reported that they had employees with skill gaps, equivalent to 1.4m staff or 5% of the workforce, according to the BBC. Rapid technological change and changing consumer preferences are the main cause, as well as increased demand. Many students prefer academic to technical courses, which adds to the problem.

However, only a minority of employers report skills gaps. Most workplaces report that they have a fully proficient workforce with no skills gaps, and a large proportion of employers feel they underutilise their workers' skills, with 4.3m people (16% of the workforce) overskilled or overqualified for their current roles.

The risk is that businesses hire people – the wrong people – in haste and live to regret it. Nor will higher unemployment solve the problem, for the unemployed may not have the right skills.

Mitigating Measures: skills shortages

Provide training courses across the organisation to upskill the workforce. IHG, the hotels group, has its IHG Academy which trains staff, and provides a pipeline of high-quality and motivated recruits. The academy involves hotel owners working with a local college to set up training programmes that include work experience.

Consider hiring from overseas.

Outsource some work. According to KPMG, 59% of IT outsourcing is due to a skills shortage, caused in part by job cuts.

Optimise the number of trainees and apprenticeships.

Offer older workers benefits to stay on, including flexible working.

Ensure that any labour shortage is not caused by the organisation's paying low wages. It may be that workers are available but unwilling to work at the rates on offer.

Check that your organisation's expectations of workers' skills are realistic. It may not be easy to find manual staff who can resolve technical problems, require minimal supervision and work fast.

Ensure jobs and conditions are attractive. It is hard to attract employees for jobs that are part time, temporary or casual, require undesirable shifts, are in locations lacking public transport or where the workers must provide their own tools.

Be prepared to hire underskilled staff and then spend time training them.

Provide golden handcuffs and improved working conditions to deter employees from being poached after having been trained.

Ask staff to work longer hours, as a short-term solution.

Loss of key employees

Having key staff leave unnecessarily leads to many problems:

- loss of knowledge
- the expense and uncertainty of recruitment
- the need to retrain new staff
- delays while new staff become effective.

No business can stop employees from leaving, nor would it want to. It's healthy to have a turnover of staff, especially if it brings fresh blood into the business. Nevertheless there are some staff that any organisation will want to retain, and their unexpected departure represents a risk.

This could be the loss of knowledge (for example, how a specific task is performed), or the risk that the employee will take your customers with her when she goes.

Mitigating Measures: the loss of key employees

Identify your key employees. Understand the outcome of the threat. What might happen to them? Is the risk that they might die – for example a company founder or a knowledgeable member of staff? Or will an employee take the company's engineering secrets to another business? Will a sales person go to work for a rival business and poach key accounts? If the financial director leaves, will anyone know how some obscure aspect of the company's finances work?

(continued)

(continued)

For cases involving the loss of knowledge, document the information. Ensure the individual communicates their special knowledge to others.

Where the risk relates to losing customers, build a relationship team. Ensure that the client has many touch points, from the receptionist who greets clients to the senior managers who engage with them.

Conduct exit interviews with key staff, to identify what has prompted them to leave.

Ensure that you have suitable structures for new entry-level employees such as apprentices and graduate trainees. Review the progress of these candidates to ensure that your schemes are contributing to the company's goals. If too many of these new staff members leave, you will have simply paid other businesses' training bills.

Create succession plans for senior and key staff.

The talent gap

Failing to *bring on* talent means the business will underperform. Senior positions will be occupied by employees whose sole claim to success is their longevity. Failure to *retain* talent means the best will leave. These individuals will see opportunities in competitor businesses, and will take knowledge with them.

The net result is a lack of capability and a shortage of people to fulfil key roles. One major UK organisation has a small specialist design department which is mission-critical. It consists of three long-serving men who are about to retire, their leader who is in hospital suffering from alcohol-induced liver failure and one female, a talented and experienced young graduate. The latter, who has long asked for promotion, has just been secretly flown by a competitor to the United States for an interview (such is the shortage of this skill). When she leaves, as she undoubtedly will, the UK business will face a small crisis.

Unfortunately the organisation she currently works for is preoccupied with cost reduction, which means reducing head count, and this makes it hard for managers to think about more positive or longer term HR needs.

Some companies are inevitably worried about training staff to the point where they go to work for another business. This issue can be overcome by ensuring that you are not relying on a single individual. Keeping remuneration consistent with industry standards is another way to keep talent.

Mitigating Measures: talent management

Identify talent. Create personal development plans.

Identify training needs and provide training to meet those needs.

Invest in leadership development programmes. Facilitate mentoring and coaching which allows for cross-departmental debate and enables key employees to gain an insight into higher-level thanking.

Ensure key employees are able to move between units and countries. Reduce the reluctance of departmental heads to allow the movement of able staff by making them aware of the opportunities that fresh thinking will bring. Encourage them to see the organisation's wider goals.

Ensure diversity in race, gender and sexuality; lack of diversity is associated with a failure to foresee the future and to gain insight into new consumers.

More than money. Recognise that engagement and loyalty is built on giving employees responsibility, autonomy and challenge. This is especially true of younger staff. For creative staff it might mean freedom from administrative or managerial work.

Use appraisals as an opportunity to identify and motivate key performers, rather than a box-ticking exercise.

Ensure knowledge is consistently identified and transferred. Make sure best practice is spread to other business units. Identify why safety, output or sales are higher in one plant than another, and ensure this knowledge is spread.

Document all mission-critical processes as a safeguard against experienced staff leaving unexpectedly.

Demographic change

In many developed nations, the population is both ageing and declining, as women give birth later and to fewer children. In Japan, more incontinence pads are sold than nappies. By 2047 developed countries will have more 60+ year-olds than children.

This poses serious risks to the business. Knowledgeable workers will retire, leading to a loss of skills and knowledge. And there may be a lack of candidates, with the result that the organisation may be unable to undertake some processes.

Long waiting lists have developed at some GP practices, for example, caused by insufficient doctors wanting to be general practitioners, and a growing number of women doctors who want part-time work.

Similarly, some engineering skills take years to acquire: staff cannot be simply taken off the street. Writing in the *Harvard Business Review*, Rainer Struck comments that training a German master electrician takes seven years.

Mitigating Measures: demographic change

Review the age profile of your employees. Ensure the data is sufficiently granular to identify the age profile of employees working on specific processes or types of job. Project that forward 5 or 10 years. An ageing workforce will demonstrate that you need to take action.

Encourage older staff to transfer their knowledge of company processes to younger ones.

Facilitate reverse mentoring where younger staff teach older ones new skills.

(continued)

(continued)

Consider hiring staff from abroad. The UK's National Health Service has long been recruiting nurses from Africa and Europe.

Help older staff to remain in work by making their work less onerous. This could mean shorter working hours, job sharing, reduced responsibilities or even physical aids such as chairs.

Provide fitness and health care programmes, targeted at retaining older staff. This can include vaccinations and return-to-work programmes following ill health.

Increase productivity by better training and additional automation, IT or robotics. This will reduce the number of staff needed.

Outsource specific roles that are harder to fill. Outsourcing companies will, however, face the same problem, so it isn't a panacea.

Be ready to transfer people from abundant departments to roles where people are in short supply.

Reduce employee churn by providing better conditions of work or by improving engagement.

Work with local or specialised schools or colleges. They can introduce new programmes of study that will support your recruitment needs, while you provide apprenticeship or work experience programmes. This will provide a more assured supply of staff.

Sponsor selected undergraduates, in return for future work.

Consider helping mothers to return to work as their children grow up. These individuals sometimes have outdated technical or IT skills, and may lack confidence; and they can be overlooked by recruiters.

Recruitment failures

Some 46% of new hires fail, according to Leadership IQ's Global Talent Management Survey. It's an indictment of the recruitment process. In the survey, during which the respondents hired 20,000 employees, 82% of managers reported that in hindsight their job interview process with these employees had provided subtle clues that the chosen candidate would fail. But during the job interview managers were too focused on other issues, too pressed for time, or lacked confidence in their interviewing abilities to heed the warning signs.

It's well known that interviews are flawed. They tend to favour the well spoken and the extroverts. Interviewers meanwhile have preconceptions, talk too much and some even fail to ask questions. But the real problem is that interviews and the whole recruitment process are about talking, whereas the job is about doing.

One candidate was appointed to a general management, C-level job. He'd done similar work at a smaller organisation in the same industry, and was personable and intelligent. A month after his appointment a colleague at his former employer said, 'Round here, people don't think he achieved very much', and 12 months later this had become apparent. The executive constantly deferred decisions, and wanted to be liked. The organisation became paralysed: 21 months later they fired him.

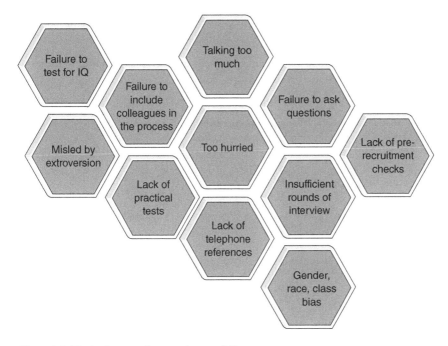

Figure 4.2 Typical causes for recruitment failure.

A meta analysis by Frank Schmidt and John Hunter on interview techniques that produced successful employees showed that the best predictor of success is the work sample. It involves candidates doing a piece of work that reflects the actual job, to see how well they do it.

For many jobs this is a successful technique. But some roles (especially senior ones) can't easily be tested in this way. Leadership and decisiveness are hard to assess.

IQ tests also work quite well, because intelligent people perform better than the less able. However, these tests disadvantage women and ethnic minorities. Actual outcomes are higher for these groups than the tests predict.

Mitigating Measures: better recruitment

Use standardised lists of questions. They help to compare candidates, ensure that the right questions are asked and allow the interviewer to compare answers with those of previous candidates for similar jobs.

Ask competency-based questions that demonstrate what the candidate has done to solve certain problems. These take the following form: 'Describe a situation where you had to get others to work together' or 'Have you ever failed to complete a project on time, despite planning to do so?'

(continued)

(continued)

Ask behavioural questions ('Tell me about a time when you had to defuse a disagreement . . .'). They examine past behaviour, and assess whether a candidate has relevant experience.

Ask situational questions. These ask the interviewee to imagine a hypothetical problem in the future ('What would you do if you . . . ?').

Set candidates to complete work samples, to see how well they carry out their job.

Seek opinions from bosses or colleagues in the candidate's current or most recent workplace. Do this by phone, where people are less guarded. Use open-ended questions, forcing the other person to respond with a sentence, rather than yes or no. Essential questions are:

- What were they like as an employee?
- How did they get on with work colleagues?
- Did they have any weaknesses?
- Is there anything else I need to know about them?
- Would you hire them again?

Get co-workers to interview the candidates. They know what work needs to be done. They will also have a better insight into whether the candidate will fit the organisation's values and culture.

Conduct more than one round of interviews, the first for competency and the second for values. At one selection process the candidate seemed excellent. By the second interview, apparently more relaxed, he started passing remarks about the legs and body of one of the interviewers from the first interview.

Pre-recruitment and pre-employment checks. Pre-recruitment checks should verify that the candidate:

- is who they say they are;
- has the qualifications they claim;
- has not concealed any information such as convictions or dismissals;
- is legally permitted to take up employment;
- has an employment history as stated on their CV.

Request original copies of qualifications. But recognise that many people will not have them.

Do an online search and check their profile on social media. This may tell you whether their behaviour at interview is consistent with their real personality.

Check contractors' recruitment policies. If their staff are to be on your premises, or working for you, you need to ensure the contractors' recruitment policy is robust.

Audit the recruitment policies of overseas contractors, such as outsourcing firms.

The disengaged workforce

According to Gallup two out of three US employees (68%) are either not engaged or are actively disengaged. A demotivated workforce will perform badly, ultimately leading to customer defection, bad publicity and lower sales.

Low engagement can result from poor communication, poor remuneration, bad terms and conditions, failure to listen, weak management, a sense of injustice or a belief that management doesn't care about staff.

Mitigating Measures: building engagement

Identify employee attitudes through surveys, possibly biennial. These must be sufficiently granular as to identify specific problem departments.

Benchmark the results against similar businesses in the industry.

Take steps to rectify the problems identified in the survey. This could involve the following:

- training staff adequately, so they know more about the business,
- re-designing jobs to make them more rewarding,
- removing barriers to satisfaction,
- soliciting feedback, and acting on contributions,
- fostering teamwork,
- discouraging bullying,
- reducing bureaucracy and hierarchy.

Repeat the survey to monitor progress.

No-show employees

Hospitals, customer services, emergency services and manufacturing all have high absentee rates of between 6 and 11%, according to Circadian, a workforce scheduling business. It reckons that absenteeism costs a company with 500 shift workers an extra $1.3m a year over the costs of a day-work business.

High levels of absenteeism are a drain on the business. They lead to inefficiency and low output, cause firefighting as managers try to keep the operation moving, and may be a sign of low morale or poor working conditions. If allowed to continue, absenteeism can become an accepted part of work life, especially in organisations with large numbers of clerical staff.

Arriving late, leaving early and taking long lunch breaks are all examples of absenteeism. Employees mostly cite sickness as the reason for unscheduled absences. But family issues, personal needs, stress and a feeling of entitlement can also be causes. Absenteeism is greatest where staff see themselves as cogs in a wheel and undervalued. Equally, an increasingly elderly population and a decline in government support services will see more burdens being placed on the workforce and therefore more absenteeism.

A study by West Chester University of Pennsylvania found that those with high rates of unscheduled absences had different behaviours than those with moderate absenteeism. This included dissatisfaction with their job, health problems, use of alcohol and drugs, and a 'liberal' attitude towards time off.

Mitigating Measures: cutting absenteeism

Measure the extent of absenteeism. Compare this with the industry average. Are you better or worse?

Set a standard for absenteeism. This might be: arriving 30 minutes late and/or non-attendance twice in five weeks.

Create a policy for absenteeism. This should include disciplinary action. Ensure everyone knows what the procedure and penalties for absenteeism are.

Require each manager to conduct return-to-work interviews. The interview should try to ascertain the reasons for absence. If the employee has simply 'pulled a sickie', the interview won't reveal anything. But knowing that they will be interviewed will reduce the frequency of absenteeism.

Focus on those with high rates of absenteeism. If left unattended, their behaviour could cause more widespread problems.

Identify and weed out new recruits with bad attendance records.

Ensure attendance records are reviewed at appraisals.

Award those who have a high attendance record.

Allow employees a degree of flexibility, including choosing and swapping shifts. This will help to reduce unexpected absences, and lets people deal with life's problems.

Give staff the option of taking unpaid leave. This avoids them having to unnecessarily tell lies.

Carry out staff surveys, to see whether management style or pay and conditions are a problem. See whether you need to improve the workplace. Do managers need better interpersonal skills?

Consider introducing wellness programmes, such as advice on healthy eating and physical fitness, counselling, flu jabs and stress workshops.

Underperformance

Underperforming employees tend to be absent more often. This reduces the department's productivity and increases stress among their peers. They generate less revenue than more motivated colleagues. Their poor attitude causes customers to leave; they make mistakes that cost money and they waste management time. They are more likely to steal, and they create an 'us and them' attitude in their work group.

Poor performers are often long-standing employees who are disengaged from the business. They feel it owes them a living, and they want to control the pace of work. Sometimes they are incompetent, either because they're unintelligent or because they lack skills or training.

They may have a grudge against the world. They may have seen management come and go, and promises not kept. They may be disillusioned about their work and have a negative mental attitude.

Managers are notorious for not dealing with underperforming staff, because they don't want to face the emotion and anger that performance management brings.

Some roles, such as sales, allow you to calculate the £ or $ difference between good and bad performers. But for many roles, even customer-focused ones, poor performance manifests itself as clock-watching, sullenness and low productivity. It can be hard to quantify.

Underperformers won't seek another job, because they aren't motivated by work. So unless you deal with the individual, they will be with you forever.

Mitigating Measures: improving underperformance

Identify the causes of poor performance. If it's a problem of attitude, how can that be overcome? If it's a training issue or the person is unsuited to the work, you will need to find other solutions.

Give clear feedback. The employee deserves to know what is expected of them.

Seek to understand their point of view and remove problems. If management has ignored them for years, it won't be surprising if they feel motivated.

Start by coaching the employee to improve their performance.

Praise improvements they make.

For the employee whose length of service gives them employment protection, begin a performance management process. This involves setting standards by which the employee will be regularly measured. In many cases they will improve.

Dismiss the employee if, given sufficient time, they fail to reach the required standard.

Consider paying them to go, by means of a settlement agreement which will prevent them from bringing a claim. This can be done with a 'protected' or 'without prejudice' conversation, the alternative being a protracted performance management process.

If the employee is a probationer, consider firing them without delay to avoid the time and effort required to improve them.

Train managers to deal with underperformance. Institute a zero-tolerance policy of accepting sub-standard work.

Toxic employees

Toxic employees have a destructive effect on the business and those around them. They bully other staff, demotivate colleagues and create an 'us and them' atmosphere in which they magnify grievances against the business and discourage effort. According to Kellogg School professor Brenda Ellington Booth, they 'suck up and crap down'. Sometimes known as 'bad apples', they cause others in their group to leave.

Dylan Minor, another Kellogg School professor, talks of rising 'toxic density'. That is, one toxic employee will infect others. There is a 47% increased likelihood that a worker who experiences toxicity will themselves become toxic. In other words, two bad employees will cause one additional person to go sour.

Mitigating Measures: prior to hiring

Avoid hiring toxic employees in the first place, by getting recruitment right. Check references on the phone. Interview for civility: ask the candidate how they might respond to a specific scenario. Watch out for negative comments the candidate makes about former colleagues or bosses. See if the candidate takes responsibility for past problems or failures. How does the candidate respond to lower-ranking staff in your organisation, such as a receptionist?

Ask other members of staff to interview the candidate. They may see a different side to that person.

Have a long probationary period for all new hires. In some cases, employees start as a contractor.

Mitigating Measures: for existing toxic employees

Isolate. You can isolate the toxic employee, by putting them in a role where they don't have the opportunity to cause damage. This is not an ideal solution: management is simply shirking its responsibilities.

Institute performance management. This is never easy because their work is rarely the worst of all employees. And they stay within the bounds of acceptable behaviour, not least because they are often savvy people.

Negotiate a settlement or severance agreement with the individual. XpertHR found that most employers have, at some time in the past year, used settlement agreements to get rid of employees. A small minority of employers make use of them on a routine basis. They're generally used when there has been a breakdown in professional relationships between staff.

Stress and mental illness

Stress accounts for 35% of all work-related cases of ill health and 43% of all working days lost due to ill health, according to the UK's Health and Safety Executive (HSE).

It is more prevalent in public service industries, such as education, health, social care, public administration and defence. The larger the business, the more stress that gets reported.

The main factors cited by respondents as causing work-related stress, depression or anxiety were workload pressures, including tight deadlines, too much responsibility and a lack of managerial support.

But a survey by Mind suggested that stress is underreported. Of those who said they'd taken time off sick with stress, only 5% admitted to their employer they were too stressed to work. The remaining 95% cited another reason for their absence, such as an upset stomach or a headache.

In addition to the causes listed by HSE, Mind added frustration with poor management, threat of redundancy and unrealistic targets.

Stress-related staff absences have the same effect as we've seen earlier. The remaining staff suffer an increased workload and come under even more pressure. Jobs don't get done and customers become frustrated.

Mitigating Measures: beating stress

Identify levels of stress from staff surveys. Seek to understand the causes of stress.

Ensure employees are supported, and avoid excessive workloads.

Train staff in setting priorities, stress management and the advantages of talking through problems. Advise staff on the benefits of exercise, eating healthy foods and getting enough sleep.

Train managers to be aware of stressed subordinates and to discuss issues with them.

Avoid a culture of bullying. Train managers in good management techniques and emotional intelligence.

Seek to give employees more control over their work. This will reduce stress levels.

The employee with an addiction

We think of addicts as being homeless or rough sleepers, but the truth is that addiction is found more often in high flyers, people with high IQ and business leaders.

Quoted in *Forbes* magazine, David Linden, a neuroscience professor at Johns Hopkins School of Medicine, suggests that the traits that make a good CEO – risk-taking, a strong drive for success, obsession, dedication and novelty-seeking – are precisely what make an addict.

While many such employees function perfectly well, their addiction carries risks for the organisation. These include accidents and injuries, absenteeism, theft and faulty decision making, as well as management time spent on disciplinary processes.

Family business members are prone to addiction, especially the second or third generation who have to live up to the high standards set by their parents or grandparents. Regeneration Partners found that 54% of its clients faced a problem of addiction among owners or managers.

Internal communication issues in family businesses could be a sign of an addiction problem at management level, according to Regeneration's chief executive, James Hutcheson, who said that addiction often played a part in the breakdown of communication in family businesses. 'Addictions dramatically magnify the risk of failure. But, like a number of issues facing family businesses, addiction can be treated,' he added. The first step to addressing the problem is to recognise it.

Mitigating Measures: conquering addiction

Recognise the symptoms. The addict may show anxiety or jumpiness; shakiness or trembling; sweating, nausea and vomiting, insomnia, depression, irritability, fatigue or loss of appetite and headaches; secretive activities; unexplained injuries or accidents and being overactive or underactive, depending on the drug.

Seek professional help. This may start with the general practitioner or specialised addiction expert.

Take expert advice before taking disciplinary measures. Be sure of your organisation's legal rights.

Beating the bullies

Workplace bullying costs British businesses £18bn a year according to the Advisory, Conciliation and Arbitration Service (ACAS). This is through bullying-related absences, staff turnover and lost productivity.

Six out of 10 employees have either suffered or witnessed bullying, says employment law firm Slater and Gordon. And in a survey by the CIPD (Chartered Institute of Personnel and Development), 91% of employees feel their employer doesn't deal adequately with bullying.

Bullying is mostly peer-to-peer (employee-to-employee) or manager-to-subordinate. Like any forms of aggression towards others, bullying can badly affect the business, infecting it with harmful values and driving out good employees. It is often subtle, with the bully contending that they were merely 'having a bit of fun', engaging in harmless banter or claiming that the victim 'can't take a joke'.

These days bullying doesn't even have to be verbal or within the workforce. A locksmith was ordered to pay a customer £7,500 for making homophobic gestures towards a customer. Southend County Court found that Peter Edwards had blown sarcastic kisses towards the victim and made more than 20 homophobic gestures over a period of several months while the victim was seeking a refund. The gestures ranged from winking to 'vile and vulgar gesturing'. The court decided this had caused distress and was discriminatory, and awarded 'Tim' (his real name was kept secret) compensation under the UK's Equality Act.

Poorly trained managers may lack interpersonal skills, and this can lead to accusations of bullying. If they are promoted because of their technical skills, or even length of service, they may lack leadership know-how.

And even the most sensitive manager can be accused of bullying if they set standards of work for an employee who has never experienced performance management, and who therefore feels victimised.

Mitigating Measures: stopping the bullies

Create and publicise an anti-bullying policy and associated procedures.

Train staff to be aware of bullying. Include diversity and respect for others as part of the training programme.

Foster a work culture that is participative and supportive, not autocratic.

Seek detailed information about any incident before taking action. Be aware that what can seem like bullying to you may not be regarded as such by the victim, and vice versa.

Avoid setting an unduly competitive environment which can reduce collaboration and cause conflict.

Train managers in how to manage poor performance.

Prevent substantial imbalances of power which can lead to bullying.

It's hard to be a woman

A Credit Suisse study of 3,000 large companies found that where more than 15% of senior management were women, the business generated profits that were 50% higher than those reported by companies with fewer than one in 10 women in the top team. Stock market valuations, share price performance and dividend payouts were also higher.

Unconscious bias is frequently the problem. Sometimes managers don't necessarily recognise their own thought processes. At other times there may be a conscious bias against women, with outspoken criticisms of their work style. As we saw with bullying, sexist comments and banter may be claimed as merely 'having a joke', but can be used as a weapon against female members of staff. The investment banks have had a particularly poor track record in the past, often facing unfair dismissal tribunals.

The *Financial Times* undertook a study which showed that in London, despite a near 50–50 gender balance in overall staff numbers, just 19% of senior roles across the top City employers are held by women. One woman said: 'The City is peppered with men who have fundamentally sexist attitudes. It's a pretty bleak place for a senior woman.'

This is exacerbated by women waiting until they are completely ready for a promotion, while men will seek advancement even when they lack sufficient experience. Women also leave work to have children, miss out on several years' promotion and find it hard to get back to where they were. In addition, a culture of late-night or weekend working and after-work drinking can also exclude women who have greater child care responsibilities.

Mitigating Measures: gender issues

Measure the percentage of women at different levels in the business. Compare your business against the industry.

Create a mentoring programme for high-potential women. BAE Systems launched such a programme, with a cohort of 24 women, followed in the next year with a second cohort. Seventy per cent of the first cohort were either promoted or moved roles.

Use search firms that have a record of inclusive recruitment processes and that source from a wide pool of applicants.

Instigate a culture change if necessary. This may require training programmes. Senior management must set an example. Publicise the work of female members of staff. It is important to have women in high-profile roles to act as pathfinders and role models for more junior women. Encourage them to give talks to junior females.

Foster a work experience that discourages unnecessary evening work and understands that after-work drinking sessions may exclude women.

Facilitate flexible and part-time working arrangements. Providing nurseries will also help.

A wider pool

Recruiting and promoting staff from a limited pool of candidates will lead to groupthink (bad decisions brought about by conformity) and a loss of cross-fertilisation. It cuts the business off from everyday life, and restricts its future. A wider range of backgrounds, including race and LGBT, will lead to more critical thinking and fresh perspectives.

The lack of women in senior positions is well known. A survey by Diversityinc of 1.7m employees in 28 countries found that although women made up 41% of the global workforce, only 19% of executives are women. Women approach problems and see solutions differently from men, and this is a valuable resource for it widens the range of business possibilities.

This lack of diversity is not only prevalent among mature industries: high-tech businesses are renowned for their inability to recruit and promote women.

Mitigating Measures: diversity

Demonstrate a willingness to consider candidates from a range of backgrounds.

Seek talent from emerging markets and from minorities. In a flatter, globalising world, it will help your organisation stay relevant to new consumers.

Accept that new employees may have different values and attitudes, and seek to accommodate them. While it may be difficult in the short term, it will benefit the business in the longer term. A case in point is the UK police. At the time of writing, four UK police forces didn't have a single black officer.

Adopt mentoring and coaching programmes for minorities and other groups.

Choose recruitment agencies that are seen to attract a wide range of candidates.

Being a discriminating employer

According to the charity Macmillan Cancer Support, almost half of people who were in work when diagnosed with cancer say their employer did not discuss sick pay entitlement, flexible working or workplace adjustments. This was mostly due to ignorance rather than discrimination, the charity said. Employers have an obligation to discuss changes with sufferers because they are covered by equality legislation.

It's one example of the scope of legislation that can catch employers by surprise, and lead to penalties and bad publicity. There are many kinds of discrimination. Stress is a common risk for employers these days. An employer can be legally at fault if they don't take action to support an employee who has shown signs of stress.

Even when an organisation is avowedly anti-discrimination, employees have a tendency to misbehave. Sgt. David Bonenberger of the St. Louis, Missouri police force won a case against the city, saying he was passed over for promotion because he was white. His suit alleged that the director Lt. Michael Muxo told him not to apply for a job because it was going to a black woman under the orders of Lt. Col. Reggie Harris, who was also black.

Muxo and Harris were found to have conspired to commit discrimination, and a jury awarded Bonenberger $800,000 damages against all the defendants. US District Judge Catherine Perry ordered Muxo and Harris to undergo at least one three-hour session of anti-discrimination training every year for three years.

And if employees are hard to control, it is more difficult still to know what spokespeople might say. When world champion boxer Manny Pacquiao made anti-gay comments during a TV interview in the Philippines, Nike dissolved its relationship with him the following day, calling his comments 'abhorrent'. *Fortune* magazine said it was a sensible move for Nike, calling it 'an aspirational and inclusive brand that doesn't want to be pulled down into the mud of discrimination'.

Retaliation has become a common complaint, whereby an employee claims that the employer took retribution after they had taken some lawful action. In the USA there are more retaliation claims lodged with the Equal Opportunities Commission than about discrimination by race or gender (38%, 34% and 31% respectively). This may be because retaliation cases are easier for the employee to win, and they produce higher damages.

Activities against which the company might be seen to retaliate are where the employee has:

- filed a claim against the employer;
- blown the whistle;
- made a complaint to management;
- protested against discrimination;
- expressed support for co-workers who have complained about harassment.

In any case of alleged discrimination, senior managers may find themselves accused of supporting discrimination, and could be personally liable despite being merely an officer of the business. For that reason, as well as the need to provide a decent and lawful workplace, discrimination must be carefully managed as a risk.

Mitigating Measures: overcoming discrimination

Define discrimination clearly. It should include all behaviour that creates an intimidating or offensive work environment.

Provide company-wide training about discrimination.

Set the grievance procedure in writing, and ensure all employees have access to it, including in the employee handbook.

Once an allegation has been received, act promptly to resolve the issue. Failure to act leaves the organisation open to litigation.

Follow written procedures scrupulously.

Investigate all claims thoroughly. Interview all concerned, in the presence of a trusted witness. Take statements. Be cautious about making a judgement where it is one person's word against another.

Consult an expert where there are complexities, including when a false claim has been brought.

Document your findings in writing, and send them to all parties.

Buy insurance. You can protect directors and managers against claims of discrimination on grounds of race, sex, religious and disability discrimination.

Step away from the biscuits: obesity and health risks

The US Department of Labor estimated the overall annual cost of poor health in the workplace at \$1.8tn. Nearly 50% of Americans have one or more chronic health conditions.

This includes overweight employees who reduce profits due to lower productivity and increased time off.

Compared with normal-weight individuals, obese workers are estimated to cost US employers an additional $11.7bn per year as a result of increased absenteeism and presenteeism (being at your place of work for longer than is needed, often due to job insecurity). On the basis of the costs of absenteeism and medical expenditures, obese men in the USA cost their business $322 to $6,087 a year depending on the scale of their obesity. The figures for women range from $797 to $6,694.

- 'High health risk' employees are 18% less productive, which amounts to 7 hours per week or 2 months per year in lost productivity.
- Smokers lose their employer 33 hours of work a year according to the UK's National Institute for Health and Care Excellence (NICE).
- Mental health problems cost employers in the UK £30bn a year through lost production, recruitment and absence, says ACAS, the UK's arbitration and conciliation service.

Helping employees to improve their health pays off. US employers have seen their absenteeism costs fall by $2.73 for every dollar spent on wellness programmes.

Programmes can start small. This will allow the business to test the response to health improvement, and offer a foretaste of how a more comprehensive plan might work. Some activities, such as providing fresh fruit, can demonstrate that the business treats employee health as important.

Mitigating Measures: employee health

Encourage employees to take more exercise. Provide secure, covered bike parking. Offer shower facilities and locker rooms for employees. Introduce a lunch time walking club and incentivise employees to participate. Encourage employees to use the stairs. Offer discounts on membership of a local gym.

Offer seminars on healthy living. These could be lunch or break time events on cooking healthy meals or how to manage stress. Hold lunch time classes in tai chi, yoga or aerobics, and incentivise employees to attend.

Provide an on-site doctor or nurse. This will reduce time away from work for doctor's appointments, especially for routine care.

Incentivise staff to be more healthy. Help overweight employees to cut their flab by rewarding them for achieving certain targets, such as a good body mass index, blood pressure or blood sugar level.

Provide healthy food. Audit your cafeteria's food. Stock vending machines with fruit, nuts or dried fruit.

Introduce online, phone or face-to-face counselling. Such programmes can give employees longer-term help to lose weight, stop smoking or manage stress. BAE's Employee Assistance Programme has over 11,000 interactions with employees a year.

Offer a flu vaccination programme during the winter. This will reduce the amount of sickness. Alternatively, reimburse employees for their vaccination fees.

Pandemic threat

Ebola, H1N1 and Zika are all viruses that have threatened at one time to become pandemics. AIDS meanwhile will have killed 90–100 million people in Africa by 2025, according to the United Nations.

A pandemic is a widespread infectious disease that spreads quickly among humans. It sometimes originates in animals and crosses to humans. Virulent new strains can have a major impact because our autoimmune system isn't prepared for it.

Pandemics are a risk that is all but forgotten until the news media report about a sudden flu bug that has broken out in some distant land and is threatening the country. At that point managers start to consider the implications of having a quarter of their staff off sick or worse.

The effects of a pandemic could be catastrophic. The government may suspend public transport and close schools. Staff may not be able to get to work, or may have to care for their children. Between 30% and 50% of staff might not turn up. Many would be very ill and some would die. Faced with a loss of staff, suppliers might be unable to deliver items that the business needs. As the recession grows the demand for your products might dwindle.

A pandemic may last 7–10 months and come in successive waves. This is unlike most other crises that are short lived. The business must be able to survive this threat for months.

Mitigating Measures: in the event of a pandemic

Monitor the threat on TV, radio and the internet, and follow advice from health professionals and the government. Learn how the virus is spread, whether by droplet infection and/or by touching.

Communicate well with staff, customers and suppliers. This will reassure them.

Operations. Consider scaling down operations or restricting the products or services you provide. Decide which services you would offer, and to whom. At some point, you might even close the business if you can't get staff or supplies. Decide in advance what would trigger that decision. What key performance indicators (KPIs) would you set?

Suppliers. Identify the impact of a loss of a major supplier. Could you get supplies elsewhere? Stockpile vital resources. Help key suppliers to cope.

Contracts. Review your contracts. Revise them if necessary to reduce your liability and increase those of your partners.

Finances. Protect your cash. Cut investment. Instigate tighter credit control, but identify whether you will need to cut prices or offer longer credit terms in order to survive. Seek payment in advance if necessary. Ensure your borrowing is not subject to revision. Be aware that banks will seek to reduce overdraft limits and recall loans.

Customers. Reduce face-to-face customer contact (and the risk of infection) by increasing email and phone support and service.

Staff. Take action as follows:

- Cope with staff absences by training existing staff to do other jobs. Re-hire retired staff. Share staff with other organisations. Consider who could be promoted. Help staff to work from home.
- Provide information on how to stay well. Tell staff to stay home if they're sick. Introduce more stringent hygiene and infection control, depending on government advice, such as

(continued)

(continued)

handwashing, paper towels and no-touch waste bins. Put up posters and provide training on how to avoid cross-infection, including techniques for handwashing and how to manage coughs and sneezes.

- Minimise cross-infection by ensuring staff stay at least one metre or more apart and avoid face-to-face meetings and socialising. Use barriers or screens where face-to-face contact with customers is essential.
- Maintain an up-to-date contact list of all staff members and their next of kin.
- Make recommendations for staff travelling to or from affected areas.
- Extend working hours so that fewer staff arrive and depart together.
- Provide more car parking if public transport is reduced.
- Allow more flexible leave options for staff who are ill or have ill family members, or who have been in contact with sick people.

Redundancy: the risks

Making employees redundant is fraught, even for those who have a lot of experience in this area. Employees become anxious when they realise they might lose their job. Work quality declines, productivity falls and customer service plummets. Worse, good employees may leave, while others, feeling let down or mistreated, may resort to theft, fraud or sabotage. Trade unions may plan industrial action.

At the moment of redundancies, other risks come into play. Employees may sue the business, or the government may take legal action. Dave Forsey, the chief executive of Sports Direct, the UK's biggest sports retailer, was charged with failing to notify authorities of plans to lay off staff. He also faced criminal charges over his alleged failure to give employees adequate notice that they were losing their jobs. If found guilty, Forsey could be fined only a modest £5,000, but he could be banned from holding directorships for 15 years.

Mitigating Measures: managing redundancies

Take legal advice and follow the required procedures when announcing redundancies. The selection pool must be identified, the criteria for redundancy must be objective, and due consultation must be carried out. Suitable alternative employment must be considered. Steps must be documented in writing. The right payments must be made.

Consider the alternatives to redundancies such as short-time working, temporary lay-offs, natural wastage, unpaid leave and terminating temporary and contract workers.

Avoid a long period of uncertainty. While the law may require lengthy consultation, management should avoid unnecessarily long periods.

Cut deep enough so that no second round of redundancies will be needed. The survivors should feel they are not at risk, enabling them to concentrate on their work.

Seek to part with ex-employees on good terms. They will remain in the local area, and will affect people's opinions of the business. Treat those being made redundant with respect: redundancies are not their fault.

After the redundancies have been made, motivate remaining staff. Present the future as a fresh start.

The workforce revolt

The number of working days lost from industrial action has fallen substantially across the West. In the UK it has dropped from 7.2m days lost annually in the 1980s to 650,000 in the 2010–2014 period. In Italy, days not worked fell from 160 per 1,000 workers in the 1990s to just 80 in the 2000s. In Australia, it reduced from around 50 per 1,000 workers in the 1980s to 2 in 2014.

This has been due to the decline in manufacturing in the West, the globalisation of business and the outsourcing and offshoring of jobs, with a resultant decline in large unionised workforces.

Two-third of strikes now last only one or two days, so these days the risk of strikes is less severe than in the past. But disputes are not uncommon in public administration, public transport and education, with pay usually being the principal cause of labour unrest.

Sometimes employees take action short of a strike, including a 'go slow' or 'work to rule'. This can be more difficult for the employer because the behaviour of staff may be less clear cut and difficult to identify with any clarity. It might involve taking time to read emails, and refusing to accept overtime or fill in for absent staff.

In education, staff may refuse to set examinations, mark students' papers or deliver marks on time, all of which are disruptive. Legally an employee is not allowed to choose which parts of their contract they are willing to undertake. Hence in the latter cases the employer may be legally allowed to withhold payment since the employee is refusing to perform their contracted duties.

Since industrial action can have a major impact on any large employer, it is wise to have contingency plans in place – and it is even more sensible to reduce the likelihood of such disputes happening.

Mitigating Measures: prior to a strike

Assess the probability and severity of strike action either in your own workforce or in the supply chain. Readiness ensures a confident and thorough response, which can be effective in managing the risk of a strike, or dealing with one if it takes place.

Prepare a contingency plan. This should include communications, security, law enforcement, picket line management, workforce deployment, continuity of operations and management training.

Maintain open, regular and positive communications with the workforce. Employees need to feel the business has their best interests at heart, and should be kept informed, especially about difficult decisions that must be made. Messages must be consistent. If a strike is threatened, emphasise that it will affect the company's reputation and threaten its survival. Remind employees that the company has contingency plans, which mean strike action will not be effective as a threat or bargaining tool.

Take legal advice on any steps you propose to take to ensure you stay within the law. Ensure that any action does not inflame the situation, nor harm long-term relationships.

Encourage those who are opposed to industrial action to vote against it, rather than allow it to go ahead by not participating in the vote.

Be ready to challenge the validity of the ballot if the vote is in favour of industrial action.

Mitigating Measures: if a strike takes place

Seek to maintain operations during the dispute. If output continues, it will have a negative effect on the morale of a striking labour force and encourage them to negotiate. The reverse is also true: a workforce will be emboldened if the business is paralysed.

Consider hiring new workers directly on fixed-term contracts, assuming this is legal in your jurisdiction. This is different from hiring temporary staff to do the work of striking employees which is usually not lawful.

Hire a contractor to undertake work during industrial action, by contracting out the supply of services. The contractor becomes responsible for the work.

Second employees from other parts of the business. Managers can also be used to maintain essential services.

Consider preparing buffer stocks of finished goods, or buying stocks from an overseas competitor.

Training weaknesses

If employees lack important competencies, the organisation will weaken and possibly fail. Hence the need for training, and it follows that training is vital to mitigate risk. But much training is of doubtful value, not because of the calibre of trainers, who are usually excellent at their job, but because of the ways that training is provided. The main problems are as follows:

1   *Training is unrelated to the job.* The employee may not be able to implement what they have learnt. If there is no connection between the training and the job, it will provide no benefit to the business or the employee.
2   *Once the training is complete, there is little follow up.* The information learnt in a course is quickly lost if the employee is not helped to practise it. This is why the value of much training quickly fades.
3   *Cheap e-learning is often seen as a sufficient means of training.* But it frequently fails to provide the individual with the opportunity to practise and get feedback.

Mitigating Measures: effective training

Take time to analyse who needs to be trained, and on what subjects. Don't make assumptions about what they need to be trained in, otherwise much of the training budget will be wasted. Some universities train academics how to write successful grant applications: it has immediate and practical advantages.

Avoid treating employees as numbers. While the corporation may need to confirm it has trained everyone in compliance or diversity, it won't get much value out of it if it isn't personalised.

Be aware of the limitations of off-the-shelf training. It is unlikely to provide sufficient personalisation for your organisation.

Evaluate how well employees have learnt. This means more than a questionnaire asking delegates if they liked the training. There is a weak correlation between reaction to training and actual learning. Sometimes the training is lively and fun, but the information isn't of value back at the workplace. Measure the outcomes in terms of changed behaviour in the medium term.

Ensure that the employee is able to apply their learning when they go back to their job.

Training should provide interaction between trainer and the employee. The trainer must be able to identify where knowledge gaps exist or where attitudes need changing.

Ensure that corporate values support the training programmes. If management is seen not to value either training or the subject matter, for example, health and safety, the programme will lack credibility.

Little and often is better than too much information in a short period of time. Cramming too many facts and figures into a short session is wasted effort. The learner will quickly forget them. Teach people instead how to access the information from databases, manuals or websites.

Recognise that learning takes many forms. Group learning, mentoring and coaching others are powerful training tools.

Whistleblowing

Every organisation has a tendency towards pack behaviour. The group comes together for mutual protection, and has shared aims; those with contrary views are easily ostracised and seen as outsiders or disloyal. This can prevent staff from discussing the organisation's weaknesses and can lead to acceptance of unethical behaviour. Sometimes the whistle-blower is sacked, a case of blaming the messenger.

Three directors of Compass Group, a FTSE 100 firm, had to appear in court to answer fraud charges relating to the dismissal of a whistleblower. Karim Pabani, former Finance Director of a subsidiary in Kazakhstan, brought the private case alleging the company directors had conspired over his sacking after he had exposed fraud in the company's business.

Mitigating Measures: whistleblowers

Ensure that both dissent and whistleblowing are acceptable. Adam Waytz, an assistant professor of management and organizations at the Kellogg School of Management, says: 'Whistle-blowing is often seen as the most disloyal thing an employee can do. But it can be reframed [by leaders] as an act of larger loyalty – loyalty to the community in which you operate, loyalty to society, and ultimately loyalty to the long-term success of your company.'

Make the whistleblowing channel visible. Ensure people know how to safely blow the whistle. Staff must be able to communicate their concerns easily.

Employees with a grudge

In recent years there has been a rise in the number of employees who have unexpectedly become killers. In most cases there was nothing to indicate that they would soon turn to murder. The killers have included white supremacists, Muslim extremists and employees with a grudge.

It is difficult to identify such killers in advance. They rarely give any clues of their intentions, and the attacks are vanishingly rare. Private businesses and government departments are equally at risk. Given the low probability of such an event, there seems little purpose in alarming employees by putting them through simulations or training exercises. Nevertheless businesses at higher risk, such as military and defence establishments, entertainment venues and government institutions, should have continuity plans.

In the small town of Moneta, Virginia, Bryce Williams shot dead a television reporter Alison Parker and cameraman Adam Ward on live TV. He is thought to have held a grudge against the station for firing him two years previously.

Omar Thornton killed eight colleagues at a beer distribution company in Connecticut, USA. He had been accused of theft, and had claimed the accusation was racist. Given the choice of being fired or resigning, he signed the resignation papers and was being escorted out of the building when he took two pistols from his lunch box and opened fire.

Mitigating Measures: employees with a grudge

Prepare a continuity plan for a deadly attack. This is likely to be somewhat different from evacuation in the case of fire.

Ensure that security staff are trained to respond to an attack.

Radicalised employees and members of the public

Extreme right-wing supremacist views caused 32-year-old Norwegian Anders Breivik to kill eight people by setting off a van bomb in Oslo, and then murder 69 people at a summer camp on the island of Utøya.

At Leytonstone underground station in London, a man armed with a knife attacked a 56-year-old musician, slashing at his neck, prompting fears he was trying to behead him. The attacker was fought off by bystanders and then tasered by police. He had been shouting, 'This is for Syria . . . all your blood will be spilled.'

Syed Farook, 28, had worked as an environmental health specialist for five years in the San Bernardino public health department in California, inspecting food in hotels and restaurants, before he and his wife brought assault rifles to an office party and killed 14 of his co-workers.

Farook appeared to be a normal father. He was said to enjoy working on vintage and modern cars, reading religious books and occasionally eating out. His wife was said to be a shy, quiet woman, and they had four children. They were later killed in a shoot-out with police.

His brother-in-law, Farhan Khan, said he was mystified: 'I have no idea why he'd do it,' he said. 'Why would he do it? Why would he do something like this?'

Police subsequently thought it was a case of self-radicalisation. And while the case is extreme, it is by no means rare. The question for organisations is how to avoid recruiting staff who will harm the business or its employees, and how to identify radicals among existing staff.

Some organisations have close relationships with the people they're in contact with and are therefore better placed to assess whether they have become radicalised. This includes the education sector, religious groups, political groups, charities, NGOs and those in the criminal justice system. But businesses outside those groups have much less hope of identifying employees who might turn rogue.

Since the number of people who murder colleagues or the general public is infinitesimally small, the risk of working with such an individual is almost zero. The chances of identifying that person prior to an attack are even more slight. Nevertheless some organisations will want to reduce the risk and take precautions.

The list below highlights some behaviours that have been associated with killers, including radicalised religious ones.

Signs of radicalisation

Individually most of these signs amount to nothing. Collectively, they're more serious, especially the first few.

1   Spends extended periods in Pakistan, Syria or other jihad locations. This person may be going to a training camp where they can learn how to kill.
2   Types terrorist-related terms into Google. Such people often seek information about how to make bombs. They may download articles about jihad. Some have even asked for advice about this on social media.
3   Is offended by anti-Muslim or anti-Christian cartoons.
4   Is intolerant of other cultures and disrespectful of women.
5   Has a need for adventure and excitement. Young people with a high need for adrenalin are at risk of radicalisation.
6   Needs a father figure. Identifies with a charismatic figure and wants to be part of a group. Such individuals may seek the approval of a family substitute.
7   Makes frequent use of a video camera. Radicalised people film themselves and then post the videos to social media.
8   Holds homophobic views. Those who are opposed to gay marriage could be at risk of being radicalised.
9   Is isolated. Loners are more likely to become extremists.
10 Falls out with old friends and finds new ones. Someone who stops social intercourse and finds friends outside school or work may be on the way to becoming a radical.
11 Make changes to their appearance. Someone who grows a big beard or by contrast adopts a crew cut could be showing signs of a change in their outlook.
12 Holds rebellious views. Someone who is opposed to authority or is hostile to the government could be at risk.

The signs of radicalisation are often not obvious, because terrorists are not stupid. A document written by Al Qaida but now translated and published by Isis/Daesh says that lone terrorists should seek to fit in. Entitled 'Safety and security guidelines for lone wolf mujahedeen and small cells', the booklet advises them not to 'look like a Muslim'. It recommends shaving off their beard, wearing Western clothes, and not attending mosque too often. They should not wear new clothes 'as that can be suspicious'. It also explains how to use encryption software to hide the content of emails.

Right-wing white-supremacist killers may be identified through their comments on social media sites. They typically use numbers, symbols and pictures that are popular among white supremacists. The number 88 is used by neo-Nazis as code for 'HH' or 'Heil Hitler', H being the eighth letter of the alphabet.

They may also declare intended violence, saying that a named public target is going to die, or use phrases such as 'Now it's time to fight for my blood and my land,' according to the Anti-Defamation League. They also have a focus on national issues rather than local grievances.

Many white supremacist atrocities are 'bottom up' actions caused by lone wolves or small groups, making them difficult to spot, according to Joshua Freilich, professor of criminal justice at John Jay College.

Mitigating Measures: identifying potential killers

Install software that will identify an employee who types radical or murderous phrases into Google. Check that this is within the law.

Check employees' social media accounts for radical comments figures, symbols and images, along with threats of violence.

Be alert for employees whose behaviour changes, or who has several of the characteristics shown in the box on the previous page.

5   Ethical questions

Would your mother approve?

Legislation and regulators have been catching up with the problem of ethical breaches. Issues that could once be discounted as the actions of rogue employees are now the legal responsibility of senior management, and fines and other penalties are increasingly common. The main ethical risks are as follows:

- anti-competitive behaviour, collusion
- bribery
- conflicts of interest
- mistreating employees
- environmental damage
- extreme lobbying
- underhand political and social behaviour
- knowingly selling faulty or harmful products
- price fixing, collusion and other anti-competitive behaviour
- mis-selling and unethical marketing
- mistreating suppliers
- tax avoidance.

There are also specialised *industry-specific* ethical guidelines such as the USA's International Trade in Arms Regulations.

Companies have been responding to the new challenges. BAE has dismissed 265 employees over a 12-month period for ethical breaches. These were mostly for 'personnel and workplace issues' it said.

In the sections that follow, we look at the main categories of ethical failure. But first a set of general Mitigating Measures relating to business ethics.

Mitigating Measures: improving corporate ethics

Evaluate the likely areas of ethical risk: Assess the areas where the organisation would be vulnerable to ethical failure.

Create an ethics Code of Conduct. It will help employees who might otherwise misunderstand what is expected of them. Ensure this code is obeyed rather than ignored.

(continued)

(continued)

Ensure that senior team accept the corporate values. There is no value in mission statements if people at the top don't buy in to those values.

Provide staff training in ethics. This needs to be given to all new staff, with regular refreshers.

Audit against ethical failings.

Set up an ethics hotline. Also known as a compliance hotline or whistleblowing hotline, this can come in various forms. It can include a 24-hour, multi-lingual, local, free phone line where staff can take details and prompt for more information. It can also be run as an automated answerphone, or on a website with a contact form. BAE gets over 1,000 reports a year to its ethics officers or to the anonymous hotline.

Support whistleblowers. Staff should know that if they report concerns or violations in good faith they will not be victimised.

Be alert for macho characters. They will aim to set the corporate culture in their own image. They will see honesty and transparency as being for wimps. Senior management has to set an example and talk to them clearly about the organisation's values. But it can be hard to distinguish between entrepreneurial individuals who have little time for bureaucracy and those who want to achieve success at all costs.

Emphasise that delivering bad news is the only way to rectify problems. Issues cannot be rectified if they are hidden. Staff must know the business wants to hear about problems.

Join a suitable body such as the Institute of Business Ethics.

Smoke-filled rooms

'People of the same trade seldom meet together, but the conversation ends in a conspiracy against the public or in some contrivance to raise prices,' wrote Adam Smith in *The Wealth of Nations*.

Price-fixing is remarkably common, judging by the fines levied by the European Union, the US government and many others around the world.

China's anti-monopoly regulator fined five domestic drug firms a total of close to ¥4m ($608,000) for fixing the prices of medicines. In the USA, Apple was found guilty of fixing the price of ebooks. And the Japanese car supplier Inoac pleaded guilty to rigging bids on parts sold to Toyota over a period of eight years. The company paid a $2.35m criminal fine, while its website proclaims that it's a good citizen that sponsors opera and ballet.

Collusion takes many forms, including 'gentlemen's agreements' not to compete, bid-rigging and sharing sensitive information such as price fixing.

Abuse of a dominant position is a similar illegal activity. This can include restricting the price at which others can sell your products, and agreeing not to sell to certain customers. Organisations are more at risk if they:

- have contact with their competitors, for example at conferences;
- have joint ventures or partnerships with competitors;
- have few customers or competitors, such as dairies who supply to supermarkets;
- have a dominant position in the market.

Mitigating Measures: anti-competitive behaviour

Identify where the business might be at risk of anti-competitive behaviour.

Set a clear policy on collusion, and promote it to all staff. Make it known that collusion represents gross misconduct and could result in dismissal.

Ensure employees know how to report illegal activity.

Report anti-competitive activity to the authorities.

The temptations of bribery

With huge contracts up for grabs, it's not surprising that salespeople seek to bribe the government officials who sign off the documents.

Enterprise software giant SAP paid $3.7m in fines after a senior executive was found to have bribed officials in the government of Panama in order to win contracts. SAP paid out without admitting or denying the claims made by the regulator, the USA's Securities and Exchange Commission (SEC).

Even Denmark, the world's least corrupt country, is not immune. A managing director of the Danish National Police was dismissed, while 13 other arrests were made, following a bribery scandal at the Danish IT company Atea. Public services account for half of Atea's business in Denmark, amounting to 5.7bn DKK (£0.6bn).

Although bribery is still common, governments and enforcement agencies around the world are taking more active steps to identify and prosecute offenders. In the UK, there is a maximum penalty of 10 years' imprisonment and an unlimited fine.

Mitigating Measures: beating bribery

Conduct a risk assessment. Risks include the awarding of contracts, fostering relationships with government officials or the involvement of intermediaries. The assessment should be carried out whenever circumstances change, such as entering a new market.

Issue an anti-bribery statement that unequivocally commits the business to preventing bribery.

Avoid doing business with partners who will not commit to anti-bribery measures.

Introduce anti-bribery training.

Set explicit limits for entertainment and gifts, for example £100 per head for meals and £25 for a gift.

Communicate your policy to intermediaries and overseas partners. Ensure that this is followed and not merely acknowledged.

Provide a hotline for reporting bribery and other ethical failings.

Take quick and transparent action when any cases are discovered.

Conflicting loyalties

JP Morgan Chase paid $307m to settle charges that it steered its clients into buying its own investment products, rather than those of other companies. Its wealth management people allegedly failed to disclose that they preferred to invest clients' money in hedge funds and mutual funds that were operated by its affiliates.

The bank paid the fine to the US Securities and Exchange Commission (SEC) and the US Commodities Futures Trading Commission (CFC). It said the weaknesses were 'unintentional'.

Conflicts of interest can occur where an organisation's behaviour towards to a client is influenced by a secondary motive. This typically occurs in the following areas:

Universities are given research grants by controversial organisations, such as tobacco, alcohol or munitions suppliers, and then find it hard to be critical of their funders. This impairs their academic independence. In 176 studies of Bisphenol A, a compound used in plastic, 86% of government-funded research found some harm, compared with 0% of industry-sponsored studies.

Regulators are at risk of capture by those they are regulating. This happens when the firms, often bigger and better resourced than the regulator, provide staff, research data and facilities to the regulator. Regulators may come to identify with the firms' needs, and become their supporter, rather than protecting the consumer.

Regulators are less likely to pay much attention to special interest groups unless they are well organised, and may regard them as radical or extreme, in contrast to the modulated tones of the besuited industry lobbyists.

Procurement officers may prefer to give contracts to suppliers they like.

Education: when students are paying for their studies as opposed to receiving free state education, their teachers and professors come under pressure to award them higher grades.

Accountancy practices are reluctant to issue audit opinions that would scare investors, for fear of precipitating their client's bankruptcy. A qualified audit report may create a self-fulfilling prophecy, because lenders will decide to call in loans and not extend them, thereby causing the client to fail. Moreover, the auditors are dependent on their clients, since they are hired and fired by them. This leads them to sign off sometimes doubtful financial statements.

Research analysts can come under pressure from their own firms to issue positive research reports or recommendations for fee-paying companies, or those who might become clients.

Rating agencies such as Moody's are paid by organisations to rate them. They're at risk of overvaluing them, for fear of upsetting their client.

Charities can become reliant on major donors and sponsors. It was found that Age UK has received £6m a year for encouraging pensioners to buy electricity from energy company E.ON despite cheaper rates being available from other firms.

The revolving-door phenomenon: senior figures in regulators or government departments anticipate gaining employment inside the regulated industry once their government service finishes. An over-representation of clients in an organisation's policy making will result in a policy bias in favour of these interests.

Tech: Google has been accused of ranking its own products higher than is justified, a claim it has denied.

Self-regulation: Industry groups are more likely to be protective of their members than are independent regulators.

Beyond corporate conflicts of interest, individual employees often have the same risk. Examples might include hiring a relative, accepting a favour from a client or recommending a supplier who is a personal friend.

Mitigating Measures: preventing conflicts of interest in the corporation

Identify where conflicts of interest might occur.

Include conflict of interest as an issue in the ethics policy, or code of practice. There should also be written procedures for preventing it and steps to be taken if it occurs.

Create an ethical gifts and entertainment policy that bans all but the most minor gifts and hospitality, and requires them to be declared.

Seek an independent opinion where a conflict of interest might occur, such as where the business might buy or sell an asset owned by a director.

Ensure executives explicitly disclose external interests. Make sure they abstain from any decisions where they have a personal involvement. Maintain a list of employees' or advisors' interests.

Ensure the audit committee assesses conflicts of interest.

Set up an ethics committee, as found in universities.

Have sufficient independent directors on the board.

Set up a robust 'Chinese Wall' between departments that have the potential for a conflict of interest.

Mitigating Measures: conflicts in not-for-profits and government

Be aware of the financial and other pressures emanating from funders or clients.

Build in design features that prevent capture. These include: the organisation's funding source; qualifications for appointment; post-employment restrictions for employees and the organisation's relationship with other agencies.

Identify whether and how vested interests can become part of the organisation.

(continued)

(continued)

Insulate policy making and report writing from the organisation's commercial needs.

Remain distant from partisan lobbyists who might seek to influence the organisation.

Ensure that funding is not overly reliant on special interest groups. These funding sources should be isolated from strategy development.

Put restrictions in place to prevent senior staff members from taking up employment with special interest groups after leaving the organisation.

Scrutinise senior appointments for outside influences.

Require staff to disclose conflicts of interest.

Ensure decision makers recuse themselves from decisions where they have a personal or commercial interest.

Treating employees badly

No company sets out to treat its employees unfairly, but some organisations are harsher than others.

The BBC reported that ambulances were called out to ill workers at the headquarters of Sports Direct, one of Europe's largest sports retailers, 65 times in two years. Many of the calls were for 'life-threatening' illnesses. Former workers said some staff were 'too scared' to take sick leave because they feared losing their jobs. Some 3,000 agency staff work at the site, and a document produced by one of the agencies states: 'Any person who exceeds six strikes within a rolling six-month period will have their assignment at Sports Direct ended.'

Workers can receive a strike for a range of 'offences' including a period of reported sickness, excessive chatting, excessive or long toilet breaks and using a mobile phone in the warehouse. The document adds that the agency can end an assignment 'at any time without reason, notice or liability'.

The local authority reported that there were 38 accidents reported at the warehouse over the two-year period, including a fractured neck, when somebody was struck by a moving object, a crushed hand from moving machinery and back and head injuries.

At the firm's annual meeting, Keith Hellawell, the chairman, told shareholders he was satisfied the company complied with health and safety regulations and any concerns were investigated immediately. The Unite trade union said the company's employment practices were Dickensian.

Mitigating Measures: taking care of employees

Put a values statement in place that commits the business to respecting its employees. The statement needs to be sufficiently detailed as to be meaningful. It should include health and safety, respect for statutory rights, the fostering of diversity, the opportunity to increase the employee's skills and the creation of an ethical, supportive environment where staff are treated fairly and with respect.

Ensure that the statement is adopted consistently.

Adopt and publicise KPIs relating to employee welfare such as accidents and staff turnover.

Seek to continuously improve the performance indicators.

Environmental damage

All products have an environmental impact, including the raw materials extracted from the ground, the energy used in their manufacture and the emissions caused by lorries taking them to customers. Businesses seek to reduce their environmental impacts because that reduces waste and avoids criticism.

And when unexpected environmental damage is done, it is usually an accident. Some businesses, however, have a track record that suggests a cavalier attitude toward pollution.

Barrick Corporation, a Toronto-based gold-mining company, has been voted as Covalence's 12th most unethical company in the world, according to Business Pundit. com. It was accused of torching up to 300 homes in Papua New Guinea in order to make room for its mining operation. Landowners were given no time to gather possessions and were reportedly physically attacked by armed guards if they attempted to protest about the eviction. Barrick Corporation is also accused of manipulating land titles in Australia and Chile, and of dumping toxic waste with high levels of arsenic in Tanzania.

Trafigura is another high-profile business that produces toxic waste from its metals business, and is known for its role in tipping toxic waste in the Ivory Coast. On hearing that the disposal of some waste was going to be more expensive than predicted, it hired Compagnie Tommy, a new and inexperienced business, to get rid of the material. Compagnie Tommy illegally dumped the toxic waste without processing it, resulting in 108,000 people falling sick and 10 people dying. When it heard that *The Guardian* newspaper was planning to publish evidence that Trafigura knew of the dumping, the company applied for a super-injunction to prevent publication.

Mitigating Measures: protecting the environment

Introduce an environmental policy that commits the business to respecting the environment and reducing its environmental impacts.

Set procedures in place that comprehensively support the policy.

Lobbyists at work

Activists regularly gain headlines for anti-commercial protests, and behind the scenes they can be active in discouraging road construction, housing development, power stations and other projects.

It's reasonable therefore that companies in these fields should put their own voices forward. But limits should be set on tactics aimed at changing opinions. It's one thing to communicate the company's case, but there are lines that shouldn't be crossed.

Hiring politicians or senior civil servants as soon as they leave office (the revolving door) gives the impression that the company is paying for services rendered, or that the individual will use their influence in government to give the business an undue advantage.

When the UK's Digital Economy Bill was being prepared, the MP Tom Watson said there was 'unprecedented and relentless lobbying' in its favour. He said 100 people were probably working full-time to 'bounce it' through parliament.

It's dangerous and probably ethically wrong to use methods that would look bad if published in the media. This includes excessive political contributions, deep infiltration of protest groups, setting up ostensibly independent lobby groups and suborning academics into writing less than honest papers.

Mitigating Measures: lobbying

Have a lobbying policy that sets out the limits of acceptable behaviour.

Political and social programmes

Corporate and social responsibility (CSR) programmes routinely give money to charities and communities to demonstrate that the business has a conscience and to improve its brand image. Generally these donations are uncontroversial.

Good governance makes publicly quoted business less likely to make donations that could represent a questionable use of shareholders' money. However, privately held businesses are sometimes at risk of straying into political and social controversy, particularly when the founder has strong views.

US retail chain Target became the subject of a boycott by gay rights campaigners after the company donated funds to a lobby group that supports US Senator Tom Emmer, a strong supporter of anti-gay legislation.

Businesses sometimes engage in politics when they feel it is in their interests to do so. Ian Taylor, chief executive of oil trader Vitol, was criticised when he donated £500,000 to a campaign to keep Scotland in the United Kingdom, in the lead-up to a referendum on the subject. However his company's track record includes fines and controversial deals in Iran, Iraq, Serbia and Libya, according to the *Daily Record* newspaper. A Scottish MP, Angus Robertson, even linked Vitol to 'murder, wilful killing, rape, and other inhumane acts', because it paid a reported $1m to the notorious Serb warlord Arkan 20 years ago.

In the USA, Las Vegas Sands, a casino and resorts business, contributed $69m to Republicans and conservatives between 2002 and 2015. In the same period, AT&T gave $25m to Democrats and liberals.

Mitigating Measures: corporate and social responsibility

Create a public policy stating what kinds of organisations the organisation will give funds to and those it won't.

Ethical products and services

The massive power of the corporation places upon it a responsibility to mitigate any harmful effects of its products, and to be responsible when marketing it. Ethical criticisms come under the following categories, which we examine next:

- *products* that harm users, or cause unnecessary harm to animals;
- *business dealings* that harm customers or the public, or are not in their best interests.

Harmful products

There are few products that are entirely harmful. Alcohol abuse brings illness and misery to a few, but alcohol in moderation gives untold pleasure to many. Cars pump out global-warming gases, but take us in comfort to where we want to go.

The problems caused by online betting are serious, though moderate gambling provides excitement to some. Previously illegal drugs are becoming lawful in some jurisdictions, though the criminal drug trade causes corruption, addiction and death.

Tobacco is the only product destined to shorten lives by ten years, causing one in five deaths in the US and killing one in three smokers.

The use of animals

Some medical research requires tests to be done using an 'animal model', that is, testing drugs and treatments on animals. The public, however, sees the testing of cosmetics on animals to be less essential, and many businesses have now pledged to be 'cruelty free'.

Similarly, the treatment of animals can be controversial. Only 7% of Americans are vegan or vegetarian, but this compares with 1% in 1971. In the UK, 20% of 16- to 24-year-olds are vegetarian. Although these numbers are very small, they represent a committed and savvy population who will seek to highlight any mistreatment of farm animals. Beyond that there is an ethical imperative to treat animals humanely.

Business dealings that harm customers or the public

There was an outcry when Volkswagen Group was found to have altered its engine software to reduce CO_2 emissions during its diesel cars' annual test. VW shares lost a third of their value in the first few days of trading following the scandal. Governments and investors prepared to sue the company, and owners of VW cars prepared law suits over the loss of their cars' resale value. Liabilities were expected to reach €30bn.

Reckitt Benckiser agreed to pay the UK Department of Health up to £90m following claims it had overcharged the NHS for its indigestion remedy Gaviscon. The department said that Reckitt had kept profiting from it after the product's patent had expired. It allegedly did this by promoting a new variant of the treatment, called Gaviscon Advance, which was still under patent, and in this way it made it harder for rival companies to launch their own versions of Gaviscon. The payment was made without Reckitt admitting liability.

It is not unusual for a business to seek to maintain its revenue stream by launching a new version of an older product. But it may then be challenged in court for abusing its dominant position. And with governments having both time and money on their side, the outcome may not be a good one for the business.

Power generator EDF has been criticised for its involvement in the construction of nuclear power plants in the UK, on the grounds that future generations will have to guard the company's spent fuel. Others, however, believe nuclear is justified for its role in replacing coal, oil and gas.

Company wrongdoings sometimes seem related to mistakes and incompetence, rather than wilful ethical failings. Power company E.ON was fined £7.75m by its regulator Ofgem for incorrectly charging customers exit fees and overcharging on bills. The previous year it had been fined £12m for mis-selling energy contracts to customers. Up to half a million households were affected.

Mitigating Measures: ethical products and services

Ensure that the organisation's products and services are fit for purpose, and cause no harm when used properly.

Pricing and fees must be easily understood, not mislead and not take advantage of vulnerable sectors of the population.

Whiter than white: the problems of mis-selling

Sometimes it's only after a scandal erupts that a business or industry looks back and wonders why it engaged in controversial promotional activity, and why no one sounded a note of caution.

The financial services industry has an unparalleled record of mis-selling its products. This includes insurance cover that will not pay out and mortgages sold to people who will not be able to keep up their payments. To outsiders, the industry seems to veer from extreme caution to wild behaviour and back again.

Other industries also come in for criticism. The War on Want charity has called for a boycott of Caterpillar for selling bulldozers to Israel in the knowledge that they will be armoured and then used to destroy Palestinian homes, infrastructure and agriculture in the Occupied Palestinian Territories. This influenced the Church of England's decision to divest its £2.2m holding in Caterpillar.

When large sums of money are at stake, the competition is strong and senior people are willing to condone questionable sales methods, ethical failings are likely to occur. If everyone in the industry is doing it, such activities seem normal.

Incentivising salespeople to sell services at a higher price, and thus gain a bigger bonus, can also cause an ethical risk. This can happen in the mortgage market where loan officers may be paid a percentage of any fees they collect over the company's established base rate. This is known in the US as an overage, the amount by which the upfront fees are over the lender's minimum rate.

It seems only sensible to stand back and ask what the headlines will look like when the news gets out about the organisation's tactics. While businesses are inevitably concerned to generate profits, they also need to think about the effect on the corporate image.

Mitigating Measures: ethics in marketing and sales

Give clear guidelines to salespeople.

Set policies for advertising and promotions to ensure they do not overclaim or mislead.

Ban incentives that encourage the recipient to behave unethically.

How to treat suppliers

There are two types of ethical risk when it comes to treatment of suppliers:

1   The organisation might treat its suppliers badly. For example, it might use its bargaining strength to force suppliers to provide goods at too low a price.
2   A supplier might itself behave unethically, such as mistreating its employees. We examine that risk in Chapter 8.

Tesco deliberately delayed payments to its suppliers, in order to boost its own profits, according to the UK's Groceries Code Adjudicator (GCA). It took the company more than two years to pay back a 'multi-million pound' sum owed to a supplier as a result of incorrect price changes. Another supplier waited for more than a year for a £2m repayment caused by duplicate invoicing. Tesco unilaterally deducted a seven-figure sum from a third supplier in order to meet a margin target. Describing the company's practices as shocking, the adjudicator said every supplier she spoke to had suffered as a result. Tesco said it had apologised to its suppliers and has now 'fundamentally changed'.

An unequal balance of power can lead to the business behaving unethically towards its suppliers. Forcing down prices, delaying payments and reneging on agreements are three examples of bad behaviour.

While businesses are quick to require their suppliers to adopt codes of ethical behaviour, and are alert to their buyers behaving fraudulently, some are slow at ensuring they themselves behave well.

Mitigating Measures: ethical treatment of suppliers

Adopt a code of conduct towards suppliers and business partners. This should include the following requirements:

*   Pay suppliers promptly.
*   Agree fair terms of business that allow the suppliers to make a reasonable profit.
*   Respect the intellectual property and confidential information received from suppliers.

Ensure that the code of conduct is applied consistently.

How much tax should you pay?

Some companies, especially those in the tech sector, adopt aggressive tax avoidance measures. There are various ways of reducing taxes, such as ascribing sales to a low-tax country or claiming high fees for the use of intellectual property.

The *Sunday Mirror* reported that in 2014 six firms paid tax at the rate of just 0.3% in the UK: Amazon, Apple, Facebook, Google, eBay and Starbucks. Google's UK CEO Matt Brittan said: 'Google plays by the rules set by politicians.' But MP Margaret Hodge said: 'We are not accusing you of being illegal. We're accusing you of being immoral.' The following year Amazon announced they would begin to pay a fairer rate of tax.

Apple secured tax advantages with the Irish government on billions of euros of sales but, like other tech companies, came under pressure from the European Union to cease doing so. Meanwhile the UK's Revenue and Customs (HMRC) planned to 'name and shame' companies that pursued aggressive tax planning.

In short, the clamour against such practices has been growing, leading to campaigns against some companies. A Starbucks campaign on Twitter to 'spread the cheer' of Christmas backfired after protesters hijacked it to complain about the coffee chain's attitude toward tax.

Such campaigns can damage the company's reputation and reduce sales, and where a business sells to government bodies, or needs government approval for export sales, high-profile tax avoidance is even more risky. While tax avoidance can achieve a short-term increase in profits, there is a risk to the brand image.

There is evidence that tax avoidance is declining as governments get tougher. All but two UK-registered banks have signed up to a government scheme encouraging lenders to avoid using tax planning schemes. So far 303 lenders have signed up to the Code of Practice. The scheme is expected to be widened to large businesses generally. HMRC said that the amount of money in tax avoidance schemes has fallen from £3.2bn in 2013 to £1bn in 2015. In the 15 months to March 2015, banks referred 30 deals that could be tax avoidance schemes to HMRC to check whether they broke the spirit of the law. The Revenue said that all but four were acceptable.

Mitigating Measures: tax payment

Set a clear policy on how aggressive your taxation planning should be. It should not employ structures that are against the spirit of the law.

Consider accreditation with the Fair Tax Mark (fairtaxmark.net) which demonstrates that the business has an open and responsible tax policy.

---

6 When the money runs out

Mitigating financial risks

Finance has not traditionally been the concern of the chief risk officer. There are three main reasons for this:

1 The numbers can seem too complicated for people to get their brain around: it's hard to see what the costs and revenues actually mean, especially in statutory accounts which are complicated by tax issues.
2 Organisations don't like to disclose too much detail about costs and revenues: it sheds light on individuals' salaries and on loss-making units.
3 Finance is locked up in the finance department, a place from which ordinary staff are excluded.

But finance is one of the major risks in an organisation. It's also the most easily understood, because it consists only of numbers – money coming in and money going out.

There are two types of numbers: the first are the statutory (or financial) accounts that are prepared for the tax authorities. These rarely provide useful figures because they have been mangled beyond comprehension.

The management accounts contain the genuine truth. Produced each month, they tell the reader where the organisation is making and losing money. And this is where the big risks lie. You can have a small environmental footprint, high-quality products and customers who adore the business. But if the numbers don't add up, the organisation will fail.

In this chapter we categorise finance risks as follows, and set out Mitigating Measures for each:

- narrow margins and insufficient profit
- weak cash flow
- high costs – in overheads and people, energy, transportation, buildings and IT
- excessive debt
- inadequate financial control
- lack of liquidity
- bad debt
- commodity prices
- access to capital
- flotation
- take overs
- exchange rates
- investment choices
- overexpansion
- the pension fund.

The unprofitable business

Lack of profit (or exceeding the budget in the case of non-profits) is the one sure route to insolvency. For commercial organisations, a fall in profits stems from three causes:

- rising costs
- declining sales
- prices set too low
- or a combination of these.

Businesses with *high energy costs* or that buy *commodities with volatile prices* will be familiar with the risks associated with those costs.

Companies facing *high competition* can find themselves cutting prices to retain volume, and will start to lose margin. Firms that lack innovation can find customers start to buy on price rather than brand loyalty.

The same is true for not-for-profit organisations. Hospitals and NHS Trusts in England have been overspending by a record £2.45bn a year. This is the result of hospital costs rising faster than their income. Unless the trusts get more money, they would have to slash head count, cut services and delay operations.

Not-for-profits may see their revenue decline in times of recession when donors and sponsors find themselves short of money. The same applies to organisations in markets that are subject to the business cycle. Lancashire councillors voted to cut spending on museums from £1.3m to less than £100,000, which would lead to the closure of five museums including the last surviving nineteenth-century steam-powered weaving mill.

Mitigating Measures: staying profitable

Conduct an analysis of revenue and costs. Are you at risk from revenues sliding or costs rising, with the result that the business could become loss making? If so how can revenues and costs be managed?

Identify trends in costs, revenues and margins. Develop a strategy to maintain or improve each over time.

Gain additional revenue by seeking new markets for existing products and services, and by launching new products.

Look for ways to cut costs, including head count, automation, cost control, efficiencies and removal of loss-making units.

Move to higher value added products and services in order to improve margins.

Narrow margins

The bigger your profit margins, the longer you can survive a squeeze.

Businesses that trade on slim margins seem smart in the good times, because customers flock to them. They seem to be the face of the future: savvy businesses that provide value for money for customers, and take market share from less entrepreneurial competitors.

But when revenue falls, as it does in a slow down, such businesses find their income isn't sufficient to meet their costs. They all too quickly fall into loss. Margins are determined by only three things:

- *Price charged*. Prices are controlled by how much your customers are willing to pay. But as brands like Apple and Louis Vuitton show, some companies manage to charge much more than the average.
- *Sales volume*. Sales are in large part determined by your brand identity or product positioning, and by how smart your competitors are.
- *Costs*. This is the one element you have most control over.

Mitigating Measures: boosting margins

Seek to increase your margins. You can only do this by cutting costs, raising prices or getting more sales.

Enough cash to pay the bills

Cash flow is about getting money in from customers faster than you pay your bills.

If you get it the other way around, and pay out faster than the money comes in, you eventually go bust.

Cash flow is particularly risky in capital intensive industries where the investment is huge, and revenues only come at the end of the project. House builders have to borrow large sums of money from the bank, and spend it on building houses and paying contractors. Only when the houses are completed can they sell them and pay back the bank.

Cash flow is sometimes related to debtor management. Healthy profits can disguise sloppy debt collection processes. It is only when revenues decline and margins get tighter that companies discover the need to actively manage their debtors.

'Businesses need to be savvy about who they trade with,' says Philip Sykes, president of R3, the insolvency trade body. 'If a business isn't paid upfront, or pays in advance for its own supplies, it is essentially lending money to those with whom it is trading.'

Mitigating Measures: improving the cash flow

Monitor cash flow, whether you do it on a spreadsheet or a more sophisticated program is up to you. You need to know how much cash you will have several weeks ahead.

Collect debts efficiently. Get your finance department to engage with sales. Phone outstanding debtors. Make debtors realise you take this seriously.

Be aware of the potential for customer fraud. Taking on a customer who fails to pay is worse than not winning that customer in the first place.

Ask for some money before delivery. This can apply not just to unknown customers but even to existing clients where there will be a long gap between the execution of the service and your getting paid. This means the customer shares some of the risk with you.

(continued)

(continued)

Be aware that existing customers can become bad debtors. Their circumstances can and will change. According to Dun & Bradstreet, 80% of bad debt is caused by customers a company has supplied for more than a year.

Aim to be cash positive every month of the year. Take whatever steps are necessary, by cutting discretionary expenses. Beware of lean months caused by seasonality. Consider compressing your tax and other payments into 11 months of the year, and take a holiday in the leanest month. You might also cut advertising and other expenses in that low-revenue month.

Close or dispose of loss-making units. Businesses are often emotionally attached to units that are part of the organisation's history, or are closely associated with the founder.

Sell assets to improve the bank account, if necessary.

Have a backup plan. How will you deal with a period when cash continues to flow out? Push payments out to 45 days. Have credit facilities in place. Ensure you have reserves you can tap into.

High costs: the big, big risk

High costs are a quick route to insolvency. Fixed costs are particularly troublesome, for you can't easily get rid of them in the bad times. All organisations add cost during the good times.

It's therefore essential to keep this major risk under control, by keeping costs low and variable.

There has to be a balance between investing for the future and avoiding undue debt – between having enough people and buildings, and allowing costs to get out of control.

Mitigating Measures: cutting costs

Cut strategically, not across the board. Identify which areas need investment and which are overweight.

See this as an opportunity to restructure. According to Heywood, Layton and Penttinen at McKinsey, businesses should examine market trends, and decide whether to exit from a low-profit or declining area and invest in high-growth ones.

Renegotiate supplier costs. Sometimes suppliers continue to maintain the price of goods in long-term contracts, even though the market price has fallen.

Consider the 'Make or buy' question. Decide whether it is better to buy in a service or product that is currently performed in-house. Or the reverse may be true: some previous outsourcing decisions may have proved to be poor ones.

Review supplier costs. Long-standing suppliers tend to raise their prices. New suppliers may be more inclined to offer keen quotes.

Assess whether some operations should be offshored. See Chapter 9 on offshoring.

Sales. Identify whether smaller accounts could be serviced by telesales rather than field staff, or even self-service online ordering. But the less contact you have with customers, the more they will defect to competitors.

Seek to cut travel costs. Allocate a budget to each member of staff and incentivise them to beat it.

Automate parts of your business, especially those where manual tasks are carried out. This will cut your costs.

The overhead problem

Fixed committed overheads, such as salaries and office rent, are a risk because you have to pay them each month, whether or not you sell any product or bank any money.

If your overheads are £1m a month, and your gross margin is 10%, you have to sell £10m worth of goods just to pay the rent and the salaries of people who sit at desks. That's before you buy any stock or ship any goods.

Anything that can be cut from overhead goes straight into net profit, assuming no effect on sales. Alternatively, reduce overheads from £1m to £800,000, and the amount you need to earn drops from £10m to £8m. That allows for more wriggle room during weak sales periods.

Mitigating Measures: lowering your overheads

Get more granular information on overheads. Don't allow them to be lumped together. Seek to allocate costs by building or department. This may tell you where costs are high or savings could be made.

Identify where there are unnecessary people in the business, and remove them. Most organisations add staff when things get busy, and fail to remove them when life quietens down, as it always does. Most businesses have flab.

Reduce the number and size of premises. This can save all the ancillary costs of running a building such as heating, maintenance and security.

Look for entire departments or products that could be closed down.

Maximise your use of tax benefits. Tax breaks vary by jurisdiction, and are complex and sometimes short lived. But they typically support R&D, hiring and training employees, reducing energy use and investment.

Add IT, automation and more efficient machinery to bring down the cost of labour.

Focus on saving costs in high-cost areas. This varies from industry to industry. It may be energy, IT, people or supplies. There are strategies for reducing the costs of each.

People costs

People are often an organisation's biggest cost, with staff costs accounting for 40–70% of expenses. So reducing head count is one of the best ways to reduce cost.

It is easier to hire people than to fire them, which is why companies always have more staff than they need. It follows that every business has staff it needs to get rid of.

The maxim is 'hire slow, fire fast'. In other words, avoid hiring people unless you really need to, and make sure you get the right person. And don't delay when it comes to getting rid of people. It's a job that everyone prefers not to do, so it happens less often than it should.

Mitigating Measures: managing employee costs

Consider removing management layers. Identify whether there are levels of management that are not needed. Insurance company Aviva removed its regional layers for both Europe and America and got the country heads to report directly to Aviva's chief executive. Similarly, supermarket giant Tesco took out two layers of management. This removed around 1,000 people from the payroll. This kind of cost cutting gives a business a flatter structure, with faster decision making and letting people feel closer to the top. But there's an added risk that managers end up with too wide a span of control, stresses grow, opportunities get missed, quality is affected and inefficiencies start to appear.

Use seasonal staff to even out the peaks and troughs. Hire enough permanent staff to meet only normal demand.

Use fixed-term contracts where future work is reliant on the winning or renewal of contracts.

Instigate home working and hot desking. Review the potential to reduce space needs by promoting hot desking and working from home.

Review the centre. Head offices easily acquire bloated functions. Expansionist managers get extra staff, and when they are replaced by less vigorous successors, the need may no longer be there.

Examine the effects of previous acquisitions. Identify whether earlier acquisitions have left some duplication. Are there separate HR departments, payroll or finance departments?

Transfer fixed costs to variable by outsourcing whatever staffing you can, while retaining strategic skills in house.

Assess whether some functions are no longer needed. Sometimes departments were created by a previous project and have continued to exist after the need has passed. One business had a 'lean' team which after years of activity had failed to create any change in the organisation, nor any lean processes.

Automate manual processes. Identify which manual processes could be replaced by self-service computer-based ones. This might include stationery orders, recruitment, appointment setting or room booking.

Consider whether some functions could merge. Can you combine security and building automation? It might make sense for the same people to provide physical security, control visitor access and be responsible for surveillance cameras, fire alarms, air conditioning, lighting and water. Rather than having separate employees in front of monitors at different locations, you can have one centralised point of command and control. This would allow mobile employees to respond faster to reports of an intruder or a basement water leak.

Cut fast and deep, rather than little and often. Downsizing is demoralising for staff, which translates into reduced productivity and disengagement. Staff need to know that the blood-letting is over, so they can concentrate on their work again.

Don't re-hire past staff. Organisations routinely re-engage staff soon after making them redundant.

Avoid cutting critical job roles: those which are critical to generating revenue and/or future growth. This might include salespeople and R&D but not estates or finance staff. However, sometimes departments with critical job roles can be overstaffed, and some individuals will be incompetent. Gallup found from its studies of 170 different companies (all well-known, well-run, major organizations) that 35% of salespeople lacked the requisite talent, and the bottom 25% of most sales forces produced nothing. It also discovered that 19% of the salespeople were actively disengaged from their jobs. Not only did they produce few sales, but many of them actually alienated customers.

Reset the pay structure. Over time, pay scales can rise faster than the market; and some jobs become bigger while the value of others shrink. Re-setting pay scales can reduce costs in the medium term, though where a job is downgraded you may have to keep the incumbent's pay the same, while reducing it for future hires.

When costs start to build up

Moving from prestigious or city centre buildings to lower-cost ones in a more provincial town will reduce the cost of real estate and the cost of staff.

For every one dollar spent on living in Phoenix, Miami or Dallas, it costs $2.21 in New York, according to Payscale.com. Staff will settle for lower pay in cheaper cities. According to KPMG, Manchester has the lowest business costs of 10 major European cities it compared, while London is the most costly.

Amalgamating into one office from several can save a considerable amount, because of the overheads that get removed along with the lease, such as the cost of IT, air conditioning and other building services.

Check for unnecessary regional offices which could be culled. Can staff work from home and hold meetings in hotels?

Mitigating Measures: putting a ceiling on building costs

Consider jettisoning buildings, or getting rid of regional offices.

Consider moving to a cheaper location.

Tech isn't cheap

Estimated at US$3.5tn annually, global IT costs are growing at an annual rate of 5%, which means they double every 15 years. As a percentage of corporate revenue, IT costs have grown 50% since 2002, putting a strain on IT budgets. Seventy-five per cent of IT budgets are recurrent costs, used to 'keep the lights on' in the IT department.

Many organisations outsource their IT. But that adds risk and may not deliver the anticipated savings. However, there may be some part of a company's IT spend that can usefully be outsourced.

Some costs, such as the cost of implementing an ERM system, may be substantial in the short term but could improve productivity. Access to better information may also make for better and faster decision making.

Leasing is invariably more expensive than buying, especially if you can keep the equipment for a few years longer than planned.

Software can take up to 30% of a corporation's IT budget, according to OMTCO, with licensing costs taking up the biggest element. Vendors have increased their maintenance rates, shortened release cycles and differentiated support in order to increase their revenues.

Mitigating Measures: computing your IT costs

Use free open source and off-the-shelf software, such as LAMP (Linux, Apache, MySql and Php). Find free equivalents of applications like Word. Companies like Roche are now using Google Docs, while 80 million people are using Libre Office, though this is tiny compared with the 1.2 billion who use Microsoft Office.

Standardise systems to gain greater interoperability, more flexibility and fewer conflicts.

Implement a future-proofed architecture which will reduce the number of new systems that get introduced, and will therefore cut costs.

Avoid cloud-based subscription services where possible. Although vendors promote subscription services as a good idea, they are a way of keeping you permanently in thrall to them.

Look to online storage rather than in-house. Costs have fallen with the advent of Amazon's AWS and similar services, and require little or no maintenance.

Consider outsourcing some of your IT.

When energy costs heat up

As shown below, energy costs can be a large proportion of some industries' costs, and energy prices are frequently volatile. This can have a big impact on the profitability of industries such as hauliers. Fuel can represent 15–20% of a short-haul operator's costs but 50% of long-haul operators' bills, according to Chainalytics.

Energy as % of total production costs, by industry

- industrial gas production 70
- aluminium smelting 40
- airlines 28
- steel making 25
- glass, paper and cement 20
- automotive 10

Taking proactive action can reduce price volatility. This normally involves hedging a proportion of the company's fuel requirements for a specific period of time.

Mitigating Measures: reducing energy costs

Understand the context: your current and future business environment, financial position and budgets, objectives and predicted fuel consumption.

Identify and quantify your fuel-related risk.

Determine your tolerance for energy risk.

Develop a fuel price risk management policy.

Create a strategy and implement it. This might include fixed-price physical contracts, take-or-pay and hedging or derivatives such as swaps, extendables and collars.

Ensure there are adequate controls and procedures.

Monitor the results and modify as necessary.

The costs of moving stuff

Freight costs have jumped as much as 14% for US consumer packaged goods companies in three years, driven largely by a truck-driver shortage and deteriorating transportation infrastructure, according to a report by the Boston Consulting Group.

'That's surprising because we did the same work two years ago and nobody mentioned transportation,' said Elfrun von Koeller, one of the report's authors. In the USA, the packaged goods industry spends about \$15.5bn a year on transportation. 'It used to be one of those things like air, you just breathe it,' said von Koeller.

But in the last few years a freight capacity shortage, particularly in US domestic truck and rail transportation, has badly affected supply chain managers. Drivers have been lured away to work in the construction industry, while the oil and gas industry is requiring more truck and rail capacity.

At the same time ageing infrastructure has been adding further delays. Between 2012 and 2014, on-time arrival industry-wide fell by nearly 5%, according to the survey.

Mitigating Measures: putting a brake on freight costs

Consider relocating your manufacturing and warehousing to reduce the miles driven.

Maintain good relationships with logistics companies to ensure you can more easily get goods delivered to where they're needed.

Too much debt

Debt is a good thing, because it allows you to expand in ways you couldn't if you relied on your profits alone. But it carries risks.

Gearing (the ratio of debt to revenue or debt to capital) is a measure of solvency. In other words, the more debt you carry, the more chance you'll go bust. Excessive debt carries three inter-related risks:

1   *It's harder to reach break even.* More of your revenue goes to paying loans. Debt makes the business especially vulnerable in a downturn when sales are lower.
2   *Less money is available to be invested* in research and development or new products. The business may become overly reliant on old products.
3   *The company may reach its overdraft or loans ceiling,* or breach its commitments, and be prevented from getting further borrowing. The bank may decide to reduce its or overdraft limit.

When things are going well, taking on debt seems logical. But circumstances change, and when a decline sets in, it exposes the risk that the company has exposed itself to. Talking of the problems that the falling price of oil caused, Colin Welsh, chief executive of oil financiers Simmons & Co, said 'What looked like sensible levels of debt a year or 18 months ago now look ridiculous.'

A business is heavily in debt ('highly geared' is the euphemism) if its debt is more than half the shareholders' capital (that's a debt : equity ratio of 50%).

For the reasons quoted above, excessive debt should be reduced. This can be done quickly, by selling assets, or slowly, by making more profit.

But as indicated earlier, few organisations can fund all their development from their current profits. It doesn't allow you to acquire major assets, such as businesses, land or property. And as long as you make profits from the money you've borrowed, it makes sense to borrow. In other words, if you can borrow £1,000 and convert that into £1,200, it makes sense to continue borrowing.

Excessive debt is either a sign of a bright new future or a failed strategy. Until or unless the debt comes down, or the business goes bust, it's hard to know which is the truth. Here are some causes of debt:

Expanding too fast or incautiously: A new CEO may scorn the slow and steady methods of the past. They may borrow money to hire expensive staff, launch into new markets and open new offices. A case in point was the Yuanzhou Fibre Technology Plant, covering 2,000 hectares in Jiangsu, China. It ceased operating, according to the *South China Morning Post*, after investing ¥100m (£10m) in new workshops and equipment. The bulk of the investment came from banks, microcredit companies and underground loan sharks. The expansion took place just as China's economy slowed. 'When business turned bad,' said one banker, 'the interest payment, especially the annualized 40 to 50% interest paid to loan sharks, became a heavy burden and finally killed the company.'

Failed acquisitions: The business may have bought companies which then failed to live up to their promise. Now it will owe that money to the bank.

Being the victim of private equity deals: The business may have been bought and sold several times by private equity. Each month the business has to repay its owners a lot of money.

Long-term lack of profit: This is creeping death. The business is reliant on ageing products or a declining market. It's slowly decaying.

Mitigating Measures: driving down debt

Ensure your debt : equity or debt : assets ratios are within the norms for the industry.

Reduce excessive debt by increasing sales, reducing inventory or cutting costs. You could also re-finance existing debt at lower interest rates, or dispose of unwanted business units.

Stagger debt maturity (the dates on which debts are due to be paid), so that the company has more time to re-finance. This reduces the risk that the company will find it hard to raise new finance, or may only be able to finance it at high rates.

Seek to have an undrawn revolving credit facility, in case times get bad and you need extra cash.

Consider converting some debt into asset-based loans (ABL). These are loans, typically for working capital, against which easily realisable company assets are pledged. ABLs usually involve lower costs and have fewer covenants than more traditional financing structures, which is an advantage to borrowers. Your receivables and inventory are typical assets for such purposes. Capital equipment might be secured through senior loans, that is, debt which takes priority over unsecured loans.

   However, if your assets fall below an agreed value, an ABL creditor will take over your deposit accounts, take control of the cash and repay itself out of funds it receives in the account. So it is not to be undertaken lightly. But in cases of acquisitions or if the business is expanding and its growth is accompanied by an increase in receivables, it's worth considering. Ashtead Group has extended the maturity of its borrowing facilities to an average of six years and uses an ABL senior facility which is free of conditions (or covenants) as long as the debt remains below an agreed threshold.

Inadequate financial control

Research by the Turnaround Society found that insufficient financial control and accounting weaknesses, especially in financial planning, are contributory causes in 36% of business failures.

   'Young companies often find that when they grow quickly and cash keeps rolling in they don't keep track of every dollar spent,' says the organisation. 'More money comes in, then goes out without control.'

   It adds: 'Mature companies often have trouble implementing rigorous financial controls because it means changing old and longstanding processes, curtailing some freedom and investing in expensive experts and changes.'

   A study of 9,000 annual audits showed that firms with material weaknesses in internal controls in their inventory management had a lower return on assets than those without. When the weaknesses were remediated, the companies gained a higher return on assets. The study by Feng, Li and McKay was designed to assess whether internal controls had an impact on operations. The authors concluded many businesses don't recognise that good controls provide better-quality management information.

Mitigating Measures: instituting financial control

Identify the risks associated with expenditure, fraud and loss. These will be found in areas where payments and the acquisition and disposal of fixed assets are made, whether in sales, payroll, operations or suppliers.

Create policies and procedures to control expenditure and avoid fraud and loss. Examples include the separation of duties, posting of entries, approval of expenditure, setting of budgets and the need for trained staff with appropriate seniority. Inventory, reconciliations and the provision of credit must all be controlled.

Set controls to assess whether the procedures are being followed. These should be formalised in documentation, and duly audited.

Staying liquid

Liquidity is a company's ability to pay its current bills. Lack of liquidity is a sign that you're paying out money faster than it's coming in.

Sometimes this can be resolved by chasing money that's owed to the business. At other times you need to cut costs so they remain below your income. For startups it can indicate that you have to invest before you get revenue, or it can demonstrate that the business model doesn't work. For established businesses, it's often a sign of long-term decline.

Mitigating Measures: improving liquidity

Collect your debts fast. Offer a discount for faster payment.

Cut costs, especially where they aren't contributing to revenue. Reduce your manufacturing or service costs, for example, by cutting your raw material, packaging or transport costs. Cut staff and use the rest more efficiently, or seek a reduction in salaries.

Reduce your inventory. Carry less stock.

Reduce the number of lines offered.

Sell off unused assets. Make existing assets work harder.

Dispose of unprofitable business units.

Negotiate with suppliers either a reduction in prices and/or slower payments. Seek alternative, lower-priced suppliers.

Review the prices and discounts given to customers. Where possible, reduce discounts and raise prices.

Seek a capital injection, increase your borrowing or get an increased overdraft from the bank, providing that all other steps have been taken and the business will henceforth be profitable.

Writing off bad debt

Technically a bad debt is one you can't recover, and which you've decided to write off as an expense. Every organisation faces a certain level of bad debt; it's part of the cost of being in business. Retailers of low-value goods don't give credit, but almost everyone else does. Business-to-business industries often do substantial amounts of work before getting paid.

There is a risk in giving customers too much credit, unless you use a third party to provide credit or factoring, in which case the credit provider takes the risk. In some industries, customers are lured in with offers of a 5% deposit, but getting them to pay the remaining 95% of the price is harder. Those who are attracted to such a low entry price often struggle to complete their payments.

Minimising bad debt starts with controlling who gets credit and how much; and chasing debt when it falls due.

Mitigating Measures: calling time on bad debt

Before accepting a new credit customer, check their credit references. Unknown customers should pay in advance.

Never allow a customer to continue receiving credit beyond their agreed limit.

Be cautious about the customer whose orders grow, and each time gets more credit. They may disappear or file for bankruptcy.

State your terms and conditions clearly and prominently on invoices and your website.

Specify in the contract that the goods belong to you until paid for. Include the right to charge interest on late payments.

Offer a discount for speedy settlement.

Require customers to report problems promptly on delivery. Resolve disputes fast: you won't get paid if issues are outstanding.

Require written purchase orders or a contract before starting work or delivering goods.

Phone the person who placed the order when it's overdue. Don't rely on letters or emails: they can be easily ignored.

Set agreed time limits for action. This includes sending letters before action, taking court action or handing the invoice to debt collection agents.

Get stage payments, rather than wait until the work ends.

The commodity price roller coaster

Commodity prices are a major risk to companies who buy raw materials. In 2015 crude oil fell from $100 to $43, while oats fell from $375 to $237. In the ten years to 2015, copper has plunged and reared from $1/lb to $4.50 and then back to $2.

Interest rates, geopolitical risk and the demand from worldwide economies affect the price of 'hard' commodities such as gold or oil. Weather and climate change impact 'soft' or harvestable ones.

According to a PwC survey of leading manufacturers, 86% of senior executives said commodity price risk was important to their financial performance, and agreed that they hadn't managed commodity risk well over the previous two years.

The commodities to which they were most exposed were: gas and oil (68%), metals such as steel and copper (67%), and electricity (33%).

Fewer than half (46%) of these organisations were able to alleviate price increases by passing them on to their customers. Forty-seven per cent could pass on only some or very few of their price increases.

As a result, many turn to other strategies to manage their risks, namely procurement contracts (83%) and cost reduction (84%). A large minority (48%) were reformulating their products or substituting the commodity, while one-third were hedging.

Mitigating Measures: smoothing commodity prices

Maintain margins by passing on price rises where possible.

Fixed-price contracts will give you an assurance of price stability. But they require a commitment to buy in volume, and will reduce your flexibility in pricing and sourcing.

Ensure that commodity pricing is done at a higher level than at the local plant purchasing department. Leaving the decisions to a purchasing manager risks failing to understand the wider risks and opportunities.

Hedge the commodity you need to buy. But prevent rogue trading activity by implementing controls; and require measured behaviour and transparency.

Consider vertical integration – as in acquiring a raw material producer – to ensure continuity of supply. Unilever invested in palm oil plantations, while BASF moved into oil and gas extraction. But be aware that running these upstream businesses requires different skills and therefore poses additional risks.

Get counterparty risk insurance. Determine how exposed you are to the risk that customers will fail to buy or pay for pre-agreed volumes, which could leave you with a commitment to pay for commodities for which there are no customers.

Lessen your dependence on major suppliers, in case they renege on commitments or contracts.

Credit lines. In the increasingly uncertain global conditions, make sure your credit isn't going to be limited, which could restrict your trading activities.

Check that your assumptions about volumes and revenues will remain valid in the light of changing circumstances. If prices were to rise or customer demand were to fall, what threats would that pose to the business?

Consider proprietary trading, where you trade in the commodity, in order to create profit and have more control over the process. But it isn't for widows and orphans. Businesses that lack expertise in this area risk major losses from trading.

Use less energy, especially less carbon fuel through better insulation, more efficient lighting and controls, and the use of renewables such as solar. Get equipment that can run on different fuels, and change to vehicles that use low-cost energy. Reorganise distribution networks so as to reduce fuel.

Reduce your reliance on commodities. Adapt plant to use a variety of inputs such as recycled raw materials. Decrease waste. Change the raw materials used in finished goods, such as plastics in place of steel.

Access to capital

Industries such as construction, ship building and automotive need access to capital. Their revenues often arrive at the end of a project when the product is finally built and sold. It follows that in a downturn banks may stop lending, which can halt the activities of such businesses.

A worsened credit rating is another risk. The cost of credit will rise or the company's overdraft facilities may be reduced.

Contractors can be asked to provide a bond or security for up to 25% of the contract price to protect the employer against the work not being completed. This is often met by a bank providing a guarantee of the money. If the banks cease to provide bonds, or the price increases, the contractor may be unable to bid for work and thus lose revenue.

Mitigating Measures: getting access to capital

Avoid over-dependence. Ensure that you are not overly reliant on a single lender.

Get long-term guarantee finance. Make sure that some of the finance is long term and guaranteed.

Spread renewal dates. The renewal dates should also be spread to avoid the risk that all your borrowing could be restricted all at once.

Time to float

Floating a business can bring in cash to grow, and release money to the founders and early investors.

But there are also many risks. These relate to whether the shares will be picked up. Later, people may cast aspersions about whether the price was set at the right point. And if shares fail to stay buoyant, investors may sue the business on the grounds that the prospectus was misleading or information was withheld. Investors alleged that Facebook failed to reveal that, since more people were accessing the app on mobile phones, its ability to sell ads would be hampered.

IPOs are hard to predict, being volatile in nature. The number of shares being subscribed can depend on the state of the stock market, on other companies' flotations and even on unrelated events such as US interest rates. Comments in the media, whether positive or negative, can also have an effect on the outcome.

How the business will change after flotation is another uncertainty. A public company has two masters: the customer and the shareholders. The latter, at least in

Anglo-Saxon markets, have short-term goals and are intolerant of what they see as poor performance.

Investors prefer to invest in businesses with the following attributes:

- a good record of delivering profits and growth;
- a business plan that indicates how earnings growth will be delivered;
- a professional and competent management team;
- is based in an attractive sector, capable of growth and with a stable long-term future.
- investors like mature markets but are also dazzled by high-tech opportunities.

Companies that don't conform to those criteria should avoid a public offering and should consider a trade sale instead, where the owners can sell the business to a third party such as a hedge fund. This will be cheaper and less fraught, though the future opportunities may be more restricted. Other risks include the following:

- The costs of flotation will be high.
- Flotation can distract the managers from running the business. After the float, shareholders will demand attention.
- Owners and directors will lose some control of the business. Shareholders may ultimately oust them. The business may be taken over.
- The firm will be subject to additional governance and auditing requirements.
- The business will have to continually disclose information to the public, which includes its competitors. The scrutiny can be intense.
- The organisation will face regular, sometimes ill-informed, criticism from the media and investors.

Mitigating Measures: a more buoyant flotation

Ensure that the timing is right. Floating when the market is bearish may lead to failure.

Ensure that the business has been prepared for sale, so as to maximise its attractiveness to investors.

Make sure that all due diligence questions can be answered.

Get insurance. You can buy cover for both the business and the individuals involved, against legal costs incurred in the event of a claim being brought by new shareholders or the government. This will cover you against claims of misrepresentation in the prospectus, and allegations of mismanagement by the board after the flotation.

Be prepared to cancel the float. It may be undignified, but this will be better than facing a disaster.

Underprice the offer rather than overprice it. This will encourage investment and allow new investors to make profits. If the price falls after flotation, investors may form a negative opinion of the business.

Get the right advisors on board at an early stage.

Choose the right size market on which to float. Larger stock markets have more investors but higher conditions of entry.

When another business thinks it can do better

There are several reasons why a company might be the subject of a takeover bid:

- The bidder might want to expand into that product line or geographical market.
- The target is in a fashionable market, such as internet businesses, though these have suffered bubbles at least twice.
- The bidder hopes to get a bargain: it believes the company will be worth a lot more in the future.
- The bidder wants to build a larger business, one that is able to compete more widely.
- Both parties want to reduce capacity.

Bidders look for businesses they think can earn more in the future than they're currently achieving.

McKinsey says acquirers in the most successful deals have 'specific, well-articulated value creation ideas going in. For less successful deals the strategic rationales, such as pursuing international scale, filling portfolio gaps or building a third leg of the portfolio, tend to be vague.'

The consultancy adds that bids claim to add value through five possible routes:

1 improving the performance of the target company;
2 removing excess capacity from an industry;
3 creating market access for products;
4 acquiring skills or technologies more quickly or at lower cost than they could be built in-house;
5 picking winners early and helping them develop their businesses.

But it goes on to say, 'the stated strategy may not even be the real one: companies typically talk up all kinds of strategic benefits from acquisitions that are really entirely about cost cutting.'

Mitigating Measures: bidding for a business

Get the target board's agreement. Board support will lead to almost certain acceptance, while a hostile board leads to only 22% success, according to Fasken Martineau.

Articulate a strategic benefit to the target's shareholders.

Mitigating Measures: defending against a hostile bid

Strategies depend on finding alternative buyers, making the business less attractive by increasing its price or lowering its value, or by causing delays in the bid.

Find a different, more attractive buyer, known as a white knight. This may incidentally serve to raise the bids, which will benefit current shareholders.

(continued)

(continued)

Sell assets that the bidder is known to be interested in. This will make the business less attractive to the buyer.

Take the bidder to court, alleging financial, legal or anti-trust (monopoly or unfair competition) issues. This will entangle them in legal action.

Set up a poison pill. Give original shareholders the right buy extra shares at a discounted price. This right is only triggered when a new shareholder acquires a specified percentage of the stock. This increases the number of shares, dilutes a hostile bidder's stock holding and makes it prohibitively expensive for the hostile bidder to acquire the business.

Adopt a bylaw requiring a higher percentage of company shareholders (say 75%) to approve new owners. This makes it easier for the board to prevent a takeover.

Stagger the election of board members. This will delay the appointment of board members favourable to the new regime, and make the acquisition less attractive.

Introduce large severance packages ('golden parachutes') for directors. This will also increase the cost of acquisition and thereby discourage a hostile takeover.

Some of these measures are banned on some stock markets, and a regulator may declare them illegal. They also serve to protect weak and undeserving boards.

Fair exchange: the problem of exchange rates

Most businesses of any size are exposed to changes in exchange rates. If you cost your goods in one currency (notably your home currency) and price them in the country where they are sold, you will either make extra profit or losses, depending on which way the two currencies move.

If you're importing into a country whose currency is declining you will either have to keep increasing your prices, which could make your goods uncompetitive, or you might keep prices level, and find that when you convert the income into your home currency it's worth less than before, and therefore your profits are reduced.

The risk is especially high for goods supplied on credit. If you export goods on credit you will set a value for the goods in your accounts. The amount you finally receive depends on how the exchange rate moves from the date you sold the goods to the date you got paid.

Hence your revenues may be adversely affected by income from weaker currencies. Reckitt Benckiser lost £363m in one year from exchange rate losses. As the company said mournfully, this makes it more difficult for investors to understand the relative strengths or weaknesses of the business on a period-to-period basis. In other words, some of the ups and downs in profit are simply exchange rate movements.

You may also work in currencies that impose exchange controls. These have included Argentina, Brazil, China, India, Russia, South Africa and Venezuela. This means you will not be able to repatriate your earnings from such countries. Not only did Reckitt Benckiser, as we saw above, lose £363m in one year on exchange rates, but at time of writing £109m of its earnings was locked up in some of those countries due to exchange controls.

If you import and export between the same currencies, you can match receipts and payments in the same foreign currency due at the same time. You are then left only with the balance of the transactions that are not matched.

Some companies accept they will lose on some transactions and gain on others. This saves on costs and risks of hedging, as well as management time. However, if the business has consistent flows, for example manufacturing the product in a strong currency and selling in a weak one, the losses will continue to grow. The reverse is also true.

If you're *selling* goods and you think the customer's currency will depreciate, you can try to get immediate payment, possibly by offering a discount for speedy payment. If you think the currency will appreciate then in theory you would be in no hurry to get paid, but few firms are relaxed about delays in payment.

If you're *buying* goods from a country whose currency is likely to depreciate, you may try to delay payment. You might achieve that by simply not paying within the supplier's terms. In the longer term the customer may refuse to do business with you, or expect payment when the goods go on board. And this all presupposes you can accurately forecast which way the currencies will move.

Mitigating Measures: exchange rates

Hedge large transactions. This means paying to ensure that you won't lose money from any variations in the exchange rate.

Require foreign customers pay you in your home currency. You can also insist on paying for all imports in your home currency. This avoids any exchange rate problems. This passes the risk to your customer. But they may not be willing to agree to that. They may decline your business or, if they're the customer, seek a different supplier. This tactic only works if you're in a dominant position.

Make and sell in the same currency area. This keeps costs and revenues level. It requires local production facilities.

The right investment

Investment is about forgoing cash today in favour of more cash tomorrow. It allows the organisation to:

- be more productive (new plant or a new IT system);
- win new customers (acquire a business);
- reduce competition (acquire a competitor);
- gain new knowledge (buy a promising startup);
- create new products (hire researchers or developers, or invest in design or engineering).

Sometimes the CEO sees a bank account full of money, and falls to wondering what they could spend it on; investments and acquisitions are fun, if risky. Investments can be designed to acquire the following:

- plant and equipment;
- a business;
- people. One university set up a fully staffed laboratory containing multi-million pound equipment, in order to lure one valuable researcher;
- design, R&D or new products.

Investments should be proportionate to the size of the business. If the investment is too large, you may not be able to support it financially, nor have the resources or expertise to manage it. If it is too small, it won't have any measurable impact on profit. There are exceptions, however. Buying a small startup could produce big profits in the future. However, any startup with a highly promising future will have been spotted by other investors; and its founders won't sell at anything like a reasonable price.

When EDF, the French energy business, was planning to spend £18bn on building two nuclear power stations in Britain, an association of employee shareholders said it could bring down the business. EDF Actionnariat Salarié (EAS) said, '[We] ask the management of EDF to stop this risky project, whose financial risks are too big for our company, and which could put EDF's very survival at risk.' EDF had reluctantly agreed to finance the project on its own already stretched balance sheet after other partners pulled out.

Mitigating Measures: wiser investment

Identify how well the investment fits into your core business. Read between the lines when managers become creative at explaining how a business in a completely different market will provide added strengths.

How necessary is the investment? Could it be just an adventure?

How risky is it? Would its failure endanger the business?

What return on capital will it bring? And how reliable are the forecasts?

Overexpansion

Overexpansion can cause a business to run out of money, or be left with unsupportable debts, if the expected favourable outcomes do not come about.

Among mature businesses, overexpansion often happens when a new boss takes over, an appetite for risk grows, and cautious voices are silenced. The organisation goes on a spending spree. It buys more businesses than it can absorb, and it pays too much for them.

The phase is characterised by management unable to keep track of events, firefighting, lack of internal control, money wasted on fruitless projects and some business units being overly autonomous.

Not all expansionist phases are wrong. Where an organisation has been lagging behind trends, with management failing to take advantage of opportunities, it needs an injection of risk-taking. But it can be difficult to judge when an entrepreneurial attitude has turned into risky overexpansion.

When aggressive expansion led to disaster

HBOS management pursued rapid and uncontrolled growth in the lead up to the 2008 financial crisis. This made it overexposed to commercial real estate at the peak of the economic cycle. As the market deteriorated, the bank found itself short of money.

Peter Cummings, head of HBOS's debt-fuelled corporate arm, was fined £500,000 by the Financial Services Authority and banned from working in the banking industry.

A parliamentary commission found that HBOS had engineered its growth by 'accepting more risk across all divisions of the group', a strategy that 'created a new culture' in the bank's higher echelons. It said HBOS had believed its growing market share was due to a special set of skills which HBOS possessed and which its competitors lacked.

But the effects of the culture were all the more corrosive when coupled with a lack of corporate knowledge at the top of the organisation, said the Commission. Cummings's division ended up with £25bn of impairments, equivalent to 20% of its 2008 loan book and far above rival banks.

Apart from the failings at the corporate division, its international unit ran up £14.5bn of bad debts from reckless expansion in Australia and Ireland alone. Its treasury function incurred £7.2bn of bad loans. 'The roots of all these mistakes can be traced to a culture of perilously high risk lending,' the report said.

The company was taken over by Lloyds Bank, aided by the British taxpayer, which bailed it out by taking a 41% stake in the business.

Mitigating Measures: expansion

Be aware of how the failure of new projects could affect the business. Carry out a sensitivity analysis that explores what alternative outcomes might occur if expected revenues were lower or if costs were higher.

Beware of 'betting the farm'. If the risk could lead to business failure, don't take it.

Be alert to people with vested interests. Those who prepare analyses will usually produce forecasts that support their case.

Set trigger points for debt. These will be points at which certain actions must be initiated, such as abandoning the project.

Listen to the naysayers. Paul Moore, head of Group Regulatory Risk at HBOS, warned his senior colleagues about excessive risk-taking. He was dismissed and his concerns were not acted on.

Keep the cost of new projects low until proven. Make use of existing resources and staff, take on temporary workers, and use existing facilities.

Share the risk by finding joint venture partners, or use sub-contractors.

There's a hole in our pension

Many pension funds have a shortfall between the future value of the assets in their fund and the amount they'll have to pay pensioners. At some point in the future, therefore, the pension will run out of money, with dire consequences for pensioners and the business.

These pension deficits may increase, due to lower returns on the stock market, reduced long-term interest rates and pensioners' increased longevity. In some cases deficits have been made worse by payment 'holidays' some businesses took during the good years.

Some businesses continue to top up their pension fund, to enable it to pay members in the future. This reduces the amount of money available for investment and dividends.

Most companies have closed their defined benefit schemes to new members. Others have closed it for payments to existing members.

For most businesses, pension contributions don't affect managers' current budgets or the profit and loss account – they're simply a promise to pay in the future. And it is hard to know whether the amount being funded each month will be enough to pay for future liabilities. Most managers realise this, but the impact of pension payments will occur many years' hence, probably when they've left. So it doesn't always seem a pressing problem

---

Mitigating Measures: the pensions time-bomb

Move to defined contribution benefits. New UK employees should be on a defined contribution scheme rather than a defined benefits one. In the USA employees should be offered membership of a 401(k) scheme and not get a salary-related benefits scheme. These will pay out less.

Take out insurance. Insure against the risk of increased longevity of existing members in old loss-making schemes.

Offer a pension increase exchange. This can offer pensioners the option of exchanging part of their pensions for higher immediate, non-increasing pensions. This removes the future inflation risk from those who take up the offer.

Encourage members to transfer out of the scheme, with cash rewards.

Annuity buyout deals. Pay an insurer to guarantee the future payment of members' pensions. This will be expensive.

Longevity swaps. This transfers the risk of pension fund members living longer than expected from the pension scheme to an insurer or bank provider. But it will cost the pension fund more in the short to medium term.

Contingency assets. Pass assets such as the organisation's intellectual property rights to the pension fund, in place of company contributions. The pension fund can use the assets to produce cash in the event that the company ceases trading or the scheme needs funding.

Hedging. You can hedge against inflation or interest rates.

7   Ever more regulation

Managing governance and the law

Good governance seeks to ensure that the organisation has integrity and makes wise decisions. It does this by implementing systems that ensure transparency, fairness and accountability.

It therefore follows that weak governance allows for the opposite: corruption and bad decisions. Activities may be opaque, people can be treated unfairly and senior people may not be held accountable for their actions.

In this chapter we examine the symptoms and consequences of weak governance, the need for a capable audit committee, a stronger internal audit department and a more knowledgeable board.

We then consider the risks of compliance failure and how to control them. We end up by considering the burden of regulation, and how to deal with it.

Symptoms of weak governance

Bad governance often has the following characteristics:

- The board is dominated by a single individual, usually the founder or CEO. Management is autocratic, and overrides procedures.
- There is a lack of succession planning.
- Management is inexperienced.
- The board lacks financial training and doesn't understand what the numbers mean.
- There is a lack of independent board members. This deprives the organisation of input from people who would be dispassionate and who could bring wider perspectives to decision making.
- Auditing is limited and hampered. Reporting is not on time and responses to audit committee enquiries are limited.
- There is a lack of KPIs (key performance indicators).
- Financial information is restricted to specific members of the board. Financial reporting is limited. Budgets are not set. Financial controls are weak or missing.
- Decisions are made without the support of evidence.
- The organisation makes major spending commitments without reviewing the alternatives or considering the consequences of failure.
- There is insufficient delegation by key board members. Organisation charts are either not in place or are not followed.
- Departments are not subject to any oversight.
- Inappropriate 'tone at the top'.

- Frequent organisational changes. High turnover of senior management.
- Excessive or inappropriate performance-based remuneration.
- Overambitious growth goals. Unusually rapid growth. Unusual trends or results.
- Lack of transparency in the business model.
- Overly complex organisational structures or transactions.
- There are late surprises.
- Ongoing or prior investigations by regulators or others.
- Cash flow problems. Poor financial position.
- Continuous loss-making operations.

Keeping it in the family

When Mike Ashley, owner of publicly quoted Sports Direct, needed someone to run the £250m investment team that identifies sites for the company's stores and gyms, he chose 26-year-old Michael Murray. This individual turned out to be the boyfriend of Mike Ashley's daughter Anna. Murray had previously had run student club nights and festivals.

Investors queried whether he was the best candidate, but Ashley retorted that Murray wasn't being paid for the work. However, Murray would receive up to 25% of any 'increase in value', which analysts pointed out could amount to millions of pounds. How that value would be established was not made clear.

The news came after it was revealed that Sports Direct had failed to pay some staff the minimum wage, and after the company had been forced to issue four statements to the Stock Exchange responding to criticisms of its operations and corporate activities.

The Institute of Directors called for Ashley to appoint further independent directors, saying there was no 'effective check on Ashley's power'.

There are many bleak consequences – risks, in other words – of weak governance:

- Faulty decisions are pushed through at board. In due course, some of these decisions harm the business.
- The organisation borrows too much money, putting its future at risk.
- The business invests in big projects, without assessing the pros and cons. This will endanger the business if the projects fail.
- Because management is not fully aware of the organisation's financial performance, there are unwelcome surprises and financial crises.
- Credit control is lax, and so customers' debts accrue.
- Since costings are inadequate, the business underprices its products, leading to losses. But the losses are not immediately noticed, due to a lack of granular information.
- Stock levels are arbitrary and too high, leading to cash being tied up and stock write-offs.
- The business is regularly in crisis or firefighting mode. Management spends insufficient time planning for the future.
- Weak or inadequate senior people are not held to account and remain in post, which delays any recovery.
- Fraud may be taking place but there is no way of knowing.

Mitigating Measures: better governance

Board overview. There must be an effective board which is responsible for the long-term success of the company.

Division of responsibilities: The chair and the CEO should be separate people.

Group decision making. No individual should have unfettered powers of decision.

Effective non-executive directors should be in place.

The board membership must have the right balance of experience and independence.

There should be a formal and rigorous procedure for appointing new directors.

The board must have the information it needs. If the directors don't receive timely and actionable information, it can't manage.

Non-executive directors must be independent. That means they must not depend on the business for their income, nor have family employed in the business.

Directors must submit to regular re-election.

The board must have oversight of the organisation's internal controls.

The inadequate audit committee

Audit committees have responsibility for the oversight of many risks, including IT, regulatory compliance and operational risks, as well as the company's enterprise risk management process.

As the audit committee finds more risks loaded on to its agenda, many question its ability to assess them adequately.

Fifty-five per cent of attendees at a KPMG audit committee round table discussion agreed that 'it is increasingly difficult or unrealistic' for the audit committee to oversee the range of risks on its plate. Thirteen per cent said its committee did not have the time or expertise to oversee major risks beyond financial reporting.

Given the threats of digitisation, cyber risks, globalisation and changing regulatory environment, some audit committees may not be competent to handle this range of issues.

Adding a risk or technology committee may improve the company's preparedness, or it might lead to duplication and bureaucracy.

Mitigating Measures: a better audit committee

Ensure the members of the audit committee have adequate training to understand today's diverse and sometimes technological risks.

Assess whether the committee understands the organisation's risk appetite and tolerance.

Ensure that the audit committee receives and reviews the major risks from the organisation's risk register.

(continued)

(continued)

Assess whether the audit committee is considering strategic as well as operational risks. The former are harder to identify.

Consider whether the board should be supported by a risk or technology committee, if one does not already exist.

From counting the pennies to evaluating risk: internal audit

In recent years internal auditors have moved beyond their original core role of financial assessment to risk-based internal auditing. And no auditing is more important than checking for risk. This, however, calls for auditors to be more highly skilled and less narrowly based.

To ensure that risks are being managed, the audit team needs to be independent, questioning, supportive and knowledgeable.

The chief audit executive must have a good relationship with the CEO and the board, as well as with the audit committee. They must be seen as measured, intelligent and insightful; a good communicator; aware of the business' direction of travel, and conscious of its vulnerabilities.

Seventy-three per cent of companies reviewed by Bryn and Daals of Deloitte have placed risk management inside internal audit, rather than building a risk department. There is logic to that, especially in highly regulated industries. Most companies did not see a need for a high-ranking chief risk officer, preferring to embed risk at operational levels, and with risk already being managed by the CFO or CEO. Nevertheless, this approach means that risk becomes a compliance issue rather than a strategic concern for board-level debate.

But with risk increasingly being placed inside internal audit, that department must gain a wider view of risk.

Mitigating Measures: boosting internal audit

Make risk-based auditing an essential part of internal audit. Push audit beyond purely financial assessment.

Get staff to identify and control their risks, not the audit team. This means establishing a 'universe' of all risks.

Build risk-based internal auditing around the risk register, and ensure the register is sufficiently comprehensive.

Protect team members from being bullied or captured by the departments that are being audited. Ensure they get full access.

Ensure that the team is competent to assess whether controls are adequate. Provide training and hire sufficiently senior staff.

Educate internal auditors to understand the underlying nature of risk, not just the superficial outcomes. This will give them a better perspective and help them to contribute.

Encourage auditors to play the role of counsellor, and commend good practice, rather than being a constant threat to management.

Avoid excessive control and emphasis on less important risks (such as petty cash). It is easy to spend too much time on minor issues and overlook the big but less visible and longer-term risks. This can be done by identifying the organisation's risk tolerance. Risks that fall within that risk tolerance can be ignored. Figure 7.1 suggests that some risks are over-managed while others are under-managed.

Consider outsourcing your internal audit to external auditors, so the information is more independent.

Board weaknesses

A weak board is factional, lacks skills and doesn't hold the CEO to account. There can be no bigger risk than that.

Why Kids Company failed

A UK House of Commons committee lambasted the board of Kids Company, a charity that supported deprived inner-city young people, after it sunk, having gone through £40m worth of public grants in the space of a few years.

The MPs criticised the head of the trustees, the BBC's creative director Alan Yentob. He was described as someone who condoned excessive spending and lacked proper attention to his duties.

The report criticised the trustees' financial negligence and said its CEO, Camila Batmanghelidjh, was reluctant to restructure the organisation she founded.

Ms Batmanghelidjh and Kids Company 'appeared to captivate some of the most senior political figures in the land, by the force of the chief executive's personality as much as by the spin and profile she generated for the charity', the report added.

The committee also highlighted 'extraordinary accounts of luxury items and holidays or spa days being lavished on a favoured group of clients'.

The report said the charity's board of trustees ignored repeated warnings about the charity's financial health throughout its 19-year existence. It also failed to provide robust evidence of the charity's outcomes, or address increasing concerns about its programmes and behaviour of staff.

The trustees' negligent financial management was ultimately responsible for the charity's inability to survive, and its closure left many vulnerable beneficiaries without support, the report concluded.

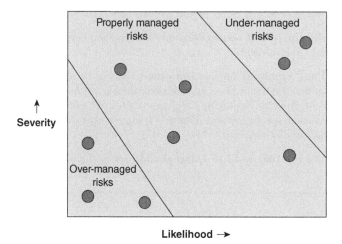

Figure 7.1 The control of risks. Some minor risks may be overly controlled while more serious risks might be not be recognised.

Mitigating Measures: improving the board

Get the board to understand the organisation's appetite for risk and know its significant risks.

Balance the board in terms of functional expertise, with diverse experience and background. Members must be trained in their duties. Enough members should be independents, who should not play an executive role.

Appoint board members after seeking applications from a wide range of candidates, and appoint them in open competition, not behind closed doors.

Re-elect board members every five years, to avoid the risk of them growing stale or complacent.

Get the board to focus on long-term value creation, rather than meeting quarterly shareholder expectations.

Scrutinise board members' performance at regular intervals. Weak contribution, a lack of expertise, failing mental faculties and poor preparedness are reasons for dismissal.

Ensure board members understand key issues: finance, cyber security, IT issues, crisis management and talent and succession planning.

Help the board to challenge the CEO.

Shareholders who want to run the show

Activist shareholders are increasingly common, and often come from hedge funds headed by strong-minded entrepreneurial individuals. They seek to change the board's strategy, sometimes through argument and if necessary by persuading other shareholders to vote them on to the board, where they can create change.

The risk to the business of successful activism is the upheaval that will ensue. This can include a change of strategy, loss of control of the business and a loss of jobs (not least among board members). A business is at risk from activist shareholders when it has the following traits. Some are negative, while others are positive.

Negative traits

The target business may have the following negative traits, indicative of weak governance and sloppy management:

- *High overheads*, sometimes due to its being in a complex or mismatched set of markets, and possibly due to over-manning.
- *Operating in a bureaucratic or inefficient manner.*
- *Financial results that are weaker* than others in the industry.
- *Undervalued shares.* A low price-to-book ratio is a symptom of an unattractive business – unattractive due to poor performance. This means there is scope for the shares to rise on improved performance, and thus the purchaser would make a profit.
- *In a market that has been slow to change.*
- *Suffered a negative 'say on pay' vote*, indicating that the board is out of touch, doesn't care about what people think, or doesn't believe that senior pay should be related to performance.
- *Failure to act on shareholder criticisms.*
- *A board whose members have not been changed for years.*
- *Zombie directors* who have not been supported by the votes of at least 50% of shareholders, but who have been kept on the board despite that.
- *Bad PR*, having been criticised or sanctioned by a regulator, or having weak corporate social responsibility (CSR). This is indicative of a board that is not paying attention or doesn't care, and which could cause a fall in share value if allowed to continue.
- *A classified board* where membership election is staggered. This means that takeovers will be delayed by at least a year, which serves to protect and insulate the existing board, and which in turn can lead to weaker performance.
- *Dominant CEO* and weak board members. This can lead to maverick decisions and autocratic behaviour, neither of which is conducive to good management.
- *No shareholder engagement programme*, which implies the board is not listening and can lead to shareholder unhappiness.
- *Low levels of management ownership.* This means management has less motivation to perform well, since their rewards are more fixed.

Positive traits

To be attractive to a purchaser, the business will also require some positive traits. These include the following:

- *A strong brand image.* This means the business has longevity, and the brand can be leveraged into additional areas.
- *Good underlying profitability*, which entails less risk for the bidder.

Mitigating Measures: defence against the activist shareholder

Be responsive to the criticisms. They may hold some truth.

Focus on increasing shareholder value. If the business produces good returns, the activist will have little to complain of. Strategies for increasing returns may include reducing costs, especially head count, and splitting off or selling unrelated or unprofitable business units.

Seek to understand the activist's background, history and motives, in order to mount a response.

Provide a strong rebuttal if appropriate, based on facts. Communicate the value that the current strategy provides. The activist will have a much more limited understanding of the current strategy, still less an insight into the plans for future growth. Don't allow the activist to dominate the dialogue. Shareholders are usually ready to give the board the benefit of the doubt and support the existing arrangements.

Seek the support of institutional shareholders.

Institute an active shareholder engagement programme.

Invite the activist on to the board if necessary and if that is their wish. Unless the individual is simply a corporate raider who wants to strip assets and sell out quickly, there is much to be gained from a knowledgeable and committed individual.

Get advice from consultants if necessary. When a takeover bid occurs, time will be limited.

Compliancy failure

Although markets have always been regulated in one way or another, there has been a growth in the scope and number of regulators. This has come about for two main reasons.

1   Decisions by governments to denationalise many of their services. From the late 1970s onwards, states sold off commercial activities to the private sector, and opened many industries to competition. The creation of large private companies providing fundamental services such as energy and water meant that more control was needed over these large entities.
2   Repeated ethical failures, whether market rigging by banks or collusion by manufacturers. It led to public mistrust and calls for increased regulation. Someone, it was felt, needed to check up on what was going on. And hence the regulators. In addition, alarm over the risk of bank failures has led to extra regulation specifically in financial services.

Regulatory risk has two phases:

1   There is an initial uncertain period when government contemplates regulating an industry or issue for the first time or adding new regulations in an already regulated sector. By way of mitigation, companies can only really lobby at this stage.
2   A second and more permanent phase happens after regulation is in place; businesses then need to conform to legal requirements.

There are broadly two main types of regulation:

1 **Ethical and moral requirements**, such as bribery and corruption, or health and safety. Organisations can mitigate the risk of penalties by ensuring their systems are robust, values are ethical and audits are independent and thorough.
2 **Operational requirements**. These are not always set in law, but the regulator may have the power to penalise a company that is providing a poor quality service.

Failure to conform can lead to lengthy investigations, financial penalties, bad publicity and in extreme cases the loss of future contracts. Few fines are likely to be terminal, though in rare cases penalties include major costs. In the wake of the 2008 financial crisis, US banks suffered fines amounting to $150bn, according to *The Financial Times*. But since this represented only 21% of the $700bn profits they had generated between 2007 and 2014, the banks were arguably the winners.

The UK's Court of Appeal has said that in the worst cases of environmental harm a fine in the magnitude of 100% of the company's annual pre-tax net profit should be contemplated 'even where this results in fines in excess of £100 million'. According to Jessica Parker of law firm Corker Binning, the court justified this approach by emphasising that the fine must be of sufficient magnitude to send a message to shareholders and directors.

Damage to company reputation is arguably more harmful. Being barred from work is another possibility. Serco was banned for six months from bidding UK government work, following the disclosure of numerous lapses. These included billing the government for monitoring criminals who were dead.

Penalties against individuals have been rare in the past, but may become more common. The Bank of England banned Barry Tootell, former CEO of the Co-op Bank, and fined him £174,000 for his role in the bank's near collapse. It also banned the bank's former head of corporate and business banking, Keith Alderson, and fined him £89,000.

Conformance failures include the following:

- bribing customers, especially intermediaries and politicians in the developing world;
- colluding with competitors;
- causing pollution or environmental damage, whether from emissions to air or discharges to water;
- health and safety failings, such as using unsafe practices; or worse, causing the injury or death of employees;
- operational failings, such as providing poor customer service;
- failure to safeguard customers' privacy and credit card details;
- financial improprieties, such as insider trading.

Regulations can either be industry-specific, such as controls on energy businesses; or they can be generic, such as the UK's Modern Slavery Act or the EU Competition Department, with the latter being able to prevent company mergers, break up cartels and ban state aid.

Although businesses complain loudly about regulations such as the US Sarbanes Oxley Act of 2002, once in place the requirements soon become absorbed within the organisation's standard procedures. Senior managers therefore need to put protocols in place to deal with new regulations, and put the issue behind them. A negative attitude by the senior team about the laws will cause a culture of hostility to the legislation, which may lead to more junior executives flouting or barely adhering to the legislation. In time this may pose a business risk.

Fighting the regulator

There are times when a business or an industry decides to challenge the regulator.

- Canada's Information Commissioner lost a landmark case over delays in the release of government documents. A Federal Court judge said she was unable to censure National Defence for taking a three-year extension on delivering records requested under the Access to Information Act, an extension the commissioner had argued was unreasonable.
- The Swedish energy regulator lost a case concerning the income allowed to energy companies. Eighty-seven out of 171 companies appealed, in a case worth SEK33bn (£2.75bn).
- Australia's securities regulator lost its action against Andrew Forrest, who runs an iron ore business. The Commission had pursued him and his business, Fortescue Metals, for allegedly misleading the stock market over public statements relating to agreements with China. As well as imposing fines of A$11m (US$9.6m), the regulator's action threatened to have Forrest removed as a director. This would have forced him to step down as Fortescue's chief executive. But the Federal Court dismissed the case and cleared Forrest and Fortescue Metals of wrongdoing, according to the *Financial Times*.

The legal costs of fighting a regulator are large, and the case will distract management from running the business. A negotiated settlement will usually be cheaper than a legally enforced one. Losing a case may incur further penalties. And being publicly accused of bad behaviour may harm the company's reputation.

However, regulators are fallible, and do not always adopt the high standards they expect from those they supervise. Staff are sometimes unprofessional or even amateurish. Every case is different, and the decision to fight should not be taken lightly.

Mitigating Measures: ensuring compliance

Identify and assess potential regulatory risks, and put controls in place to manage them.

Introduce a regulatory compliance programme. This involves knowing what the regulatory issues are, introducing corporate standards for each, auditing their compliance and instigating an improvement programme.

Have a strong audit team. Guard against auditors being captured or intimidated by local management into accepting low standards.

Introduce a code of conduct. Have it promulgated clearly by the senior team.

Train all staff in the organisation's values and standards. Those who do not adhere to them must suffer penalties.

Create a whistleblowing system. Some businesses have independent channels whereby a third party receives the information.

Ensure consistency between what the business says and what it does. Employees quickly get to recognise corporate hypocrisy, and if they believe the company doesn't really believe in its claimed values, they will disregard them.

Place responsibility for regulatory risk with one member of staff. Given the number of regulators, and their tendency to span different business units, it is not uncommon to have regulatory oversight placed in different parts of the business. This means that awareness of risk is diffused and not managed consistently.

Do not create a consistently adversarial attitude towards regulators. There may be occasions when the business must reject the regulator's findings, but this should be done only after due consideration.

Factor regulatory risk into product development. Avoid creating products that are likely to fall foul of regulations.

Build management reporting systems that will allow a fast and tailored reply to requests for information. Ensure they are sufficiently granular to permit easy response to requests for information.

Ensure that management and staff are well versed in regulatory risk.

Communicate regulators' concerns across the business, so that employees can take steps to prevent continuing problems. If they don't know, they can't improve.

Treat risk control self assessments (RCSAs) as a tool for improvement. Do not let them be seen merely as a paperwork task.

Ensure there are sufficient compliance and regulatory staff.

Over regulation

CEOs are worried about over-regulation, and with some justification. Forty-two per cent of CEOs worldwide and 65% of the US CEOs regard this as one of their top risks, according to a survey by PwC.

Government regulation usually starts when there is evidence that the industry is lacking self-discipline and is taking advantage of customer weaknesses.

The best way to avoid over-regulation is by proving that it is unnecessary. An industry needs to demonstrate that it practises excellent self-regulation. Abuses and excesses should not occur. Bad behaviour must be punished. The US chemical industry's Responsible Care Program is sometimes cited as an example of self-regulation that has pre-empted state regulation.

However, if self-regulation is overly zealous, and too far ahead of the curve, the industry risks spending too much time and money on it, and even reducing business efficiency.

At the same time, scandals caused by a few rogue businesses or free riders can cause government to impose regulation. An industry's ability to control bad behaviours may be limited to creating a responsible culture within an industry, providing information and codes of practice, and creating social sanctions, such as shaming or public exposure of miscreants.

Meanwhile governments often want to be seen to be doing something. Politicians can be suborned by social media and journalists who will whip up emotion and demand action.

Mitigating Measures: the risk of more regulation

Avoid compliance failure. Have sufficiently stringent systems and audits in place, allied to good training. Set the right culture and build motivated teams.

Gain the support of competitors to create high standards of self-regulation. You may have to take a lead on this. The industry should set independent controls in place. Businesses must be willing to abide by the decisions made by the industry body and accept its sanctions.

Promote co-regulation, devolved or joint regulation with the state, if necessary. This is a midway point between self-regulation and state regulation.

Avoid over-regulation by moving into unregulated or less regulated markets. Banks can move into non-banking areas such as hedge funds and insurance, or find clients in less regulated developing markets.

---

8 Your delivery has been delayed

Supply chain risks

Supplies risk falls into two broad categories: supplier and non-supplier issues.

Non-supplier issues comprise the following:

- depletion of natural resources, leading to price rises (see Beating price rises);
- disruption of supply due to weather or a natural or man-made catastrophe (see Chapter 17 – Stormy weather);
- price fluctuation of currencies and commodities (see Chapter 1);
- disruption of supply caused by political upheaval (see Will raw material always be plentiful).

Supplier risks include:

- regulatory and ethical issues, such as child labour (see Unethical suppliers);
- financial concerns (see Managing the survival of your suppliers);
- quality problems, including logistics (see Supplier quality failures);
- threats to your intellectual property or proprietary processes (see Chapter 13 – See you in court).

We examine the key risks in the sections that follow. But first a set of broad Mitigating Measures.

Mitigating Measures: the supply chain

Use a simple outline questionnaire to initially discover possible vendors. This will identify the certifications they hold and their claimed standards. Use more detailed question-naires for strategic suppliers to whom you expect to be committed.

Follow up questionnaires with visits to supplier sites, using third party auditors if necessary.

Segment each supplier into a risk category from high to low. This might include the quantity it delivers to you, its financial health, the importance of what it supplies, ease of switching, the extent to which it adds value, the time needed to switch and the riskiness of its geographical location. This assessment should be reviewed at least annually.

(continued)

(continued)

Ensure adequate checks at receiving inspection.

Identify potential problems with suppliers, and take action.

Use the Kraljic Matrix to assess supplier risk. This puts them into one of four squares, based on difficulty of supply and impact on profit. This categorises suppliers as Bottleneck (difficult goods to get hold of but not financially significant); Strategic (difficult to source and vital to the business); Routine (low volume and low risk) and Leverage (high impact on profit but widely available).

Supplier quality failures

Suppliers can let you down in so many ways. They can deliver poor-quality goods, fall behind on deliveries or cause a PR row by having bad working conditions.

Existing suppliers become less of a risk as you get to know their strengths and weaknesses. But the risk is higher when launching new products because the supplier's capability is uncertain.

Every raw material has different issues. Among other supplies, Whitbread is concerned about cotton, because the company uses a lot of it. The company has a policy that it will not knowingly source cotton from Uzbekistan because the Uzbekistan government sends college students and adults from schools, hospitals and local government into the growing fields every summer to pick cotton. Other concerns of Whitbread include the sustainable sourcing of timber, palm oil and fish.

There is nothing better than a hands-on inspection, but this is expensive. You can use third party auditors, especially for overseas suppliers.

Inevitably, organisations concentrate on their main suppliers. Sedex, a non-profit that provides ethical supply chain data, found that the risks increase the further you go down the supply chain. Lower-level suppliers are often smaller and have fewer formal systems, putting their customers at greater risk. Audits of second-tier suppliers reveal 18% more risks, while third-tier suppliers have the greatest number of critical issues.

Many businesses rely on published data, such as ISO 9001 accreditation, and that provides only a partial picture.

Mitigating Measures: supplier quality

Identify critical suppliers. Which are you are most reliant on? Evaluate what would happen if they were no longer able to supply you. What steps can you take to prevent or manage that problem?

Audit your suppliers, possibly using a third party organisation. Apart from reducing risk, independent audits carry more weight with NGOs and pressure groups, if that is relevant to your organisation.

Agree targets for quality with your suppliers.

Maintain stringent goods-in inspection, to ensure only high-quality raw materials and supplies go into production.

Use indemnification clauses in your contracts. If your suppliers or partners could cause you damage, require them to maintain insurance. So if your product were to contain faulty batteries from a supplier and you get sued, you could get your supplier to claim on their insurance. You will need to see the terms of their insurance documents.

The day that students had nowhere to sit

College refurbishments often take place during the summer break, while students are away, and it is essential that the work is complete when students arrive back in September. But the carefully planned refurbishment of college lecture halls was thrown into disarray when a second-tier seating supplier failed to deliver the lecture theatre seats, even though the main supplier had done the rest of the job properly.

It being the summer, senior staff were on holiday while the work was progressing, and junior staff failed to manage the second-tier supplier.

With just a few weeks to go, senior management changed the location of lectures, and took steps to speed up the refurbishment programme; and so when the students arrived they all had a place to sit.

Later, management held a review into how it had happened, what lessons could be learnt and what should be done to manage the summer break work better.

Managing the survival of your suppliers

Suppliers need to be resilient against economic hazards (such as interest rate rises or downturns), disruptive weather and their own suppliers lower down the chain.

If a key supplier goes bust, you will find yourself without goods, and therefore unable to sell your products. You may not be able to find alternative suppliers very quickly. This is important if a supplier provides scarce raw materials, or if they have processes that are rare.

If you supply to governments, as is the case with medicines or defence products, for example, they may require your suppliers to be approved. Replacing these suppliers isn't easy since the new ones will have to be quality assured under standards set by government, industry or your own business.

A supplier may seem sound, but what about the financial health of your supplier's corporate group? Is it profitable or losing money? Is it over exposed elsewhere? 'Group stability, not just supplier stability, is key,' says Louise Green, of information specialists Bureau Van Dijk, which keeps tabs on 170 million businesses. And if the owners are individuals you should make checks on them before signing any contracts.

But auditing suppliers isn't always exact. If they are privately held, their financial status may not be publicly available or easily verifiable. And if they are based in emerging economies, information may be harder to get. A lack of transparency may also impede your investigations. And you may never be sure that local indemnities will pay out.

Mitigating Measures: supplier resilience

Assess the risk. Identify how exposed you are to the failure of critical suppliers.

Seek to minimise your dependence on critically important suppliers. This could relate to scarce raw materials or how much volume a supplier delivers. At Reckitt Benckiser no single supplier accounts for more than 5% of the cost of sales.

Consider making any critically important supplies yourself, as opposed to being reliant on suppliers (the 'make or buy' decision).

Implement dual sourcing. Buying goods from more than one supplier reduces the risk of being unable to get stock. This is less than efficient, because you have two sets of everything, from invoices to quality assurance. But it halves the risk that your operation will come to a halt due to the loss of a supplier. It's about finding the balance between the administrative efficiency and the low cost of dealing with one supplier compared with the reduced risks of having two or more. Each additional supplier adds new risks, such as ethical failings.

Have your own branded goods. This meaning you control consumer loyalty, and if a supplier ceases trading you can source the goods elsewhere.

Place your equipment or templates in a supplier's premises. If you own the equipment it will be protected from being sold and thus lost to you.

Conduct supplier audits. These start with questionnaires, and are followed by site visits, sometimes carried out by third party specialists. Part of the audit will involve assessing the supplier's financial health. Are they profitable and do they have money in the bank?

Change to suppliers located closer to your home markets. Kingfisher, the company that owns B&Q and Screwfix, has invested in sourcing offices in Poland and Turkey, in addition to its Far Eastern ones.

Help suppliers with financing or investment funding, if that will enable you to get higher quality or cheaper goods. It might also make them more loyal to you, and possibly tie them to you through an earn-out system.

Let your suppliers make an adequate profit. If you keep seeking reductions in price, or go to reverse auction, you will succeed in lowering the price for a while. But in the longer term the supplier may be unable to survive, thus putting your supplies at risk.

Use trigger events to alert you to possible failure of strategic suppliers. This could include the kind used by the UK government below.

Seven signs that a supplier might be in financial trouble – UK government

1   There's a decline in the supplier's parent company's credit rating below investment grade (below Standard & Poor's BB grading).
2   The supplier's parent company lacks or ceases to have a credit rating, or suffers a decline in its agreed financial capacity.

3   The supplier issues a profits warning to a stock exchange.
4   A regulatory body investigates improper financial accounting and reporting, suspected fraud or other impropriety.
5   The supplier materially breaches its banking covenants.
6   Material litigation begins against the supplier relating to its debt or its obligations under a contract for the supply of goods or services, or from non-payment of any financial indebtedness. Litigation would be material if the value of the claim is more than 3% of the supplier's group revenue.
7   It defaults on a payment, or loans get cancelled or suspended.

Will raw material always be plentiful?

You may be unable to get hold of your raw materials due to:

- the supplier not being able to deliver due to industrial action or bankruptcy;
- government legislation;
- harvest failures;
- severe weather events, leading to transport disruption (See Is Just in Time justified, p. 138).

Several of the raw materials used by Johnson Matthey are only available from a limited number of countries or suppliers. This includes rare earth, narcotics and platinum. Most of the world's platinum is in South Africa, and the mines there have been subject to industrial unrest.

In recent times, protesters have blocked the roads leading to the large Mogalakwena mine belonging to Amplats, part of Anglo American Plc. Mine workers failed to turn up for work. Police have arrested protesters on charges of public violence, malicious damage to property and inciting violence. South African mining companies have been criticised by communities, unions and some politicians for not doing enough to raise living standards. In response to the risk of upheaval, Johnson Matthey has increased its stocks of at-risk materials.

Mitigating Measures: continuity of supplies

Encourage your supplier to resolve the problems that hinder continuity of supplies.

Seek alternative suppliers.

If the problem is likely to be long term, seek alternative raw materials, though some processes are dependent on specific inputs.

Lack of raw materials due to conflicts or government bans

Laptops and phones require rare earth, so called not because they are necessarily rare (some are abundant) but because they are only needed in tiny amounts. Eighty-five per cent of the world's rare earth is in China, which means the supply is vulnerable to geopolitical problems. In 2010 China halted exports to Japan, following a territory dispute.

Meanwhile Indonesia banned the export of unprocessed raw minerals, including nickel and bauxite, in an effort to boost domestic processing. This created anxiety in the international mineral markets. Before the ban, Indonesia was the world's top nickel ore exporter and the largest bauxite supplier to China, and accounted for around 12% of the global market in both cases, according to the *The Jakarta Post*.

Much of the world's raw materials comes from a small number of countries. Forty-eight per cent of the world's chromium is in Kazakhstan, while 79% of all manganese comes from South Africa.

Export bans could become more common in future. The Indian government announced a ban on cotton exports, aiming to help its textile industry, but this was rescinded after complaints from China.

Other substances may be banned by home countries or trading blocs such as the European Union. At the time of writing, the EU was proposing banning two more pesticides, isoproturon and amitrole.

Mitigating Measures: loss of raw materials

Identify whether any raw materials or substances are likely to suffer a ban on export or usage.

Initiate a research and development programme to identify alternative substances or changes to your processes.

Beating price rises

The price of commodities can fluctuate greatly. Demand by growing economies, weather events and supplier failure can all cause price hikes. This in turn can damage your margins.

There are many solutions to price increases, including finding supplies in other regions. In Ghana, Guinness increased its use of local raw materials (barley and hops) from 12% in 2012 to 48% in 2015. This has created additional supplies that are closer to home and easier to manage.

Mitigating Measures: supplier price rises

Don't delay in raising your price following a rise in raw material costs. If supplies across the world are affected, you must be ready to increase prices. Businesses often fear that increasing their price will allow competitors to keep their prices level and to grab a larger market share (the kinked price theory). Many businesses believe that customers are more price aware, and more ready to switch, than they actually are. Sometimes you have to be the first to raise your prices.

Agree medium- or long-term contracts with suppliers, to guarantee supplies. Alston Transport signed a ten-year exclusive agreement with Hydrogenics, a manufacturer of hydrogen power systems, for the supply of fuel cells for regional commuter trains in Europe. Similarly, John Lewis, which owns the Waitrose supermarket chain, signed a ten-year deal with Ocado, the online supermarket delivery service.

Negotiate with suppliers to keep their prices down. They may need you as much as you need them.

See if you can unbundle some of the supply. You might collect the goods yourself, or get an unimproved, untested or unrefined version.

Seek a different supplier. Some suppliers may delay their increase for a while.

Hedge. Buy futures in their selected commodity or raw material.

Add a clause to your customers' contracts, allowing you to increase the price if costs rise.

Re-design your products. In response to China restricting exports of its rare earth, companies have reduced the quantity of dysprosium used in permanent magnets and the lanthanum used in refinery catalysts.

Find substitutes. Li-ion battery makers found they could reduce the amount of cobalt needed by creating a cobalt-manganese-nickel compound. Photolytic businesses replaced indium and gallium with silicon-based cells.

Build alliances and join buying groups. Airlines have reduced costs and reached wider markets by code sharing: sharing routes, ticket sales and airport facilities.

Set up a reverse auction where the lowest price wins. This may only work for products whose quality is unlikely to reduce.

Too few suppliers

We tend to think of oligopolies (a restricted number of suppliers) as those that affect us as consumers – the banks, supermarkets chains and telephone companies.

But many B2B markets have few suppliers or even just one single supplier. Anyone who needs to buy aluminium, steel or oil will encounter an oligopoly. And when the EU fines companies for collusion and fixing the market, as it so often does, there is an oligopoly at work.

Makers of vehicle parts across the globe have also come under scrutiny from competition authorities, in what John Terzaken, an anti-trust partner at law firm Allen & Overy, called 'unquestionably the broadest and deepest international cartel case on record'. The US Department of Justice agreed to accept fines totalling hundreds of millions of dollars with a small number of car parts suppliers. Not all oligopolies are criminal, needless to say, but the fewer the suppliers the greater their power.

Mitigating Measures: too few suppliers

Be alert to the possibility of collusion among suppliers. If found, report the companies to the authorities.

Ensure that your own organisation is not seen to be colluding. Innocuous meetings with competitors at conferences can turn into illegal information sharing.

Seek alternative international suppliers.

Amend your processes to avoid a reliance on oligopolistic supplies. This can mean using alternative materials or methods.

Is Just in Time justified?

Just in Time (JIT) strategies involve having components or raw materials arrive just in time to be used. The advantages lie in having less inventory, a smaller warehouse and less risk of damage.

But JIT increases the risk of not having the required goods at the time they are needed. This can be caused by supplier failings, distribution holdups or extreme weather events. Unexpected scrap and re-work, sometimes caused by machine failure, can also add to an out-of-stock situation.

Just in Time relies on having a predictable supply and demand. If you can forecast how many vehicles your plant needs to produce, and you have reliable suppliers, there is no need to keep excess inventory.

But if sales vary from week to week, your product needs customising and you can't guarantee your supplies will arrive promptly, JIT adds risk.

In the past, catastrophes were limited to the area where they happened. An earthquake in Russia had little impact on the wider world, and many businesses had only local plants, suppliers and customers. Two things have changed:

1   Businesses have plants and customers all over the planet. We're interconnected like never before. A problem in one part of the globe will have an impact on businesses elsewhere.
2   Extreme weather events are more common, due to climate change. Other disruptive events, such as terrorist incidents, are probably no more common or severe than in the past, but they get more publicity.

Some incidents that affect deliveries are 'black swan' events – they're completely unexpected. Others, such as food crises and pandemics, are 'slow burn' events that develop over weeks, months or a few years, according to think-tank Chatham House. Slow-motion events emerge even more slowly, with the impacts building up over several or many years. These include climate change, water scarcity and biodiversity loss.

Mitigating Measures: JIT

Measure your supply chain risks. Plan investment and stock locations based on this information and on simulations.

Investigate the possibility of HILP (high impact/low probability) events occurring. What disruption could they cause to your supplies? Have a contingency plan to recover from such an event.

Regularly review the level of inventory currently in place. Consider moving some components to JIC (just in case) inventory, which involves keeping spares or extra raw materials.

Consider manufacturing critical components in-house or buying out the supplier.

Contract with more than one supplier to minimise the risk of delays.

Ensure your systems provide a fast response to changes in demand, using electronic data interchange (EDI) which will reduce the lag.

Unethical suppliers

Unethical suppliers can cause headaches for a business. Infractions include:

- the use of child labour and indentured labour (the use of unfree labourers)
- low wages
- poor working conditions (working hours and health and safety)
- corruption and bribery
- lack of human rights at work, and lack of trade union rights.

These problems are not limited to suppliers in emerging economies. *The Independent* newspaper reported that Bulgarians were being flown to Britain, where they lived in packed caravan compounds and paid just £45 a week to pick fruit for Britain's supermarkets.

Ethical failings by suppliers can adversely affect the organisation's reputation. At one time meat companies across Europe were putting horse meat into beef burgers. While eating horse is not in itself a risk, the scandal revealed that the supply chain was inadequately audited and that adulteration was taking place, while for some people eating horse is taboo. This scandal dented the supermarkets' brand images.

For a supermarket to monitor the ethics of its 2,000 suppliers – and their suppliers – is a major task. This is also a problem for industries such as apparel, where most supplies originate from developing economies.

Conflict minerals

In countries like the Democratic Republic of Congo armed groups use rape and coercion of workers in mining and selling four minerals: tin, tantalum, tungsten and gold. The minerals are used in jewellery, mobile phones and electronics, and it is hard to verify that they have been produced ethically.

Where the mines are controlled by armed gangs, their proceeds go to fund wars and war lords. Fifteen to 20% of diamonds come from illegal sources. And even where the material has not been mined by slave workers, it may have been worked by children and in dangerous conditions.

Mitigating Measures: unethical suppliers

Have a code of conduct which your suppliers must adhere to.

Audit all major suppliers. Those who give cause for concern will need extra attention or ultimately should be removed from the roster.

Join a relevant trade association, such as the Food Fraud Network. Companies in the garment trade should join the Bangladesh Accord, an agreement set up in the wake of the Rana Plaza factory collapse that killed 1,130 people. Almost 200 businesses signed up but only seven of the 1,660 factories have implemented their corrective action plans. It highlights the importance of paying more than lip service to such standards. In Bangladesh

(continued)

(continued)

78,000 garment workers produce garments for H&M in buildings without fire exits, while workers at Walmart factories suffer threats of termination, forced overtime, denial of sick leave and 10 to 14 hour days without breaks or drinking water, according to AFWA.

Consider taking control of key suppliers through ownership, in order to ensure quality. This adds more risk, however.

Supplier partnerships

Treating suppliers as partners rather than something to control should reduce risk and create better solutions. The same also applies to working with clients. Partnership sourcing involves being open about your vulnerabilities, and seeking advice on how to overcome them.

Talking about car technology, Volvo's then CEO Olof Persson told PwC,

> We didn't have the knowledge about charging stations, traffic management systems and how to integrate this into the city structures that we have. By partnering with those who have that additional knowledge we could actually get the product to market faster.

This isn't the same as operating a joint venture (JV). The latter involves a much greater commitment to the other business, including giving them a share of the profits. A JV also involves greater risks, because you are tied by a contract to the other business.

Supplier or client partnership, by contrast, allows the other business to become more deeply enmeshed in your business and encouraged to think like you. If you're the larger party, you can expect to gain the majority of the rewards. You harness their knowledge and insights. Sometimes the supplier only expects gratitude and loyalty. For them it reduces the risk of losing the client to a competitor.

Quoted in *Industry Week*, Sherry Gordon, president of consulting firm Value Chain Group, talked of a supplier day where key suppliers came to offer ideas to the customer, with the customer expected to listen without refuting what the suppliers were saying. 'This day resulted in big and small, strategic and cost-saving ideas being offered to the customer,' she said. 'So why hadn't these ideas ever come up before? Some of them had, but the customer wasn't open to them or looking to reap the value of the ideas.'

Satya Nadella, Microsoft's CEO, started to forge relationships with cloud companies, long regarded by Microsoft as the enemy. One such business was Salesforce, whose sales management programme is now integrated into Office and Outlook. Speaking to *Wired* magazine, Marc Benioff, Salesforce's CEO, said: 'Before, we were not able to partner with Microsoft. Satya has opened a door that was closed. And locked. And barricaded.'

There are risks, however. You end up giving an outsider information about where profits are to be made. There is then little to stop them from using that information to their own advantage. They could create their own competing service, moving vertically into your space. Or they could work with a competitor at some point in the future. It is a rare human who doesn't consider whether there is some personal gain to be made from new knowledge.

Mitigating Measures: supplier partnerships

Develop greater listening skills when dealing with suppliers and partners.

Set up programmes that involve discussion with suppliers and customers. Some individual, somewhere, has solutions that could provide a route to the future.

Decide how much data you need to make available to business partners. Even more importantly, decide what data will not be revealed.

Consider developing your suppliers through training and investment. This could lead to a higher-quality supply.

Consider introducing BS 11000, the collaborative working standard.

9   When the wheels come off

Operational failures

Whether you manufacture products or provide a service, every type of operation carries its own risks.

With a turnover of $28bn, Deere and Company makes huge construction equipment, which involves many manufacturing and end user risks. The company also has a leasing arm, which creates financial and debt risks. It has sales operations in the USA and in developing nations, which could give rise to ethical risks. And it services equipment, which provides operational risks. In short Deere faces no shortage of threats.

Many businesses are similar hybrid organisations, providing both services and products, which create varied risks. Operational risks comprise the following:

- A product or service may be of poor quality; customers might defect.
- Contracts might not be not delivered on time, due to staff shortages or unexpected delays.
- Output could be halted, due to fire or a lack of components.
- There might be a catastrophic failure, causing harm to employees or customers

Less immediately serious are problems relating to low productivity and excessive waste. But if left unchecked they could bring the business down.

These operational failures can be due to one or several factors, many of which are interrelated:

- bad systems, or a lack of procedures;
- lack of training;
- a single employee who makes a technical mistake or fails to do their allotted task;
- low standards, such as letting employees smoke around fire hazards;
- lack of performance management;
- inadequate risk assessment or controls: Lack of auditing;
- under investment: lack of maintenance, insufficient staffing or inadequate resourcing;
- an act of god, such as flooding or lightning strike.

Some failures stem from a gradual decline in product quality or a slow rise in accidents. These are partly self-inflicted, and could have been forecast. Others are unexpected, such as a terrorist incident. But risk assessment and putting plans in place will avert most of them.

In the sections that follow, we examine some of the major risks affecting business operations. Many other sections of the book affect operations, including Chapter 4 on people management, Chapter 8 on the supply chain, Chapter 11 on environmental impacts, and Chapter 17 on weather.

Quality failings

Given that manufacturing involves heat, pressure, fuel and toxic materials, it isn't surprising that processes fail from time to time.

Service operations are also prone to failure. Again, this is not a surprise, given that they involve large numbers of people, many not well paid or highly qualified, interacting with customers in sometimes unpredictable ways.

In Hull, UK, a woman lost her baby because of a series of errors by hospital midwives. They sent her home several times during her pregnancy, after she had haemorrhaged and had reported reduced movements from the foetus. When the mother went into spontaneous labour a day after her due date, midwives mistakenly monitored the woman's own heart rate – confusing it for the baby's.

Another patient at the same hospital received a potentially lethal blood transfusion, when the nurse administered the wrong type of blood. The type 'O' patient received type 'A' blood after nurses confused him with a patient who had the same name but a different date of birth, an incompatible blood group and who was located at a different hospital site. The investigation said it was astounded the patient didn't die as a result.

The same hospital recorded five 'never events' that year (events that should never happen), including cases where surgeons operated on the wrong part of patients' spines and left a nylon bag inside a patient after surgery. Such failings usually come down to:

- lack of staff commitment or concentration
- lack of training
- lack of supervision
- tired or overworked staff
- weak systems.

In some but not all cases these problems may be worsened by financial constraints.

Mitigating Measures: preventing quality failures

Map each process. Write a procedure or protocol for doing it right.

Communicate the procedure to staff, and train them to use it.

Give each risk an owner who will be responsible for managing it. In practice, however, the threat will lie with individual lower-grade staff.

Set KPIs to keep track of progress and identify trends.

Keep records. In particular, record failures and near misses. Seek to understand the underlying causes and rectify them.

Hold review meetings to assess how quality can be maintained and improved.

(continued)

(continued)

Develop a continuous improvement programme. Engage staff in this.

Build in some redundancy (duplicate equipment) and slack (excess staff) where possible. Machines and people tend to fail when they are pushed to the limit.

Foster an atmosphere that supports learning. Treat error as useful information rather than something to blame staff for. Avoid silos and hierarchies. Encourage a culture where staff are enabled to debate and reach out to others. Help staff to challenge custom and practice.

Be alert to weak systems and workarounds that get treated as normal, such as staff using their own equipment because the company's ones are inadequate. Staff readily get used to working around inconveniences and setting up their own methods, and fail to ask why this is happening.

Implement a management system, such as ISO 9000 or HACCP (depending on the industry), which sets out a 'plan – do – check' methodology for ensuring that products or services are consistent. Have an independent auditor check the system, or it will be ignored.

Become a highly reliable organisation (HRO). If working in a high-risk environment, such as airlines, healthcare or the military, seek to become an HRO. These organisations suffer fewer incidents than the average. Their characteristics include acknowledging expertise, no matter how junior the individual, a senior team that is in touch with daily operations, an appreciation of continuous learning and improvement, a preoccupation with the risk of failure and a reluctance to accept superficial judgements.

Plan for contingencies. An organisation whose faulty goods or an operational failure could be disastrous needs an emergency plan. A swift and effective response or recall procedure will help the problem to be quickly overcome whereas a tardy and grudging operation may lead to hostile social media comment.

Energy firm gets a record fine for poor service

Energy firm npower was fined £26m for its continued failure to bill customers properly. More than half a million customers were affected, with many suffering distress and worry, according to the regulator Ofgem.

The company's profits fell 60% as a result of customers receiving late bills, inaccurate ones or no bills at all. Over one 12-month period it lost more than 300,000 customers, and many of its remaining customers reduced their energy usage.

Problems persisted for four years when the company changed its invoicing from an old in-house system to SAP. The programme, which was installed by IBM, caused disruption to npower's billing, customer service and financial systems. Many of npower's 5.4m customers began to experience billing delays and cancelled direct debits, while some customers' accounts were never set up.

This created a backlog of complaints and longer call waiting times. The regulator, Ofgem, said there was a 'serious deterioration in service levels'.

The project was designed to improve the administration of millions of customer accounts. But Forrester analyst Duncan Jones said that the stakeholders should have expected to encounter some technical problems with such a large transformative project.

He told *Computer World* magazine: 'Customers, vendors and service partners need to ensure that project contracts give the flexibility needed to react to unplanned changes during and after the implementation process.

'These are complex projects involving a lot of changes to the way that people are doing things, and there is risk involved that you have to mitigate,' he said. 'They [npower] should have foreseen this, SAP should have foreseen this and IBM should have foreseen this.'

Mistake proofing

Mistake proofing (or 'Poka-yoke' in Japanese) is designed to stop employees or customers from making errors. It reduces the opportunity for failure.

People are only human and will make always mistakes. Quality inspection only identifies a problem after a mistake has been made. It is better to stop the problem before it starts. Here are four examples of error proofing.

- A freezer has an alarm that sounds if the door is left open for more than 30 seconds. This stops food from being spoilt.
- Some cars will not start if left in gear or if the driver is not wearing their seat belt.
- Child-proof caps on pill bottles stop children from ingesting harmful medication.
- Printers' guillotines don't work until the safety hood is in place. This stops operators losing fingers.

Poka-yoke systems start by identifying the risk. Then you put some preventative device in place. If you can't do that, you introduce a detection system, such as an alarm.

Mistake proofing is equally applicable to service businesses. Computer forms often require the user to answer all the questions before the form is accepted. The form may also check that an email address is formed correctly.

Mitigating Measures: introducing mistake proofing

Identify errors, whether made by employees or customers.

Prioritise these errors in order of seriousness.

Create systems that prevent those errors, where possible.

Add an error detection system if you can't stop people from making mistakes.

What a waste

In its broadest sense, waste is whatever doesn't contribute to customer satisfaction. Organisations should use only the absolute minimum of resources (material, machines and labour) to create its product or service. Everything else is just waste. Waste adds cost, and cost is a risk.

Whenever you have to re-do some work, or discard something because it was sub-standard, you create waste. Reports have to be sent back to be re-written, supermarkets dump food which has passed its sell-by date and publishers print too many copies of a magazine.

Every time this happens extra costs are created. Some products and services – or entire businesses – become unprofitable due to the amount of sub-standard work and waste produced.

Lean, originally a Toyota system, describes seven types of waste. They are based on manufacturing principles, but can be applied to service businesses as well. They are as follows:

1   *Transportation*. Unnecessary movement. Nothing should move more or further than it needs, because each time it happens, there is a cost, as well as the risk of damage. This relates to moving goods around a manufacturing plant or transporting goods to a customer.
2   *Inventory*. Unnecessary raw materials or stock in a warehouse. Unnecessary printing of documents.
3   *Motion*. Motion relates to wasteful activity on goods being processed. This includes wear and tear on equipment. Repetitive stress injuries and inefficient production are also caused by undue effort on the part of the workforce. It can involve customers having to search many pages on a website to find information.
4   *Delays*. Goods and services should either be being worked on, or else despatched to the customer. Often parts are awaiting further processing, or are held up due to lack of parts. In service businesses, customers are kept waiting on the phone queue, at a checkout or in a restaurant.
5   *Overprocessing*. Companies sometimes produce goods and services that are overengineered or overspecified for the purpose. This can include duplicated activity, or forms that require unnecessary information.
6   *Overproduction:* Overproduction happens when the business produces more than is needed. This leads to the risk of excess inventory which may later need to be written off.
7   *Defects and scrap:* Defects either have to be binned, or require re-working or a recall. In service businesses, it's about incorrect data entry or a customer being sent the wrong product.

Consider whether activities add value (VA) or not (NVA). Activities that don't add value include the following:

- several people having to sign off purchase orders;
- getting work checked by others;
- writing reports that are never read or are not actionable;
- meetings that have no outcomes;
- looking for information that is not easily accessible.

An example of NVA might be cleaning areas that are not dirty, because someone wrote a procedure for it. A good question to ask is: What would happen if we didn't do it?

Another way of reducing waste is the '5S' system which emerged with the 'Just in Time' philosophy in Japan. 5S is concerned with ensuring the employee has the necessary tools to hand. The English version of the five 'S' words is:

- *Sort.* Identify tools; have only what you need.
- *Straighten.* Put everything in order.
- *Scrub.* Everything should be left clean and tidy.
- *Standardise.* Have standard procedures for doing everything.
- *Sustain.* Make sure things don't go back to the bad old ways.

Mitigating Measures: reducing waste

Apply the principles of Lean to the business.

Identify examples of waste in transportation, inventory, movement, delays, overprocessing, overproduction and scrap. Re-work, inconsistent output and sub-standard production can be reduced by better quality systems, whether ISO 9000, Lean, Six Sigma or some other system.

Introduce 5s as a way of improving productivity.

Document your processes, audit them and then have the findings regularly reviewed by senior management.

Low productivity

A business that suffers lower productivity than its competitors is at risk. It creates a vicious circle, producing low profits and therefore less cash for investment. Conversely, higher productivity will allow a business to survive longer: it has more scope to give discounts or invest in development. There are eight causes of low productivity:

1   *Demotivated, disengaged or disloyal staff.* This may be due to poor industrial relations, mismanagement or inadequate communication.
2   *Overmanned departments* where assistants have been added, and work expands to fill the time available. It could also be caused by an ageing, overpaid and underworked workforce that has grown complacent, padded by years of continual wage rises.
3   *Low investment in IT*, with too many manual and repetitive tasks. Or an over-reliance on a low-paid, overseas workforce.
4   *Poor working conditions*, such as noisy open plan offices which have been shown to reduce productivity.
5   *An emphasis on low prices.* This can lead to hiring cheap unqualified staff, poor-quality work, dissatisfied customers, contracts not renewed and a constant search for new business.
6   *Weak quality control*, leading to sub-standard work, reject goods and returns.
7   *Inefficient process*, such as moving partly finished goods to another building, or having slow equipment.
8   *Lack of training or competence.* Staff may need to be shown how to do a task properly. Unproductive or incompetent staff may need to be replaced.

Mitigating Measures: raising productivity

Compare your productivity levels with industry norms.

Assess where productivity is low, and understand its causes.

Analyse where manual tasks could be replaced by automated ones.

Review the extent to which staff are engaged. Understand the reasons for lack of engagement, and rectify them.

Improve working conditions, such as providing quieter offices or less disruption.

Rationalise or re-engineer operations to improve workflow.

Improve quality control.

Provide adequate training.

Why outsourcing doesn't mean your problems are over

Organisations outsource in order to hand a non-core process to a specialist, someone who can do it better and for less money. Outsourcing also allows the business to adapt more easily, being less tied by trade union conservatism. To that extent, outsourcing reduces risk.

When it works well, it solves many problems. But if the relationship later descends into acrimony, you can find yourself stuck with an organisation you can't easily get rid of, and a sub-standard service.

The risks grow as you outsource to another country. And if your supplier has a different view from you about recruitment and compensation, that too can add complications if you find that the outsourced employees lack the necessary skills.

When outsourcing goes bad

A back office outsourcing contract for an English local authority and a police authority went sour after £180m of planned savings didn't emerge, and problems developed over the quality of the service.

IBM was to take over most of the council's SG&A (selling, general and administrative) activities. This included HR, payroll, finance, procurement, customer contact, property and IT.

Along the way the contractor, SouthWest One, which was 75% owned by IBM, sued its client, Somerset County Council, for £25m. The council had withheld payments, saying the contractor had failed to deliver promised savings of £180m, and that the council was dissatisfied with the contractor's procurement quality. SouthWest One said it had met its obligations.

The matter was settled out of court with the council paying SouthWest One £3m and a further £2m to the lawyers. The council could have been faced with a £40m bill if it had lost the court battle.

Much of the savings were predicated on an ever-increasing amount of money being put into public services, whereas public funding had instead reduced.

The council ultimately brought 160 staff back to its own premises.

In its 'lessons learnt' report, Somerset County Council admitted the 'sheer size and complexity' of SouthWest One made it 'difficult to manage'. The contract was too complicated from the outset, and the partners didn't have enough staff to manage it properly.

Signed in 2007, the contract, was 'incredibly complicated' and ran to over 3,000 pages. But the detail didn't stop the project from failing. This related mainly to problems implementing a central SAP system. The system was 'plagued with problems that led to delays paying supplier invoices'. This required 'hundreds' of IT engineers to fix.

'One of the most significant lessons learnt related to the sheer size, breadth and complexity of the contract', said Kevin Nacey, Somerset County Council's finance and performance director. 'The system regime was too onerous for both sides to administer,' he said, 'and the initial team was too small to manage the contract.' SAP and other performance issues were not resolved quickly enough.

For its part, IBM had to bail out SouthWest One with a multi-million pound loan to keep the venture afloat. SouthWest One reported a £31m loss.

Mitigating Measures: outsourcing

Decide on your organisation's outsourcing maturity. Among other things, this relates to your experience of outsourcing, the extent to which the relationship between client and provider is defined, and how well the activities are measured and reviewed. The less experience the organisation has, the smaller your immediate outsourcing goals should be.

Be wary of suppliers who want you to outsource a wide range of functions and create a new IT system to provide the service.

View forecast savings with suspicion. It is in the supplier's interest to maximise the claimed savings. They aren't impartial.

Ensure that the risk is shared with the contractor. The contractor must have a vested interest in making the project work.

There must be an explicit methodology for the project. You must know in advance how the new system will work.

Involve your service managers and supervisors in the early days of the project. This will minimise disruption and iron out problems.

Identify how problems and disagreements will be resolved, and who will be involved in decision making.

Be cautious about losing skills. Outsourcing a service means you will lose familiarity with it. If that service is a core part of your competitive advantage, be extra careful.

(continued)

(continued)

Assess how easy it will be to bring the service back in-house. All contracts end some day, and by that time you may have lost vital knowledge. You may need to keep some resource in-house to retain some skills in that area.

Be aware of differences in enterprise architecture. If you're used to Microsoft SQL and the vendor is using Java, you need to be aware of the problems you might encounter on the way.

Be conscious that labour costs in low-cost countries are rising, and the expected savings might not materialise.

Find a partner that has skills in the area you lack, in addition to them offering lower costs.

Consider the possibility of keeping the work in-house. See the Target case study below.

Target goes back in-house

Target Corp aimed to hire 500 software engineers and other staff for its online communications, using open-source tools. 'Keeping the intellectual property created by in-house software engineers preserves competitive advantage,' said chief information officer Mike McNamara.

Historically, Target has outsourced significant portions of application development and backend systems to India and US firms, such as Infosys and IBM. 'We've got to a stage where almost half the team is in third parties. It's unhealthy,' he said, talking to *CIO* magazine.

'Strategic use of technology to make the supply chain more efficient and cut the time getting products to customers can boost Target's market advantage against other retailers,' he said. 'If you can get advantage through shorter lead times, you don't want a third-party provider sending it to Retailer B down the road.'

The future is another country

Offshoring is outsourcing's big brother. You could outsource work to a business in the same industrial estate, whereas offshoring implies that your contractor will be based on another continent.

There are many advantages to offshoring, chief among them being the reduction in cost and the handing of specific work to specialist contractors.

Following the wave of offshoring in earlier decades, there has been a move to repatriate or 'reshore' some services, particularly when quality was found to be lacking or savings didn't outweigh customer dissatisfaction. In a similar move, companies have been shifting resources from one low-cost country to another, such as moving from China to Vietnam, as they try to avoid higher costs.

And with the rise of Asia as a consumer society, the idea of 'offshoring' may be out of date. The business should be wherever the customer is. Asian companies build cars in the USA, and American car companies set up plants in China to serve the growing market there. And in an era of increased automation, the labour element is likely to be smaller than before, and therefore less important.

However, being one step beyond outsourcing, as we said, offshoring brings additional risks. The chief ones are as follows:

Political or cultural unrest: For something as important as a data processing centre or a manufacturing unit, you need to be assured that the country is stable. The political situation can quickly change and the world seems to be ever less predictable. That said, thousands of businesses offshore their work, and the countries where offshoring takes place have a vested interest in stability.

Increased labour rate as time goes by: Wages rates have been growing in the developing economies for many years, and with that comes the erosion of wage differences with the West.

Legal and regulatory risks: If you need to demonstrate compliance to a regulator, this will be more difficult if your operations are located 5,000 miles away.

Ethical and environmental problems: Factory collapses, child labour, indentured labour and poor working conditions are quickly unearthed by NGOs and spread by social media. Suppliers' performance is a risk.

Loss of knowledge and loss of control: If you offshore your design function, will you lose important skills? Do your designers work with customers to develop new products? The same might apply to IT or engineering. There are some business functions that you might not want to lose. Other companies find that the gap between home-based R&D and offshored manufacturing adds problems and hampers innovation.

Uncertain future transportation costs: The price of fuel can rise, making for an uncertain future.

Slow response times and slow delivery: Where goods are delivered from half way across the world, they can take 30 days to arrive. Are you prepared for that wait? How will the cost of occasional urgent air freight reduce the benefits of offshoring? If products are out of stock, how long will it take to get them into the stores?

Communications difficulties: When you need to discuss details, it's harder when the workforce is far away.

Variable quality: Vendors sometimes fail to deliver on their promises. Or the quality may decline as time goes by. Managing quality at a distance is always going to be hard.

Mitigating Measures: managing offshoring

Consider what jobs could be done better or more cheaply in a low-wage country. These start with repetitive non-customer-facing work such as data entry, but can also include more complex tasks, for example medical diagnostics.

Compare the cost of local outsourcing. Higher automation locally can mean costs are not very different from those in a distant low-wage economy.

(continued)

(continued)

Spend a substantial time studying vendors. Find suppliers who understand your industry. View the processes in operation, and at different times. Take up customer references. Don't rely on assurances.

Phase your offshoring. Don't commit to offshore everything until some of it has transitioned smoothly. In the first phase, offshore only new activities or those that are causing bottlenecks, rather than core ones. Don't give overseas staff customer-facing roles initially.

Expect problems in the transition phase, and deal with them.

Set binding standards for your vendor. Agree the detailed work processes in writing.

Agree KPIs, including those by which success or failure will be measured.

Share the risk with the supplier by building in penalty clauses.

Document roles and agree how communication and reports will be delivered and when. Ensure there is adequate support in your home country.

Audit the supplier regularly. Ensure that it is known to NGOs and conforms to third party ethical standards.

Ensure that continuity plans are in place. What will happen if the facility floods or goes up in flames?

Understand and agree HR policies, including hiring, working conditions and remuneration.

Invest in training the offshore workforce. Provide maximum documentation, webcasts and local language videos. Show videos of how it works in your home country.

IT. Ensure your IT systems are compatible with the supplier.

We interrupt this programme: major incident risks

Being unable to access your workplace is the ultimate problem for any organisation. Fire, explosion or the loss of a data centre could bring the organisation to a halt. A major incident could be one of any of the risks mentioned in this book, but on a grand scale.

The scale of an incident is measured by recovery time – how long it takes you to get up and running again. This depends on the scale of the incident and on the organisation's resilience. Being able to switch production to another manufacturing plant or to quickly restore data from backups will reduce the duration and severity of the incident.

Businesses can mitigate the loss of a plant by having a sound continuity plan, and testing the plan to ensure it works. A continuity plan often involves being able to operate from another site. It can also require a mirrored IT system.

The Costa roastery in London

Costa Coffee's 1,882 UK shops rely on the company's roastery in Old Paradise Street, London. The roastery produces the company's own brand coffee which, they say, is preferred over its rivals by 70% of consumers in blind tastings.

Its output also serves the 4,000 Costa Express machines found in garages, offices and supermarkets for people who want a quick cup of coffee on the go.

At any given time the company has five days production in hand. If a fire broke out in the roastery, the building was flooded or some other calamity were to happen – one that lasted more than five days – it would be a calamity. Owner Whitbread has placed this danger high up on its list of risks. It has plans to have its coffee roasted elsewhere, were that to happen.

Mitigating Measures: preventing business interruption

Put contingency plans in place. These should cover the main types of incident that could affect the business. This should include recovery plans for IT and operations.

Periodically review and test these plans.

10 Keeping staff safe

Minimising health and safety risks

Health and safety is a very traditional area of risk. We all know what slips and trips look like. But many manufacturing and engineering jobs have gone from the West to China and other developing nations, so the average Western workplace is less dangerous than it was several decades ago. Today, only 1 in 12 American workers is employed in manufacturing compared with 1 in 5 in 1980, according to Bloomberg. In part this is due to mechanisation, and in part due to offshoring.

Nevertheless, this still leaves a great many jobs at high risk from health and safety accidents, including 800,000 employees in the UK automotive sector alone. So in this chapter we examine the risks from fire and then from workplace accidents.

Blazing fury

When workmen came to do some routine welding outside a warehouse at Obhu, Japan, it started off as a standard job. But no one noticed that expanded polystyrene had been left outside the building. Minutes later the welding sparks ignited the material. Fire spread to the warehouse which held plastics and sodium cyanide. The conflagration took hold, and began to burn down the warehouse, generating black smoke and chlorine gas.

Half the warehouse was in flames. The fire also damaged the cargo handling area. Chemicals and fire extinguishing agents flowed into the River Sakai close to the warehouse and killed fish. The chemical fire continued to burn for 19 hours, and caused a loss of ¥800m (£5m).

Obhu City issued an evacuation order to 2,000 households which held 8,000 people downwind of the fire, though only 400 people actually complied. Fortunately no one died, though three people were injured.

The fire brigade later blamed a catalogue of failings, including organisational problems, poor management, poor safety awareness, inadequate risk recognition, poor planning of maintenance and wrong hot work methods. But it had all started out as just another routine job.

Fire is a constant risk. In any one year there can be 1,800 fires in UK industrial processing premises, with 80 casualties. There will also be 5,000 fires in commercial or retail premises, of which 40% will be in retail premises. A further 1,000 fires will happen in health and hospital premises, with 30 casualties. And there will be 600 fires in schools, more than one a day. In the USA in 2013, direct losses amounted to $2.6bn, with 65 deaths and 1,525 injuries.

In this section we examine what can be done to prevent fires at work. The first action is to assess the risk of fire, followed by taking steps to prevent it from happening.

Risk assessment

A fire risk assessment involves five steps:

1   *Identify possible fire hazards.* What could ignite a fire? It could be lights, heaters, naked flames, electrical equipment, cigarettes, matches and anything that could get hot or cause sparks. Arson might also be a cause.

    What could provide fuel? This might include:

- textiles, wood, paper, card, plastics, rubber, foam, furniture, packaging and waste materials;
- liquids, such as those containing solvents: petrol, white spirit, methylated spirits, paraffin, thinners, paints, varnish and adhesives;
- gases: lpg or acetylene.

    What work processes are dangerous? Do you have equipment with moving parts, hot working, flammable liquids or processes that give off sparks such as cutting, grinding and welding?

2   *Decide who could be in danger* in the event of a fire (for example employees or visitors).

3   *Evaluate the risks arising from the hazards.* Are your existing fire precautions adequate? Should more be done to eliminate the hazard or control the risks?

4   *Record your findings.* Detail the actions that need to be taken, and implement them. Prepare an emergency plan.

5   *Review and revise the assessment* when necessary.

Mitigating Measures: reducing the risk of fire

Carry out a fire risk assessment. See above.

Control the sources of ignition. See the hazards above.

Control the sources of fuel. They include anything that can burn.

Ensure that waste is carefully managed. Waste is a frequent cause of fires.

Take extra care with building alterations and renovations. Fires often start this way.

Provide adequate fire detection and warning, notably fire alarms.

Ensure there are suitable means of escape.

Provide suitable methods for fighting fires, including extinguishers or sprinklers.

Maintain and test fire precautions, including alarms.

Train employees in fire safety.

Minimising accidents at work

Work accidents are quite traumatic events, and the events afterwards – arrival of health and safety inspectors, reports being written and insurance claims – are unsettling because they usually illustrate what could have been done to prevent the accident.

Table 10.1 Accidents, Great Britain, 2014–2015

Type of injury	No. of fatal injuries	No. of injuries causing a 7 day absence
Injured while handling, lifting or carrying	–	16,018
Slips, trips or falls on same level	3	13,646
Other kind of accident	5	8,390
Struck by moving (including flying/falling) object	12	5,789
Acts of violence	2	3,969
Falls from a height	29	3,117
Contact with moving machinery	9	2,239
Strike against something fixed or stationary	–	2,004
Struck by moving vehicle	16	1,055
Exposure to, or contact with, a harmful substance	–	735
Injured by an animal	1	418
Contact with electricity or electrical discharge	2	230
Exposure to fire	1	169
Trapped by something collapsing/overturning	12	159
Exposure to an explosion	–	27
Drowning or asphyxiation	7	5
Total	99	57,970

Source: HSE.

Accidents also cost money. If an employee is absent due to an accident, you lose the output they would have generated, the cost of their replacement, plus the time spent training that person. Meanwhile the business will still be paying the salary of the injured person.

The European Agency for Safety and Health at Work (EU-OSHA) estimates the costs of accidents and ill health at work as being 1% of UK GDP, 5% of Australian GDP and 3% of Dutch GDP.

A bad safety record is usually indicative of many failings, including low standards and a management that is either not interested in safety or puts profit above it.

In some organisations, there is a culture that condones the non-reporting of incidents involving safety. This occurs in sites where there is a high failure rate, which then treats failings as inevitable.

As Table 10.1 shows, lifting and carrying are the biggest cause of non-lethal accidents. This is followed by slips, trips and falls. Being struck by a moving object is also common. Falling from a height is the biggest cause of death.

Apart from the hazards on this list, commercial building users and owners need to be aware of the risks of legionella, asbestos and hazards where children and vulnerable adults are present, such as cleaning chemicals.

Studies have shown that better safety records are associated with a specific management culture. This includes:

- safety officers having high rank;
- senior managers participating in safety activities;
- frequent re-training for existing employees;
- a participative management style;
- harmonious management-worker relations;

- provision of disability plans;
- performance appraisals relating to health and safety;
- thorough investigation of accidents.

Don't try this at home

The UK's Cranfield University was fined £80,000 with costs of £75,000 after a worker was nearly killed while dismantling a cluster bomb. These bombs contain hundreds of metal fragments which are designed to penetrate tank armour within a radius of 25 metres. There could be few activities more hazardous than bomb disposal.

Three university employees were working to deactivate the bombs, so they could be used in demonstrations. One of the bombs exploded, causing serious injuries to one of the workers. He suffered severe abdominal injuries and his right colon, which was penetrated by a shard of metal, had to be removed in surgery. An investigation by the Health and Safety Executive found that – remarkably – no risk assessment had been carried out. The university's management team were unaware that the dismantling process was being carried out.

Risk assessments are vital, but organisations sometimes don't carry them out even where the risks are high. And sometimes staff do stupid things without senior management's knowledge.

Mitigating Measures: improving safety

Enforce safety standards. Actions speak louder than words. Policy statements aren't sufficient. Managers must be alert to breaches of safety.

Log all incidents, no matter how inconsequential they appear. The organisation needs to learn from these errors.

Make part of the senior team's remuneration dependent on the health and safety record. BAE links 5% of top salaries against the safety record.

Encourage employees to look after their own safety, and that of their colleagues. Ask staff to identify health and safety hazards.

Carry out safety risk assessments on all sites. Audit the workplace for dangerous processes. Identify who might be harmed. Seek to avoid the hazard where possible (for example replace manual handling with lifting aids). Institute controls and precautions for remaining hazards. Ensure the controls are followed.

Maintain good housekeeping. This includes mopping up spills and keeping walkways clear of obstructions.

Review the quarterly recordable incident rate (RIR) where an employee requires medical attention beyond first aid. It should be set as an important performance indicator. Hold each business unit to account, especially those with poor records. Reward those who improve.

(continued)

(continued)

Set up a confidential whistleblowing hotline so that employees can report areas of concern or non-compliance.

Employ external consultants to report on safety issues. Internal auditors can be captured by operational staff or not notice problem areas.

Have regular safety reports sent to the board, complete with standardised metrics. This lets you identify changes that may be harbingers of worse to come.

Provide safety training for staff working for business partners such as contractors and retailers, if necessary.

Identify the organisation's position on a Safety Maturity Index whose scale will range from 'Safety is disregarded' to 'Safety is an integral part of the business'.

Apply safety standards such as ISO 45001.

11 Leaving dirty footprints

Dealing with environmental mess

The making of things inevitably means extracting resources from the earth, using energy and making noise; and once used our products create waste. The task therefore is to minimise the impacts of what we do. In this chapter we look at how to mitigate our environmental risks. We examine nine main environmental risks:

1   emissions to air, including greenhouse gases
2   water pollution
3   solid waste
4   consuming scarce or non-renewable resources
5   toxic or hazardous substances
6   damage to nature through the destruction of natural habitats or amenity space
7   noise pollution
8   contaminated land
9   water shortage.

In the sections that follow, we examine each in turn. But first here's a quick list of Mitigating Measures that apply broadly to environmental issues.

Mitigating Measures: better environmental protection

Create an environmental policy.

Identify, measure and record your impacts.

Set objectives and targets for reducing your impacts.

Create procedures for minimising your impacts.

Audit your processes for compliance.

Take steps to continuously reduce your impacts.

Consider implementing ISO 14000.

Following any incident of environmental damage, take fast and effective measures to rectify the problem. Be open and cooperative with the authorities. Make speedy compensation to those affected by the event. This will help to mitigate the scale of any penalties imposed.

Huffing and puffing

Emissions to air come from boilers, vehicle exhausts, heating and lighting, incinerators and industrial processes.

For service businesses, emissions to air may seem limited – you just switch on the lights and drive to and from work. But service business can have many indirect emissions. A call centre will make use of buildings, computers and IT systems whose manufacture and maintenance involves energy and toxic processes. However, it is fair to say that emissions to air are largely the concern of industrial organisations, especially large facilities whose outputs are regulated.

Emissions to air are a risk because governments seek to reduce greenhouse gas emissions and to protect their populations from air pollution. They do this by imposing limits on emissions and by penalising those who create emissions. Workforce illness is an additional risk for industrial businesses.

Main categories of emission to air

There are two distinct types of emission:

1   *Greenhouse gases*, which warm the earth and thereby cause climate change, but don't otherwise affect us. They come largely from carbon-based energy sources.
2   *Toxic emissions*, which come from industrial processes. The most common are as follows.

- carbon monoxide
- lead
- nitrogen dioxide (one of several nitrogen oxides)
- ozone (formed from precursor volatile organic compounds)
- particulate matter
- sulphur dioxide.

We examine each in turn in the following sections.

Greenhouse gases

Greenhouse gases come from both natural and man-made sources. The man-made (or anthropogenic) sources largely come from burning fossil fuels such as coal, oil and gas, as well as deforestation. We burn the fuels in order to produce electricity and use them in industrial processes. Burning fossil fuels contributes to global warming, which results in a wide range of extreme weather events, including storms, flooding and even heat-waves. Reducing energy use therefore serves to reduce environmental damage, and saves money as well.

Alternative sources of energy are becoming more mainstream. You can install bio plants that convert organic matter into electricity or heat. Sources of energy include liquid manure, corn, leftover food and slaughterhouse waste. Or you can convert the matter into methane and add it to the natural gas network.

Photovoltaic cells are gaining wider use, from PV rooftop cells that provide space or water heating to roadside signs powered by the sun, as well as solar farms that contribute electricity to the grid.

Mitigating Measures: reducing greenhouse gases

Institute an energy policy and implement it through written procedures.

Conduct an energy audit with the aim of cutting energy use.

Monitor your carbon emissions. Track it on a per-unit-of-output basis.

Increase the use of energy management systems.

Lights. Switch off lights at night. Install energy-reducing controls such as timed switches and occupancy, daylight and motion sensors.

Heating. Insulate and draught proof buildings. Turn down air conditioning. Allow local control of heating. Service heating and air conditioning equipment regularly to maximise its efficiency.

Office equipment. Set office equipment to sleep when not in use.

Renewables. Introduce renewable energy, notably solar, wind and biomass.

Recycling. Maximise the amount of recycling, in offices and kitchens. Find ways to recycle production waste.

Travel. Support lift sharing and the use of public transport. Provide bike loans. Erect bike racks and install showers and lockers for walkers and bike riders. Use video conferencing in place of air travel.

Employee engagement. Set up local environmental champion groups to promote energy efficiency and recycling.

Paper. Use recycled paper for printing and toilet paper.

Transport. Service vehicles regularly to reduce energy costs. Use low emission vehicles. Educate drivers to drive efficiently.

Compressed air. Check for wasteful leaks. Reduce the operating pressure. Reducing it by one bar can save 7% of energy used.

Refrigeration. Keep freezer doors closed: it costs £6 ($8) an hour when a freezer door stays open. Keep the system at the right temperature. A one-degree reduction in temperature causes costs to rise by 2–4%. Avoid excessive refrigerant charge: leaks can increase energy costs by 10%.

Industrial processes. Identify the heaviest uses of energy and assess how to reduce them. Improve boiler efficiency. This starts with insulation and good maintenance, but includes devices such as economisers and turbulators.

Buy your energy from a supplier which gets its energy from renewable sources.

Manage your supply chain. Encourage your suppliers and distributors to reduce their energy use.

Toxic emissions

In the following section we examine each of the main types of dangerous emission before listing Mitigating Measures to control and reduce them. I'm indebted to the Good Guide, the pollution information site, for some of this detail.

Carbon monoxide. Carbon monoxide (CO) is a colourless and odourless but poisonous gas produced by incomplete burning of carbon in fuels. When CO enters the bloodstream, it reduces the supply of oxygen to the body's organs and tissues. In the UK, carbon monoxide poisoning, usually from leaking gas appliances, kills 40 people a year. Seventy-seven per cent of the CO emissions come from vehicle exhausts. Other major CO sources are wood-burning stoves, incinerators and industrial activities.

Lead. Having become recognised as highly toxic in the 1980s, lead emissions have fallen substantially, due to the advent of lead-free petrol; but lead remains a threat. Lead is a widely used metal that can contaminate air, food, water or soil. It can adversely affect the nervous, reproductive, digestive and cardiovascular blood-forming systems and the kidneys. Lead petrol additives, lead smelters and battery plants are significant contributors to lead emissions. In the USA, 9,600 facilities release significant amounts of lead each year.

Nitrogen dioxide. Nitrogen dioxide (NO_2) is a brown, highly reactive gas that is present in city air. NO_2 can irritate the lungs, cause bronchitis, pneumonia and reduce resistance to respiratory infections. Most combustion processes produce NO which, when it oxidises, becomes NO_2 in the atmosphere.

Nitrogen oxides. Nitrogen oxides (NO_x) comprise nitrogen compounds like nitrogen dioxide (NO_2) and nitric oxide (NO). These compounds contribute to the creation of ozone (O_3) and acid rain. They also harm ecosystems on land and in water. NO_x forms when fuels are burned at high temperatures. The major sources are vehicle engines and stationary sources such as power stations and industrial boilers.

Ozone. Ozone (O_3) is the major component of smog. Although O_3 in the upper atmosphere is beneficial because it protects us from the sun's ultraviolet radiation, high concentrations of ozone at ground level are a health concern. Ozone damages lung tissue, reduces lung function and sensitises the lungs to other irritants. O_3 is formed in the air when oxides of nitrogen (NO_x) and volatile organic compounds (VOC) react to form O_3 in the presence of sunlight. These reactions are stimulated by ultraviolet radiation and temperature, so peak ozone levels typically occur on sunny days.

Particulate matter. Particulate matter (PM) is the particles from dust, dirt, soot and smoke that are released into the air by factories, power plants, cars, construction and fires. Exposure to particulate matter can affect breathing, aggravate existing respiratory and cardiovascular disease, damage lung tissue and contribute to cancer. People suffering from lung or heart disease, asthmatics, the elderly and children are most sensitive to the effects of PM.

Sulphur dioxide. High concentrations of sulphur dioxide (SO_2) affect breathing and can aggravate existing respiratory and cardiovascular disease. Sensitive populations include asthmatics, individuals with bronchitis or emphysema, children and the elderly. SO_2 also contributes to acid rain, which causes acidification of lakes and streams, and can damage trees, crops and historic buildings. Sulphur dioxide is released mainly from burning fuels that contains sulphur (like coal, oil and diesel fuel). The main sources are coal- and oil-fired power plants, steel mills, refineries, pulp and paper mills, and non-ferrous smelters.

Volatile organic compounds. VOCs evaporate quickly in the air. They come from diverse sources, including vehicles, chemical plants, drycleaners and paint shops. VOC emissions form O_3 through complex chemical reactions with oxides of nitrogen (NO_x) in the presence of sunlight. Exposure to high levels of some VOCs can cause headaches, dizziness, light-headedness, drowsiness, nausea and eye and respiratory irritation.

Other categories of emission. Governments are especially concerned with 'dark smoke', on the grounds that the darker the smoke, the more toxic the emissions. Dark smoke was common in advanced nations in the 1950s, when 12,000 Londoners died in the smog of 1952. Since then, governments have legislated against smoking chimneys and bonfires.

Mitigating Measures: cutting toxic emissions

In order of priority, the ways to reduce airborne pollution are as follows (see Figure 11.1):

Eliminate the process. You don't have to continue doing what you've always done. Ceasing to use a polluting process frees you from health and safety risks, and from litigation.

Substitute. Find less-polluting methods of producing the product.

Reduce the use. Produce less waste, or use raw materials more sparingly.

Filter or scrub. Clean or absorb the polluting dust or gases, rather than releasing them.

Introduce controls. Contain the process, so as to minimise the harm to the workforce.

Personal Protection Equipment. Provide the workforce with face masks or respirators. By the time we have got to this level, we are tolerating the pollution, which is the least preferable solution. It is some distance from the ideal position where you eliminate air pollution through designing it out or by ceasing to carry out the process.

Muddying the waters: avoiding water pollution

When two dams collapsed in Brazil's Minas Gerais region, 50 cubic metres of polluted waste water from an open cast mine swept over the plains, sweeping away the town of Bento Rodrigues, killing at least nine people and leaving another 19 unaccounted for. Much of the aquatic life was killed along a 300-mile stretch. Water from the mine, owned by Samarco, a joint venture between Anglo-Australian mining company BHP Billiton and Brazil's iron ore company Vale, polluted the water supply of hundreds of thousands of people.

Billiton's UK shares which had traded at £20 fell to £8.83, and at the time of writing the company was expecting total losses and fines to amount to $2.6bn.

In the aftermath, critics pointed to a lack of inspection, with the regulator checking the dams once only every four years. The relationship between the government and the mining companies was too close. There had also been warnings about the design of the dam and its safety; there was a lack of emergency planning, and no alarm system was in place.

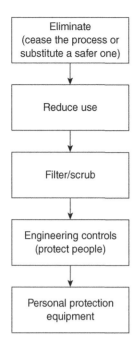

Figure 11.1 Preferred methods of reducing emissions to air.

Operating standards are a concern in all countries, but in emerging nations some risks are higher. The dangers of low expectations, lower safety standards, bribery and low pay, weaker government inspection regimes and sometimes isolated plants can lead companies to overlook or not notice risks of pollution and environmental catastrophe.

Billiton is an extreme case. Most businesses do not have the capacity to pollute on that scale. But any discharge into a river can have major – and highly visible – consequences.

Avoiding water pollution helps you reduce your operating costs and reduces waste disposal costs; avoids pollution clean-up costs; precludes higher insurance premiums; avoids bad publicity and stops enforcement action and fines.

In most countries you need a permit to discharge commercial waste to rivers and drains, and most permits will specify limits.

Turning fishing nets into carpets

Large masses of discarded nets can drift in the oceans for years, ensnaring turtles, seabirds and marine mammals. Clean-up operations are difficult and can be costly. Meanwhile, according to *The Guardian* newspaper, low-income coastal communities that depend on fishing for their livelihood often lack access to basic services.

Interface, a carpet tile manufacturer, has gone into partnership with London Zoo and yarn producer Aquafil to create Net-Works. The programme has enabled communities in the Philippines to earn extra revenue by collecting discarded fishing nets.

Aquafil recycles the waste nets into new nylon yarn, which avoids the need for Interface to purchase raw material. Some 40% of Interface's products are now made from recycled or bio-based products – up from 0.5% in 1996. Interface has also built a relationship with community banking groups to help give villagers access to secure savings and micro-loans for education or business ventures. In addition, the project has given women the opportunity to become more financially independent. Interface is looking to expand the Net-Works initiative to Cameroon and help new partners replicate the model.

Mitigating Measures: minimising water pollution

Maintain a risk register of all assets and processes that might cause water pollution.

Drainage. Ensure there is a map of drainage systems on your site. This will identify areas of risk, and help resolve problems if they occur.

Deliveries and handling materials. Deliveries and movement of oils, chemicals and raw materials are the cause of many accidents. How well managed are these processes? Ensure good working practices. Install automatic cut-off valves. Have plans for managing spills, rather than washing them down the drain.

Protect your storage. Leaks of stored fluids are a source of pollution. Be aware of the risk of leaks, failure to close valves and sensors not working. Tanks should be above ground (so as to be visible) and bunded. Keep storage of liquids away from watercourses and drains. Be aware of buildings and tanks that are beyond their useful life and could fail. Instigate planned maintenance. Protect pipes against corrosion and damage. Install overflow alarms.

Manage waste. Use resources carefully and reduce the amount of waste produced to save money and resources.

Effluent. Liquid waste is liable to leak, spill and overflow. You need to dispose of it according to regulations. Prevent it from reaching drains and waterways through raised kerbs and bunds. Install isolating valves.

Construction and repairs. Be aware of the higher risks of water pollution associated with building work. Ensure staff are managed properly.

Prevent vandalism and theft. Determine what problems might be caused by break-ins, vandalism or theft. Risks are higher in unattended buildings overnight. Store materials in secure buildings if possible. Install an intruder detection system. Keep valves, taps and hatches locked when not in use.

Substitute and minimise use. Substitute safer or cleaner processes and less hazardous materials, such as solvent-free and water-based fluids. Use materials that can be reused. Install filters or other systems to clean your waste, especially trade effluent and detergent-filled water from washing.

Training, emergency planning and response. Train staff to be aware of possible risks. Instigate incident response plans and test them. Map business processes and write procedures for each. Undertake regular independent audits of all major risks.

(continued)

(continued)

Cleaning. Limit the quantity and toxicity of cleaning materials and pesticides. Replace solvent cleaners with aqueous ones.

Adopt eco-friendly landscaping maintenance. Use less chemical fertiliser which can seep into rivers, cause eutrophication and kill aquatic life.

Down in the dumps: reducing solid waste

Disposal of solid waste costs money, so it makes sense to reduce it. Solid waste can also be a fire hazard.

Across the EU, businesses are now required to reduce their waste. In the UK, any business that handles more than 50 tonnes a year of packaging a year has to demonstrate that it is recycling and recovering an agreed amount.

Mitigating Measures: less solid waste

Conduct a solid waste audit. Discover what waste the organisation is producing, and in what processes. Decide how it can be reduced.

Replace single use products with reusable ones. Instead of purchasing and providing disposable tableware, encourage employees to bring their own reusable mugs, cups, plates and cutlery or supply reusable tableware and wash it on-site. Two middle schools in Minnetonka, Minnesota, replaced their disposable tableware with reusable bowls and utensils. They were able to prevent 3,000kg (6,700 pounds) of rubbish and expected to save $23,000 over three years.

Provide prominent recycling bins. These should allow for segregating different kinds of waste.

Manage food waste. Putrescibles can be composted.

Use returnable packaging. The car industry uses returnable racks for vehicle parts. Pallets have long been a returnable item. Steel drums can be returned and cleaned. Stackable plastic containers can be returned on trolleys.

Use raw materials that can be re-processed. The off-cuts from some forms of plastic can be put straight back into the process.

Discourage the use of printed paper copies of documents. Meeting agendas can be put on to tablets. Where you need to print, it should be double sided.

Discuss with suppliers how they might minimise the packaging on goods they send you, as long as the products are not damaged in the process.

Use air dryers or cotton towels in bathrooms, rather than disposable paper ones.

Buy recycled products. This can include toilet paper, printer cartridges and photocopy paper.

Use of scarce resources

With a growing world population, and the industrialising economies eager to enjoy the benefits that the developed nations have enjoyed for so long, many raw materials are suffering from excess demand, and in some cases we're running out of accessible supply.

These trends are having an impact on businesses, leading to concerns about a reduced access to resources. Twenty-nine per cent of profit warnings issued by FTSE 350 companies in 2011 were attributed to rising resource prices. And in a recent survey of their membership by EEG, the Manufacturers' Organisation, 80% of chief executives of manufacturing companies said that a shortage of raw materials was a risk to their business.

Forestry: Half of the world's forests have now disappeared, cleared for agriculture, for logging, and for roads and settlements. Deforestation is known to contribute to global warming when the trees are cut down or burnt. It also causes habitat loss and thus reduces biodiversity, as well as causing soil erosion and landslides. Since forests provide oxygen through photosynthesis their loss could have implications for the planet.

Farming: Agriculture uses huge amounts of water, and often in drought areas such as California. Farms also tend to grub up tropical forests, as mentioned above. Sometimes this causes degradation of the land, as topsoil is blown away through erosion.

Fishing: A growing world population and larger boats have led to bigger catches that have depleted stocks of many fish species to a point where they are endangered. A lack of property rights in the oceans has meant no one can take responsibility, and individual boats have no incentive to reduce their haul. However, governments and the EU have introduced quotas, mesh sizes and other devices in an attempt to restore stocks.

Mining: There is no shortage of minerals in the earth. We have hardly begun to dig deep into the earth, nor to explore the sea bed, which covers two-thirds of the surface of the planet. However, many fields are located in inaccessible areas, and require expertise to extract the minerals. The impacts of mining are more associated with pollution, energy use, destruction of habitats and corruption. In the future we may mine asteroids for minerals, unleashing an inexhaustible supply of raw materials

Carbon fuels: Leaving aside the question of global warming, we have allegedly passed peak oil, a point at which accessible reserves will start to reduce. Fossil fuels are non-renewable, and therefore our excessive demand for them is not sustainable. Shale oil is plentiful, though its extraction process is controversial.

Water is increasingly a scarce resource, and perhaps the most important of all. Hence we will look specifically at this problem in the section that follows, and provide a Mitigating Measures checklist for it.

Impacts relating to resource extraction include the following:

- The reserves may be scarce or finite, in which case we should seek to manage and conserve them.
- Much energy may be used in its extraction, such as bauxite mining.

- Extraction may require harmful inputs. Miners use cyanide to separate gold and silver particles from their ore.
- The waste may be substantial. Eighty tonnes of waste are produced to get one ounce of gold.
- Workers may suffer. Mineworkers can get respiratory diseases from dust.
- The resource's end use may have damaging consequences. Fossil fuels cause global warming, while nuclear fuel could cause an atomic explosion and requires future generations to care for the toxic waste.
- Violence may be employed in its extraction. Conflict minerals are one example.
- Its production may damage the environment. Logging can cause the loss of rainforest.

Mitigating Measures: the use of scarce resources

Audit your use of scarce or non-renewable materials.

Reduce overall use of materials, for example through lightweighting or waste reduction.

Substitute non-renewable materials with renewable equivalents where possible. Seek to protect their sustainability. For example, avoid overextraction which could reduce stocks.

Recover non-renewable materials where possible.

Put controls in place for protecting the environment.

Avoid using hardwoods from tropical forests, unless certified to be from a sustainable source.

Don't use peat obtained from wetlands.

Use low-carbon energy sources to extract minerals, to reduce production of CO_2 gases.

Reduce water usage.

Remove conflict minerals from your supply chain.

Thirsting for a solution

Though 70% of the world's surface is covered by water, two-thirds of that is locked away in glaciers or is inaccessible. Hence only 3% of the world's water is available to drink. And with climate change, a growing world population, changes in the demand for food and a growing use of water, supplies are drying up.

Water shortages are one of the effects of climate change, causing droughts in parts of the world. Increased demand from agriculture can extract too much water from rivers and lakes, which causes downstream rivers to dry up. According to the World Wildlife Fund for Nature, at current rates of consumption, two-thirds of the world's population may face water shortages by 2025.

Agriculture uses 70% of the water supply, but manages to waste 60% of that through leaking irrigation systems, inefficient application methods and excessively thirsty crops. This does not relate simply to the developing nations. California is highly water stressed, with big implications for food production.

Every day, Americans flush 4.8bn gallons of water down the toilet. Hot water requires even more energy, which costs your organisations money.

Water shortage has numerous impacts. Stressed water courses become polluted from fertilisers and biocides. Water shortage reduces food production and affects all other industries since almost nothing can be made without water. Hence output declines, and the area suffers economic setback. As people can't get clean water, hygiene declines and child mortality rises. So do diarrhoea, cholera, typhoid fever and water-borne illnesses. In addition, water reduction causes the loss of habitat for many species, and degrades the environment.

For businesses, it means reduced quantities of raw materials, or higher prices. It can also mean a reduction in demand among affected populations.

Many organisations practise water stewardship, some out of necessity. This involves reducing the amount of water used. Agricultural industries should waste less, while manufacturers can recycle more. Even if water is not in short supply in your locality, it is good to reduce water use. This is because clean water requires a lot of energy in reservoirs to remove pollutants and render it safe. According to the USA River Network, the US consumes at least 521m MWh a year for water-related purposes which is 13% of the country's electricity consumption. The energy required to heat water is even higher, consuming 304bn kWh each year.

Mitigating Measures: water shortage

Use percussion taps that turn themselves off.

Repair leaks.

Use high-pressure, low-volume cleaners.

Reduce the water pressure in taps.

Reduce the amount of water used in processing. Putting a water-filled container in the toilet cistern will reduce the amount of water used in each flush. Install waterless toilets.

Switch to raw materials that require less water.

Farmers and food companies may investigate switching to crops that are more drought resistant or less thirsty.

Breathless: the risks of toxic materials

Toxic materials can escape into the drains and rivers where they kill fish. Some materials give off poisonous fumes that affect the workforce. Others are nerve agents.

The most dangerous, as listed by the US Agency for Toxic Substances and Disease Registry (ATSDR), start with arsenic, lead and mercury, followed by vinyl chloride (harmless as a finished product but injurious to heath in industrial processes). After this come PCBs, known to be carcinogens and used in a wide range of products until 1979, but which are still released into the atmosphere when burnt in incinerators and dumped in landfill sites.

Then there are polycyclic aromatic hydrocarbons (PAHs), a group of 100 chemicals that occur during the incomplete burning of coal, oil and gas, as well as tobacco or grilled meat.

Many industrial processes use toxic materials. Safety data sheets will reveal whether your organisation is using any.

Some toxic materials in commercial use

- *Drain cleaner* may contain lye (sodium hydroxide) or sulphuric acid which causes chemical burns, and can cause blindness if splashed in the eyes.
- *Laundry detergent*: its cationic agents can cause nausea and vomiting, sometimes, and even coma. Non-ionic detergents are irritants.
- *Furniture polish* contains phenol, which on contact with skin can cause it to swell, burn, peel and break out in hives.
- *Motor oil* contains heavy metals which can damage the nervous system.
- *Pesticides* may have acute and/or chronic toxic effects, and pose a particular risk to children.
- *Ammonia*: a volatile chemical that is damaging to the eyes, respiratory tract and skin.
- *Toilet bowl cleaner* contains hydrochloric acid which is highly corrosive, and an irritant to both skin and eyes. It also damages kidneys and the liver. It may also contain hypochlorite bleach which is corrosive, and irritates or burns eyes, skin and the respiratory tract. It may cause pulmonary oedema, vomiting or coma if ingested.
- *Rubbing alcohol*: isopropyl alcohol is an irritant to the eyes and mucous membranes. By analogy with effects seen in animals, it may cause central nervous system depression at very high concentrations.
- *Bleach* can contain sodium hypochlorite, an irritant.
- *Battery acid*: lead is a known hazard. Batteries also contain sulphuric acid, which is corrosive.
- *Anti-freeze* contains ethylene glycol, which is poisonous if swallowed.
- *Mothballs* contain either p-dichlorobenzene or naphthalene. Both are toxic and known to cause dizziness and headaches.
- *Oven cleaner* can contain sodium hydroxide or potassium hydroxide, which are corrosive.
- *Rat poison* contains warfarin, which causes internal bleeding if eaten.
- *Windscreen wiper fluid* contains methanol which damages brain, liver and kidneys, and can cause blindness.

Workplace exposure to these substances is higher, because employees will be routinely exposed to whatever toxic materials are in use. Two workers at a UK electroplating factory had symptoms that suggested asthma. The diagnosis was confirmed by lung function tests, but the cause was unknown. Then a member of staff produced a safety data sheet describing a lacquer containing isocyanates. This lacquer was used to coat the silver-plated goods and was then cured or hardened in an oven.

Widely used in coatings, isocyanates are a leading cause of asthma among workforces. They're a 'respiratory sensitiser' – when you breathe it in, it can trigger an irreversible allergic reaction.

The company installed fume extraction, but it was too late for the employees. One of them had to take early retirement on medical grounds, with compensation for occupational asthma due to isocyanates. The second worker had to change employment and applied for compensation.

> **Mitigating Measures: avoiding toxic materials**
>
> **Check safety data sheets** to see what toxic materials are in use.
>
> **Assess how you could reduce or replace these materials**.

Damage to nature

Some industries such as civil engineering and house building have a major impact on nature, turning animal habitats and pathways into ones for humans. For other industries, the effect is less significant. There will always be a conflict between creating human environments and supporting nature.

But even in an apparently crowded country like England only 2% of the land is built upon, despite the impression that we live in a highly urbanised world. Meanwhile the extent of UK woodland is now, at 13% of the land mass, the highest proportion since records began in 1924.

It is good practice to minimise the environmental impact of any construction project. There is a hierarchy of Mitigating Measures; these are shown in Figure 11.2.

Many of our purchases can harm nature. Cutting down the Indonesian rain forest for palm oil and timber is leading towards the extinction of the orangutan. Agriculture in the Amazon is threatening New World monkeys. At time of writing, there were only 20 Hainan black crested gibbons left.

Wetlands have been thoroughly drained in the past and 'improved' for farming. More than half the world's wetlands disappeared during the twentieth century. It is only relatively recently that we have begun to understand that they provide a habitat for important species. Hence the need to protect those that survive.

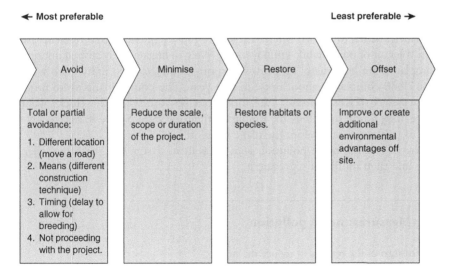

Figure 11.2 Hierarchy of actions for mitigating environmental impacts.

Mitigating Measures: damage to nature

Avoid products that threaten biodiversity and reduce the habitats of rare species.

Buy products and support organisations that actively support threatened wildlife.

Avoid products made from tortoise-shell, ivory and coral. Avoid fur from tigers, polar bears and sea otters. Don't buy medicinal products made from rhinos, tigers or the Asiatic black bear.

Avoid buying the products of uncertified logging.

Consider non-carbon forms of energy – in some places oil and gas threaten rare species and unspoilt land.

Mitigating Measures: construction work

Seek to work on brownfield land (urban, developed and possibly run-down) in preference to greenfield sites.

Carry out an environmental impact assessment (EIA) before all construction work.

Introduce mitigating environmental measures (such as maintaining habitats).

Engage in a full consultation process with stakeholders.

Noisy neighbours

Industrial processes, vehicles and construction sites all make noise. So do events such as celebrations. Licensed premises can sometimes attract rowdy customers. Universities get complaints about late night student parties.

Noise can be detrimental to health, whether at low or high frequencies, and residents are increasingly less tolerant of noise, while employees are likely to litigate for industrial injuries.

Not all complaints are legitimate. Heathrow Airport found that two individuals were responsible for 7,888 complaints about noise in one year. The complainants were using automated software. A spokesman said: 'We found out because when the clocks went back in October, they forgot to change the timing on their software. So we started receiving complaints exactly one hour before the plane took off.'

The hierarchy of treating noise pollution is to prevent it, design out the noise, then reduce its scale, and then muffle or segregate it.

Mitigating Measures: noise pollution

Change the design of the process to reduce the noise.

Get a quieter machine or component.

Segregate noisy machines from employees.

Dampen noisy machine parts to reduce vibration. Use anti-vibration mountings.

Use silencers on pneumatic exhausts.

Enclose noisy machines.

Build screens or barriers to separate noise sources and people.

Provide noise refuges for employees.

Fit sound absorbing materials in work areas.

Provide the workforce with ear protection.

Living in a waste land: the problem of contaminated land

Contaminated land is usually the result of waste from factories and mines dating from previous decades or even centuries when controls on pollution were less stringent.

It is rare for contaminated land to cause a health threat, but contaminants can leach into water courses or farm land and cause harm. Contaminated land costs money to clear up. It may be hard to sell contaminated land, get a mortgage or get planning permission for it.

You should avoid buying contaminated land unless you're sure that clean-up is possible and cost effective. If you own contaminated land, you will need a strategy for remediating it.

Mitigating Measures: contaminated land

Conduct a site assessment for land contamination. Establish the scale of contamination, if any.

Implement a plan to reduce the contamination and improve the ecological value of the land.

When acquiring land, carry out due diligence to check for contamination.

Consider requiring or providing an indemnity to transfer the liability for cleaning up the contamination. As a seller you may be able to buy a surety bond to protect the purchaser if contamination is discovered.

Check whether you can get insurance against land contamination.

If you use hazardous substances, such as oil and chemicals, ensure that you don't cause contamination.

12 Viruses and outages

How to stay on top of IT issues

Organisations have mostly cured the old IT problems that caused headlines a decade ago. In those days businesses didn't make adequate backups and hard drives would fail, causing a loss of data.

Problems caused by employees used to loom large. People would click on email attachments or send out embarrassing information. But these too, with some exceptions, have been largely reduced. Even the alarm caused by staff bringing their own devices to work (BYOD) has proved to be less of a problem than it might.

But other IT problems have grown more serious. Businesses face the daily threat of viruses, the cyber theft of personal information, massive assaults that bring down the website and errors caused by IT staff that bring business processes to a halt.

In Chapter 14 we consider the risks of IT project failure. In Chapter 15 we examine the problems of IT sabotage by staff and ex-employees. But here we consider how to mitigate the risks of outages caused by unknown attackers, along with the risks to customers' private information. We also reflect on how to overcome the problem of inadequate IT systems.

Cyber threats

After telephone company TalkTalk suffered a cyber attack, 101,000 customers left and the episode cost the company £60m. It demonstrates the impact that a cyber attack can have. There are three types of attack:

1   The website might be overwhelmed by excessive traffic in a Denial of Service (DDoS) attack. As it buckles under the pressure, the website or database stops displaying information.
2   Hackers steal information stored on the company's server, such as customers' credit card or personal details.
3   A virus spreads into the system, deleting information or corrupting the software.

Seventy-eight per cent of CEOs regard cyber attack as a major threat, according to PwC which is not surprising since we rely on computers to carry out so many tasks.

DDoS attack

A denial of service (DDoS or DoS) attack happens when thousands of computers keep demanding pages from your site, so ordinary visitors are unable to access it. This can continue for hours. At time of writing, DDoS attacks averaged 7 gigabits per second (that's seven thousand million bits per second), but individual attacks have reached 500 Gbps. Eventually the attack subsides. World-leading banks in the US and other countries have been brought down in this way.

Even teenagers and malcontents with little technical skill can use the Lizard Stresser tool, which is powerful enough to have taken down major sites such as the Sony Playstation and Microsoft Xbox gaming networks. Criminals who lack technical skills can use professional attack-for-hire groups.

DoS attacks can be initiated by nation states and political activists as well as bored youths, criminals and employees with a grudge. They're also used to extort money. The FBI gets complaints from businesses reporting extortion campaigns via email. The gang threatens a DoS attack unless the organisation pays a ransom.

Ransoms vary in price and are usually demanded in the digital currency bitcoin, because it's untraceable. Victims that don't pay the ransom get a follow-up email claiming that the ransom will significantly increase if the victim fails to pay within the given time frame. There's little evidence as to how many businesses pay, and whether the threatened attacks are carried out.

The online gambling site Nitrogen Sports, based in Costa Rica, said it had paid up:

> This particular hacker has been attacking us since July [for three months]. We actually did pay him for a while to buy ourselves some time to put additional protections in place. He has escalated his attacks and his demand for money, and we felt that it was time to take a stand.

This suggests that paying the extortionist will result in further demands for money.

When a DoS attack begins, you can't readily tell whether the traffic is malicious, since it doesn't seem to come from any particular source. Often it comes from more than 5,000 infected home and small computers, unbeknown to the owners of those computers. The business only know it's a victim when the pages begin to load more slowly and then grind to a halt. It's easy to assume, initially, that there is a problem with your internet connection.

Staff and customers start phoning, asking why the website or system is down. This adds to the workload and confusion. There's a huge cost to every minute of downtime, with customers not being able to place orders. The business loses revenue as well as suffering reputation damage.

Most DoS attacks simply crash the website. But in some cases the DoS attack is a smokescreen for an attempt to steal information or undertake some other cyber attack. Hackers can use a range of tools. A survey by Neustar Insights found that 55% of DDoS targets were also victims of theft. This included the loss of customer data, intellectual property and money, with one attack on an undisclosed bank resulting a loss of $9m in 48 hours.

And in a nightmarish twist, the same attackers can start the target company's phones ringing constantly – or ringing thousands of people from what looks like the firm's phone number.

Every business has to assume its site will be the subject of a DDoS attack from time to time. How prepared you are will determine whether your site remains in operation.

It is unwise to rely on assurances from the ISP. In the author's experience, they tend to overclaim and underdeliver when it comes to resolving attacks. Large corporations who manage their own in-house servers sometimes underinvest in protection, on the grounds that the money can't be justified since it will 'never happen' to them.

Mitigating Measures: Denial of Service Attack

Create a DDoS incident response plan. Know what you will do when a DDoS attack happens. Test the plan.

Contact your internet service provider (ISP) or your network administrator. How will you identify that an attack has begun? What steps will they will take in the event of a DDoS attack? Will your ISP take down your site if it threatens other parts of its business? It's been known to happen.

Use a DDoS mitigating service, such as Incapsula, Defense.net, Prolexic or Akamai.

Institute RPF (Reverse Path Forwarding) or similar function that checks whether the information packet could have come from where it claims it's from. This helps the system detect spoofed addresses and can delete them if their routeing appears fake.

Ensure you have ready access to redundant processing power and memory that can expand when necessary to prevent your system from being overwhelmed. CloudFlare is one such system.

Know who to phone. When a DDoS attack happens, fast reactions are essential.

Information on the loose

'Information security risk' is the risk that confidential information held by your organisation could be stolen or accidentally released, whether through viruses, hackers, careless employees or some other means.

Information security failures lead to reputation damage, financial penalties from the regulator, and lost revenue from customers who no longer trust the organisation.

We tend to think of information security as being about hackers who steal people's credit card details from our servers. But it's more than just that. One hospital found that paper records of physiotherapy clients were being used to prop open a door.

The big problems occur when a hacker attacks a major business and steals their customer information. The phone company TalkTalk was hit three times in eight months, and critics said the company had failed to adequately secure its site, something that TalkTalk denied. On the third occasion, the hackers got the bank account details of 21,000 customers, along with 1.2m customers' names, email addresses and phone numbers. These end up being sold on the dark net. TalkTalk refused to discuss its defences, as well as whether its information was encrypted. The company said that each day it blocked 170 million scamming emails aimed at its customers and 1 million nuisance calls.

Security experts reckoned that the company had suffered a relatively amateurish and opportunistic attack by 15- and 16-year-old boys. The company's CEO, Dido Harding, said the company had been the victim of a 'sequential injection' attack which experts took to mean a 'SQL injection' attack. While the CEO of even a tech company might not be expected to know technical information, the response suggested she was not sufficiently knowledgeable even after the latest in a series of attacks. The company also admitted that it did not encrypt all its customer data.

Quoted on TheRegister.com, Trend Micro's Rik Ferguson said that companies' belief in their impregnability was not uncommon and was a root cause of many breaches.

If a person or entity responsible for security fails to keep up with developments they will invariably fall behind and suffer from a misplaced sense of security. Complacency is the biggest enemy of security.

Mitigating Measures: protecting your data

Evaluate the risk of loss. How vulnerable are you to losing your data? How are paper records kept and destroyed? How tough are passwords? Who has access to the passwords? Do freelance IT people work on the system? Organisations are often reliant on contractors to maintain records or destroy waste, and their quality control may not be as robust as they claim.

Prevent the downloading or copying of some types of data from servers.

Set security controls that meet International Standard ISO/IEC 27002 (a code of practice for information security management).

Limit and monitor access to sensitive information. Continue to add enhanced security as new technologies emerge.

Comply with PCI-DSS. When taking credit card payments, be compliant with PCI-DSS (payment card industry data security standards). This means using tools and services that meet those standards, normally using a third party supplier.

Train staff in information security awareness. Educate them about the need to keep information secure.

Introduce programs that can delete documents, if stolen, or withdraw access to them.

Attacks by hackers and viruses

Viruses get access to your system rather like a burglar finds an unguarded window or weak door into your home.

Our networks are connected to the outside world via the internet. The internet is full of code that seeks to make contact with the computer ports it finds. Like a security guard at reception, the firewall at your ports will generally refuse entry to messages that it recognises as malicious. But they don't get it right every time. Infected files may creep into your system.

Anti-virus programs will then keep a watchful eye for suspicious activity. These tend to be updated daily, as new viruses are discovered and put on record.

As viruses are constantly evolving, it is a constant cat-and-mouse game. New hardware, software and protocols regularly arrive, taking advantage of more powerful memory, and so the hackers find new vulnerabilities. But 99% of viruses exploit vulnerabilities that have been known for over a year. In other words, businesses are failing to update their systems.

Attacks caused by staff and ex-employees

Staff make mistakes. They click on attachments, and they download software that contains viruses. It isn't surprising given the cleverness of some virus designers. Companies can control this though anti-virus programs, training, and application control, subjects we discuss below.

Even IT staff can unwittingly cause havoc. Many have a limited knowledge of the wide ranging systems they're responsible for. And when they are asked to do something unfamiliar, the risks grow. New systems and changes make them vulnerable. Even when they are familiar with a system, they can be careless. Few consider the impact that a change might have, and many fail to take a backup before making a change.

Organisations are also vulnerable to malicious attacks by current and former employees. The day after sacking a coder for continual failings, one business discovered that the company's e-commerce system no longer worked. The ex-employee knew of the one disused password which gained him access to the system, where he re-numbered all the product codes so the database wouldn't recognise them. Clicking a 'Buy Now' link made the system fall over. The organisation lost at least one day's revenue; but he could have caused even greater damage had he so decided.

Mitigating Measures: staving off attacks by hackers and staff

Automate your updates of operating systems, browsers, applications and the anti-virus program.

Harden passwords. Hacker software contains directories of well-known passwords, including '12345', 'password' and thousands of others. Change important passwords often, including when key staff changes occur.

Hire ethical hackers, or develop in-house skills which will let you probe for vulnerabilities in your system and fix them.

Train staff not to download software, and not to click on suspicious attachments. One business sends its own staff fake emails, asking them for their user name and password. If they do so a web page appears, telling them they've just been the victim of a phishing attack, and reminding them never to give out their password.

Take regular off-site backups.

Whitelist named applications. This is the opposite of 'blacklisting'. It refuses to allow any program that has not been approved in advance. This stops malicious software and unapproved programs from running. Whitelisting prevents 'zero day attacks' – viruses that damage a computer on the day they are released, because they aren't recognised as viruses. But it has drawbacks: it stops legitimate but unknown programs from working, and you have to manually add the names of permitted software.

Run only the current version of all applications. You do this by updating your programs as soon as they become available. The developers of Java, PDF viewers, Flash, web browsers and Microsoft Office update their products when they become aware of vulnerabilities. Using the latest version of these programs is essential. These programs account for 83% of virus vulnerabilities. At the time of writing, the applications with the greatest number of vulnerabilities are, in descending order: Microsoft Internet Explorer (still widely in use despite being no longer updated by Microsoft), Google Chrome and Mozilla Firefox. In other words, the browser is a dangerous gateway. Staff should use only a supported version of their browser.

Use only the most up-to-date version of your operating systems. At time of writing the operating systems with the greatest number of vulnerabilities, in descending order, are Apple OS X, Apple IoS, Linux Kernel, Microsoft Windows Server 2008 and Microsoft Windows 7. Microsoft products are no longer the sole or main targets.

Restrict administrative privileges. Do not allow ordinary staff or their computers to have access to operating systems and applications.

Install application control systems. These are security measures that stop unauthorised applications from executing in ways that could damage your computers. The functions vary according to the application, but the aim is to ensure the security of data used by your applications. For example, most data-driven websites use MySql, and hackers can persuade the database to give up its entire contents by typing simple instructions into the browser address bar. Application control will stop the database being subverted in this way.

Regularly scan your system for vulnerabilities.

Ensure that IT staff have sufficient training to carry out their tasks. Be aware of their limitations.

Employee revenge costs £2m

Andrew Skelton, a senior internal auditor at supermarket company Morrisons, leaked details of 100,000 members of its staff after being reprimanded for using the company mail room to send out parcels for his personal eBay business. As a result he bore a grudge against Morrisons, and decided on revenge.

He was subsequently jailed for eight years after being found guilty of gaining unauthorised access to company data and uploading it to the internet. The details included salaries and bank account details of Morrisons' employees. After uploading the information to a data sharing website, he sent information about the breach to several newspapers using a fake email account in a colleague's name. It cost the company £2m to rectify the problem.

This kind of problem is difficult to guard against because many members of staff need access to such data, and disgruntled employees are hard to identify. Almost any employee with access to the data is a risk. And which of us has not grumbled about our employer from time to time?

A survey by the SANS Institute found that despite insider risk being a major concern, 32% of 770 businesses polled had no systems in place to protect against it. Companies spend time focusing on external attacks, but the risk of insider action is huge.

When the system goes down

Every major business is reliant on its IT. We use it to process orders, identify stock levels, plan production, keep accounts and carry out a host of other mission-critical tasks. So if the IT system goes down, either through accident or a deliberate act, the business comes to a halt.

The IT Process Institute's 'Visible Ops Handbook' says that '80% of unplanned outages are due to ill-planned changes made by administrators [in other words, IT staff] or developers.'

A Gartner study agreed: '80% of outages impacting mission-critical services will be caused by people and process issues, and more than 50% of those outages will be caused by change/configuration/release integration and hand-off issues.' In plain terms, IT people cause problems.

Below we consider the specific problems caused by updates and change. But first, it's important to consider the wider issue of IT reliability, and what factors will militate against failure.

Mitigating Measures: reducing the risk of IT disaster

Continuously review your IT infrastructure for vulnerabilities.

Multiple centres. Have more than one data centre. Ensure they mirror each other, and maintain the ability to switch your data between them.

Devise workarounds so that you have alternative, possibly manual, systems in case of failure.

Have disaster recovery plans in place. Keep them updated, and test them at regular intervals.

Agree an IT strategy. Get it documented, approved and communicated. Put IT road maps in place.

Consider having IT represented at board level, rather than having the head of information report to a director.

IT changes and updates

It can look innocuous, but making a small change to a website or software can crash the site. In large systems that have been in existence for a long time, updates can cause another part of the system to fall over. It can then be difficult to trace the root of the problem.

Many businesses update their systems regularly to meet changing needs and to stay up to date. This puts the system at risk on a regular basis. Moreover, systems are frequently interdependent, and not all IT staff realise that a change in one system can have knock-on effects. Worse still, changes can be made by new, junior or inexperienced IT people.

A computer glitch at the Royal Bank of Scotland left millions of customers unable to access their accounts. The error occurred after a software update froze part of the bank's computer systems, affecting 17 million customers. Although the problem was resolved within two days, it created a backlog of more than 100 million transactions that were not paid in or out of bank accounts as they should have been. An RBS source said an 'inexperienced operative' had accidentally erased data while performing the relatively routine task of backing out of an upgrade. Deleted information then had to be painstakingly re-entered into the bank group's computer system.

Such problems are commonplace. Amazon accidentally sold new LG smartphones for one cent each. Virgin Blue's reservation system went down for 11 days. In 2014 emergency services were unavailable for six hours across seven US states: 6,000 people made

911 calls that were unable to connect. In the latter case the Federal Communications Commission found it was caused by an entirely preventable software error.

Sometimes it is better to replace legacy systems with new code. This involves a step-wise change, rather than incremental improvements. And that adds further risk. The US National Grid Gas Company introduced a new ERP system in 2012. The software was incorrectly implemented, resulting in inaccurate wage payments and unpaid supplier bills. The cost of fixing the problem was reported at $945m (£607m).

Mitigating Measures: avoiding problems during changes and upgrades

Apply project management controls to all changes and upgrades.

Establish a Change Approval process, to ensure that decisions are made at a sufficiently senior level.

Update during low trading periods. Do not allow changes to take place at critical trading periods.

Be aware of cross-program dependencies, where a change in one system may cause another to cease functioning.

Backups. Ensure there is a fast way back to the previous build.

Batch your updates. Rather than make small and frequent changes to an IT system, group them into batches with release dates. Test the change in a 'sandbox' before making it live.

Inadequate IT systems

A 2016 report by the UK's HMIC (Her Majesty's Inspectorate of Constabulary) found that 'ICT systems remain outdated and cumbersome across the police service.' Calling them 'primitive' and 'inadequate', the report gave some examples:

- Some forces can't undertake even relatively simple tasks, such as call operators being able to directly book appointments between officers and victims. The report said 'This undermines the efficiency of policing.'
- In only a minority of forces are officers able to complete all the tasks required while on patrol without needing to return to police stations.

And this isn't just a problem exclusive to government. McKinsey says,

Banks have tried to hot-wire ageing systems to improve their performance, but that's becoming an uphill struggle. . . . The core systems installed in the 1970s and '80s are ill-equipped to support the range of functions, modularity and scalability that today's financial institutions need.

These problems are often caused by a lack of IT experience at board level. This leads to businesses having outdated and ineffective information systems. It would be absurd to imagine a board that is unable to make sense of financial reports, yet many boards are helpless when considering IT strategy. As a result businesses suffer from the following problems:

- complicated systems that are hard to use;
- processes that require a workaround, or where employees store information using pencil and paper;
- time-consuming data entry systems which could be improved by letting the computer automatically get the information from a database;
- disconnected systems: many systems are not joined up. Production planning is divorced from marketing, which is separate from finance.

A university found that it couldn't take a booking for a major conference because its room booking system only permitted users to schedule rooms two years in advance, even though conferences – which generate income and prestige – need to be planned at least three years in advance.

In NHS hospitals, consultants speak their patient notes into a dictation machine, which is sent to a secretary who types out the report, prints it and posts it to the general practitioner or other department – just as they did thirty years ago. The patient's file is a bulging folder full of hand-written notes. Computers are locked in cupboards because otherwise they would be stolen, while many nurses are IT-phobic, fearing that they will accidentally delete information.

Mitigating Measures: the problem of outdated IT systems

Ensure the board is IT savvy. This means more than just having a solitary IT representative, not least because they may be an operations person. It involves educating board members in different aspects of networking, enterprise applications and the digital economy.

Benchmark the organisation's IT systems. Identify where work processes are slow, manual, unwieldy or require workarounds.

Devise a strategy that will give you a best-in-class system.

---

13 See you in court
Mitigating legal risks

Most risks carry some legal penalty. And while you don't need lawyers in every small department to manage them, staff need to understand the legal requirements and the impact of failing to meet them.

There are, however, some risks that are more properly managed by the company's general counsel or chief legal officer, such as:

- intellectual property (IP)
- company administration, company secretary
- governance
- compliance.

Some businesses also add tax to this list. The major legal risks are as follows:

- new legislation and regulations
- anti-trust and competition law
- bribery
- fraud
- environmental issues
- data protection
- contractual problems.

Many of these are covered in the relevant chapters of this book, and can be found in the index at the back.

Compliance has been a growing issue for many years, as regulation has become ever more pervasive. Whether the senior in-house lawyer is the right person to manage compliance is an issue for debate.

Crisis communications are an important issue. In Chapter 3 we saw how the handling of a crisis had very different outcomes for two firms.

Mitigating Measures: pre-empting legal risks

Assess your legal risks, possibly by hiring outside consultants if there is insufficient expertise in-house.

Consult all areas of the business when assessing legal risk. This includes the different jurisdictions where you will need to seek local advice.

Provide training on legal risks, especially on compliance issues.

Have general counsel attend board meetings as an observer or adviser, especially when risk and governance issues are discussed. Many believe that general counsel should not have a seat on the board, in order to maintain independence.

Provide Directors and Officers liability insurance (D&O), to protect them in the event of legal action against individuals. This could protect them against claims for employment practices (typically failure to enforce company rules against discrimination), shareholder claims, reporting errors, inaccurate disclosure in company accounts, decisions that exceeded the officer's authority or a failure to comply with regulations.

Have policies and procedures in place to control legal risks, and provide audits to assess compliance. This can be a defence in the event of non-compliance.

Provide a procedure for actions required if you find the business is non-compliant with legislation or regulations, especially if this might involve penalties.

Consider separating the responsibility for legal risk and compliance, especially in highly regulated markets, due to the weight of work. However, the two will need to work together.

Being sued by employees

There is a growing risk of litigation from current and former employees. A typical cause of litigation is redundancy or sacking. If the employee feels they've been unfairly treated or have a grievance, they may resort to the law. Personal injury can also lead to litigation.

Any controversial employment strategy carries risks. At time of writing, Uber drivers had filed a class-action lawsuit against the company, claiming they had been misclassified as independent contractors and were entitled to be regarded as employees.

Several tech companies, including Google, Apple, Adobe, Intuit, Intel and Pixar, violated anti-trust law when they agreed a 'no poaching' agreement. They had undertaken not to 'cold call' each others' workers. A class-action suit brought on behalf of affected employees resulted in a $415m payout.

There have been numerous cases where women bankers have taken their employer to court over discrimination. Shreya Ukil filed a complaint alleging gender discrimination and sexual abuse at Wipro's London office, demanding £1.2m as compensation. Ukil, the company's sales and market development manager, alleged she was a victim of a 'deeply predatory and misogynistic culture' at Wipro. She said, 'The culture within Wipro requires women to be subservient. Women who are confident, capable and express their viewpoints are often called "emotional", "psychotic" or "menopausal". Women who supported women are called "lesbians".' The firm, which has 160,000 employees across the world, strongly denied the allegations, and said it would initiate legal action to defend itself.

According to the US Department of Labor, employee litigation has grown 400% in the last two decades, in part due to new laws covering discrimination and protection against wrongful dismissal. It says for every dollar paid to employees through litigation, a further dollar is paid to lawyers.

Even in a business with good employee relations, it only takes one disgruntled employee to take a case. And even if the case if groundless, the company can receive bad publicity from it.

One in eight US companies have an employment charge filed against them each year, says insurance firm Hiscox. Most don't end up in court, but Alison Geary, a lawyer at Wilmer Hale, said, 'Private prosecutions are becoming increasingly common.' She says a magistrate will grant a summons unless there's a compelling reason not to do so.

Mitigating Measures: dealing with employee litigation

Have a comprehensive employee handbook. It must cover all company policies that an employee might use in litigation against you. In addition to harassment it should include discrimination in recruitment, promotion, termination, compensation and redundancies.

Ensure that policies cover all types of discrimination and harassment including sex, race, colour, disability and religion.

Train all staff to follow these policies. This action will provide a defence if an employee sues the business on the grounds of a manager's behaviour.

Have a complaints procedure that allows victims of discrimination, victimisation or bullying to make a complaint. The procedure should require employees to put their claim in writing, and within a specific time frame from the date of the problem. This will lessen the chance of you being ambushed by claims about past activities.

Allow the employee to report a problem to any manager. This will lessen the likelihood that an employee will be deterred from reporting it to their own manager, who may be part of the problem.

Ensure that managers follow company policy when it comes to recruitment, promotion, termination and pay awards.

Be aware of the risks posed by managers who do not buy into company policies, for example those who make racist or sexist comments. They are the ones who will attract legal problems.

Have a detailed written job description for each employee. This can act as a defence if you're called upon to demonstrate that the employee was terminated due to unsatisfactory performance.

Conduct annual appraisals for all employees, and minute the results. Ensure managers cover all performance problems.

Have documented performance management measures for any employee who is likely to be terminated.

Document all employee incidents. The business will lack a defence if it can't demonstrate what actions were taken.

Follow legal requirements and company policy when terminating employees.

Head off action by being proactive. Involve a senior HR member of staff, a mediator or a lawyer.

Protecting your precious assets

Alan Greenspan, former chairman of the Federal Reserve, said that 75% of the value of companies now lies in intangible assets, up from 40% in the 1980s.

According to a US Department of Commerce study, industries that are 'intellectual property intensive' were responsible for over 22m jobs and 35% of US GDP in 2010.

And when Google bought Motorola Mobility for $12.5bn it was because it wanted the company's 24,500 patents which Google's Android system could use in its battle against Apple and Microsoft. The purchase price valued Motorola at 63% more than its closing price, which highlights the value of IP. Three years later, Google offloaded Motorola to Lenovo for a mere $2.9bn – but hung on to 90% of the patents.

So it's clear how important IP is. Patents and brand names are hugely more valuable than mere factories. This is particularly true for business whose products are digital, and which could be stolen and passed around on the internet, notably software. But it's also true for organisations whose technology gives them a competitive advantage. There are four main risks:

1   *Loss of technology secrets*. If an employee goes to work for one of your competitors and takes company secrets with them, the competitor may benefit enormously. The same applies if a competitor reverse engineers your product and works out how to emulate it, your supplier passes information to a competitor or a hacker steals a blueprint or research document from your server.
2   *Counterfeiting*. Where you have strong brands, criminals may sell counterfeit versions of them, resulting in a loss of revenue.
3   *Genericisation*. Where a brand becomes well known, it can suffer 'generocide.' That is, it becomes the generic name for the product category, such as 'hoover' for vacuum cleaners. Erosion and genericisation will cause a loss of competitive advantage. Otis lost its use of the word 'elevator' for its moving staircase. Google struggles to stop people 'Googling' the net, while Adobe fights to stop its Photoshop software from becoming a generic verb, 'to Photoshop'.
4   *Failure to maximise value*. Licensing the brand name can earn substantial revenues. Disney sells $45bn worth of retail products each year, while Caterpillar earns $2.1bn by putting its name on footwear, phones and even jump leads.

Not such a happy birthday

Losing IP rights can deal a blow to the company's profit stream. The song 'Happy Birthday to You' has rarely been sung on movies or TV shows because Warner owned the copyright to the words, stretching back to 1935. Or so it claimed. According to Newsweek, the company earned $2m per year from licensing fees. That was until a film maker, who wanted to make a documentary about the song, and was asked to pay a $1,500 licensing fee, decided to challenge it in court, and won.

The US District Court ruled that Warner was unable to prove that the songwriter, whose name was anyway in doubt, had ever signed the rights over to the firm. So the copyright registration Warner had filed way back in 1935 was invalid.

At time of writing, the ruling, which was still open to challenge, meant that companies could seek the reimbursement of millions of dollars of licensing fees unlawfully collected by Warner over the years based on a non-existent copyright.

Both parties had agreed that the tune itself was very old and was in the public domain. The argument focused exclusively on the lyrics of 'Happy Birthday to You.'

Mitigating Measures: protecting your IP

Set up an anti-piracy and infringement monitoring programme. This should identify areas of IP theft, review weaknesses and mend breaches.

Monitor the sale of counterfeit versions of your products. Work with law enforcement to take such products off the streets and bring the culprits to justice. There are many ways to achieve this: Burberry uses criminal and civil legal action but also negotiated settlement. Not all jurisdictions provide the same level of enforcement or protection, and new criminals will arrive. This means your efforts will never be perfect, nor can you cease being vigilant.

Take vigorous legal action to enforce your IP.

Restrict strategically important documents relating to IP, including recipes, formulae, systems of work, designs, methods and customer lists.

Ensure that contractors and other partners sign non-disclosure agreements.

Include IP risks when assessing suppliers. How much valuable information are you putting into their hands?

Make staff aware that taking documents to a new employer is theft and will be treated as such.

Carry out security checks to ensure that IP is safeguarded. Company secrets should be available only to staff who need access to them.

Maintain the integrity of your brand names. Refrain from cutting quality or extending the name into unworthy products. Once a brand name loses the trust of its customers, it is hard to regain it.

Assess whether your IP could work harder, by extending your brands into new fields, including through licensing.

Take steps to protect against industrial espionage. This is covered in Chapter 16.

Ensure you have robust information security measures in place, something we cover in Chapter 12.

Products that harm

In safety-critical applications, such as defence, aerospace or automotive, the consequences of failure are serious and possibly catastrophic.

The same can be true in the service sector. Medical negligence is one of the top three causes of death in the USA, after cancer and heart disease, while in the UK the National Health Service faces a £4bn bill to cover medical negligence claims.

If a company's products or services are in any way controversial it may face class action, as happens in tobacco, pharmaceuticals, mining, automotive and almost any industry with apparently deep pockets.

Manufacturing faults that find their way into the supply chain will lead to costly recalls. In the USA, Natural Selection Foods had to recall its fresh spinach after the FDA found it was contaminated with E. coli. Three people died and hundreds got sick. The recall cost $350m, according to Weise. It is thought that farmers had used contaminated water to irrigate the crops.

Mitigating Measures: product liability risks

Conduct a product liability risk assessment. Ask yourself what could go wrong. Include suppliers in your assessment.

Maintain stringent quality control processes that meet ISO 9000 or equivalent. It will be an aid if a legal defence is necessary.

Have product warnings on packaging. Show what uses the product is intended for, and its limitations.

Put product recall plans in place, and be prepared to launch them. This should be part of your contingency planning process.

Prepare detailed contingency plans for dealing with product liability litigation, whether threatened or actual.

Take out product liability insurance.

---

14 Back to the drawing board

Project and contract risk

In any project there are four main risks:

1 The project costs escalate.
2 The delivery date gets delayed.
3 The final product is unsuitable.

and this results in the fourth risk:

4 The project or end product gets abandoned. It never comes to fruition.

These failings are caused by a range of problems:

The initial assessment is inadequate: People are optimistic and hopeful, rather than objective. They make instant decisions. Later they will say, 'It seemed like a good idea at the time.' Managers make assumptions – that everything will go well, and there will be no holdups on the project. They don't imagine that technical problems might occur. And they don't do enough research.

Management doesn't consider the alternatives: There are always other options. You can buy instead of making it yourself. You can lease instead of buying. You could sub-contract instead of doing it in-house. Or you could spend the money on another project.

Stakeholders are not consulted: In a remarkable number of projects, the end users are rarely asked for their input. This results in software that people can't use and new products that no one wants.

Some costs get overlooked: Anyone who wants their project to be given approval will present it in the best light. This can mean minimising the possible costs. Other project leaders don't anticipate the delays and other unexpected events which lead to extra costs.

The project lacks a detailed brief: If the end result is defined in too vague a way, you may end up with something you didn't want, or that looks nothing like you expected. This is especially true of software projects, where those who commission them don't know how IT works, nor what it can and can't do. This makes it hard for managers to write a good brief.

Then as the project moves forward into the operational phase, the following risks occur:

Circumstances change: Projects take a long time to come to fruition. During that period, management discovers new facts or the market changes.

Management is not engaged: This comes in two forms. Sometimes senior management was never really interested in the project, and hence delays decisions about it. As a result, the team lacks the support to create change and can't get buy-in from staff. There is also the 'shiny object' problem: management gets bored and distracted, and finds a new project to get excited about.

Managers sometimes think that once a project is underway it will be self-supporting. But this isn't true. Senior management needs to guide and support the project if it's to reach a successful conclusion. This is because only senior management can 'knock heads together' and insist that staff support the project.

The project people lack skills: The organisation may lack the expertise to drive a project forward. It's easy to decide that you will build a world-beating smartphone, quite another to deliver it.

Suppliers cause delays and are found to have failings, such as overpromising. Supplier salespeople will often promise a lot, only to find that operations people can't deliver it. One client asked whether an HR system could be tailored to their needs, and was assured it could. Three years on, the system is in place, but the modifications haven't been made, and the client can't easily start again with a different supplier.

The project is under-resourced: When this happens, staff can't give enough time to it. There is insufficient money to meet development costs, and requests for funds are delayed or blocked. Any worthwhile project will involve large costs, and management has to commit to it.

Change requests and project creep: As more people get involved with a project, they're likely to request additional features. This happens with software, where managers can always think of one more function they need. Apple's Steve Jobs was insistent about paring down any new device to its bare minimum to keep things simple.

Mitigating Measures: project planning phase

Control the number of projects. Management should be aware that the more projects it takes on, the fewer will be implemented successfully. People have a limited span of attention. Something has to give.

Ask for evidence. All projects should be based on facts.

Define the brief clearly and in detail. State what the project should do. How will it compare with similar objects? What are the measures of success?

Cost the project thoroughly. Include a contingency element.

Get buy-in. If you communicate with everyone, and get them on board, they are less likely to be obstructive. 'Not invented here' is why many projects fail. Too few people are committed to making the project work.

Mitigating Measures: project development phase

Put an able team in place. The team leader must have sufficient authority. Junior people will not be able to persuade people outside the team to support it. The rest of the team must be balanced to ensure a full range of skills, whether that's financial, technical, administrative or client-focused.

Control new feature requests. Require new feature requests to be itemised and rigorously discussed before being added. The team should consider how much time and cost this will add.

Allocate management time. The senior team must be supportive of the project, and provide guidance and input when necessary. The project must be scheduled at suitably senior review meetings.

Provide enough resources for the team. Ensure there's an adequate budget for purchases, travel and pilot work. Team members should not be asked to do other work which would put the project back.

Work with end users. If the project could be rejected by the client or end users, ensure they're engaged and consulted. This will ensure that the project meets end users' needs. When the project is delivered there will be no surprises.

IT project problems

IT projects are the same as any other kind of project, but with technology added as an extra risk.

The outcome of many IT projects is unknown, unlike building a bridge or a factory. Managers and end users find it hard to clearly define how the software should work, mostly because they don't know.

Senior management often has no understanding of coding, and is therefore unable to contribute useful opinions. The work is therefore in the hands of experts, who may hold idiosyncratic opinions or have strong views. A woman who had a short-term IT job in the UK's Treasury Department said sadly,

> I had a project manager who said to me 'I don't understand technical things' and yet she was making technical judgements on the project, which I quickly realised were just random and without judgement. I was quickly forced to leave when I made it clear that serious mistakes were being made. From others I talked to, this culture is endemic in the civil service where actual expertise counts for nothing in getting to be a manager.

Yet another major IT failure

An IT system known as GPES, which was designed to get information from general practitioners' computers, was criticised by UK MPs for being late, over budget and inadequate.

(continued)

(continued)

It was due to be delivered in 2009 but didn't go live until 2014. Its cost rose from £14m to £40m. The commissioning department was closed during the project, and responsibility passed to another section.

After the project went live, the Department of Health admitted it wasn't value for money and that the system was only delivering half of what it was specified to do. The department was considering whether to try and improve the system or just replace it.

The MPs' committee said the original project team didn't have the right skills or experience to build GPES and the governance structure was not fit for purpose. There was 'exceptionally high level of staff turnover in key roles', with ten project managers over a five-year period and three project board chairs over three years. The department did nothing about this.

One of the eight suppliers of the service, Atos, should be banned, the report said. 'We are not satisfied Atos provided proper professional support to an inexpert client and are very concerned that it appears to have acted solely with its own short term best interests in mind.'

Mitigating Measures: helping IT projects succeed

Consider starting with a limited scope. The bigger the project, the higher the likelihood of failure.

Build IT expertise within the organisation, rather than relying entirely on contractors.

Engage users from the outset. Ensure they see each stage of the build, and that coders listen to their comments.

Start with the end in mind. Ensure there are mocked-up images of what should appear on the screens, and what functions the users will need. Vague outcomes are your enemy. There must be a sharp focus on what the final product will look like.

See if there are existing proven models in place, rather than creating your own. Visit complementary businesses to see what they do. Scan the literature. See if you can buy or lease ready-made off the shelf products. But be aware they may not fit your existing systems or procedures.

Hire a competent programme manager, someone who is able to work with coders and managers, and speak the language of each.

What am I bid? Contract pricing issues

Bidding for contracts is time consuming and expensive. Losing a bid can sap morale, and the failure to win a major order can, in the worst case, cause redundancies.

When the business needs work, it's tempting to underprice the job so the project becomes loss making. Overpromising is another risk, as is over-optimism on the chances of things going wrong.

Where fixed price tenders have little room for change, there is a risk that costs may exceed those originally forecast. This is especially likely if the contract extends over many years or the work is dependent on a number of variables. In construction bad weather can cause serious delays, which results in cost over-runs.

Design and development projects are harder to estimate than production contracts, and are therefore more risky. Some businesses use Monte Carlo simulations. While these are valuable they may simply show that if everything goes wrong, the contract could never be profitable. It may be better to limit the scope of the bid, or share the risks with the client, though this is not always possible.

Mitigating Measures: bidding for contracts

Have a strategy for targeting the right kind of bids. They must align with the company's goals, and they must have a realistic chance of being won.

Set commercial, financial and legal procedures for all bids.

Identify whether you have the experience and capacity to deliver the product or service.

Review whether all the clauses in the contract are acceptable to your organisation. Does it require financial guarantees that if executed would be ruinous?

Assess whether the time spent in submitting a tender will be worth it. Weigh up the value of the contract and the likelihood of your winning it.

Create a risk matrix that identifies each risk, its probability and severity including cost, how it will be mitigated or shared and what steps need to be taken and by whom.

Set approvals at a management level that relates to the risk. The bigger the contract, the higher up the decision must be taken.

Allocate resources to those areas where the business is likely to achieve most wins.

Seek detailed clarification from the client on any points of uncertainty.

Build uncertainty and risk into the pricing.

Negotiate risks and uncertainties out of the contract where possible.

Be prepared not to bid on a contract where the uncertainties are too high, or where the client is not willing to share the risk or remove some scope.

Avoid offering design and development contracts on a fixed price basis unless the parameters are known and unlikely to move.

Review previous bids and contracts and learn from them. Did everything go according to plan? Were there surprises? What lessons should be learnt?

Insure your contract risks where possible.

Managing the contract

Any contract is liable to be affected by unexpected events, whether they are changes requested by the client, weather problems, operational problems or supplier errors.

It isn't hard to find examples of troubled contracts. The Edinburgh tram system was budgeted at £375m in 2003, but the final cost was £776m (or £1bn if interest payments are included). It took so long to build that the rails rusted. Political change, financial crises, faulty construction and contractual disputes all took their toll.

For a contractor, failure to adequately manage the work will result in higher costs and the risk of being sued. The main threats are:

- *Scope creep*, where the client asks for more work to be done, saying it was always part of the plan, and the project team agrees to do it. This may be caused by a lack of clarity at the design stage. At other times, poor communication or failure to stand up to a client is at fault.
- *Rising costs*. The project team may ask for more staff to keep the project on track. Or the materials will cost more than expected. This can stem from poor budgeting or failure to include all costs at the time of the tender.
- *Revenue leakage*. This can involve failure to invoice for added work done, while in some industries, fraud is a source of revenue loss. A car importer failed to bill a car company for washing and valeting the vehicles. The workers had cleaned the cars but hadn't recorded the work, so management had to give the client an unexpected £65,000 bill for three years' work.

There are various phrases that contractors need to listen out for, says Tom Zender in the *Phoenix Business Journal*. They include: 'Just one more thing . . .', 'I'm sure we told you . . .', 'But we need this too . . .', 'We just realized . . .', 'That is not what we expected . . .', 'Why didn't you . . .', 'Wait, where is the . . .'.

When you hear these kinds of phrases, he says, 'dig deep into what they mean before deciding anything.' Failure to pay attention could damage your margins.

Mitigating Measures: better contract management

Manage each contract through its life. Each project has discrete stages: planning, design and manufacture, the operational stage and finally the end of the project or hand-over. Project lifecycle management will help you think about what's needed at each stage.

Scrutinise the terms of the contract. Check for contractual liabilities that could harm the business.

Control costs as the contract proceeds. This is necessary for ensuring the project stays profitable.

Maintain extensive and regular dialogue with the client. The contractor's senior staff need to be engaged so they don't rely on third party opinions.

Train project managers to understand the risks and manage them.

---

15 Criminal intentions

Crimes against the business

Coming under attack

In this chapter we examine the risks of arson, assaults on staff, extortion, fraud, kidnap and ransom, sabotage and tampering.

It's a motley range. What ties them together is that someone has decided to attack the business or its staff.

These crimes can be carried out by criminals, vandals, the public or disgruntled employees. Some, like fraud, are common, while others, such as kidnap, are thankfully rare. Each of the sections has a box containing Mitigating Measures.

Burning with a passion

Some organisations are more prone to arson attack, that is, fires set deliberately, especially at schools, farms and smallholdings.

Arson is caused by vandalism, revenge and when a criminal is covering up another crime, such as fraud. Between 20 and 25% of arson fires are drug-related. Children cause more than one third of the arson fires set in the United States.

Vandalism is the leading cause of arson. The US Insurance Research Council reckons that only 14% of arson events are motivated by a desire to defraud an insurance company, though other studies find the percentage is higher.

Over 30,000 buildings in the UK are deliberately set on fire every year, costing the UK as much as £300m.

In the USA, there were 19,000 building arsons in 2014, which destroyed $729m worth of property, according to the National Fire Protection Association, although there may be serious under-reporting. However, arson accounted for only 4% of all building fires. There were also 8,000 vehicle arsons in the same year in the USA.

The outcome of arson can include the death or serious injury to staff, tenants and visitors; damage to property, loss of equipment and records, inability to use the premises, smoke and water damage, compensation claims for injuries and the loss of business or rent.

Mitigating Measures: tackling the threat of arson

Light the outside of your buildings at night.

Have a procedure for closing your business:

- Lock external doors;
- Close internal doors to delay the spread of flames;
- Do not leave unauthorised people on the premises;
- Tidy waste and rubbish;
- Switch alarms on.

Put yourself in the mind of an arsonist. How could they start a fire inside or outside your property? Take steps to remedy any vulnerabilities.

Have adequate perimeter fences and locked gates.

Identify ways intruders could access your property, such as trees and drain pipes. Take measures to prevent them aiding entry.

Get the police or an expert to check your locks, shutters and windows.

Install CCTV and intruder alarms that ring an off-site security service.

Consider a mobile guarding service.

Use enclosed and lockable waste skips and bins to prevent them being used as a source of fuel. Move waste storage as far away from your buildings as practical.

Report anti-social behaviour to the police. Such social behaviour can be a precursor to arson. It can include gatherings of people who hang around streets, drink or use drugs, become rowdy and cause trouble. Graffiti and vandalism are also signs of future problems. Encourage staff to be on the lookout for suspicious activity and people.

Ask your local fire brigade for advice on protecting your premises against arson.

Taking it out on the staff

Threats and assaults on staff are a common risk among staff who deal with the public. According to the UK's Health and Safety Executive, staff who are most at risk are those who:

- are providing a service;
- provide a caring service;
- work in schools;
- handle cash;
- deliver and collect goods or money;
- control others;
- represent authority.

Violence at work leads to poor morale and a poor image for the organisation, making it difficult to recruit and keep staff. It can also mean extra costs, with absenteeism, higher insurance premiums and compensation payments. It causes pain, distress and even disability or death to employees.

And it isn't just about physical violence. Serious or persistent verbal abuse or threats will damage employees' health through anxiety or stress.

Lone working presents a risk. Hope Jahren, winner of three Fulbright awards and author of *Lab Girl*, said she kept a spanner in her back pocket for protection. She explained,

> I was working alone at night, and I knew there were a lot of other people who had a key, and some of them creeped me out – the wrench made me feel safer. That is the reality of all women's lives. We negotiate risk while we lead our lives. I think men are surprised when I say that, and women are not.

Mitigating Measures: minimising assaults on staff

Undertake a risk assessment. Identify who is at risk. Seek to predict what might happen.

Consider the heightened risks at night or at weekends when staff are less likely to have support.

Seek the views of members of staff who are most likely to suffer.

Introduce measures that will reduce the risk of attack. This can include changing:

- training and information
- the work environment
- work procedures.

We detail each of these next.

Ensure adequate training and information

- Train employees so they can spot the signs of aggression and either avoid it or deal with it.
- Make sure they fully understand how to use any system you have set up for their protection, for example panic or alarm buttons, or what procedures to follow.
- Provide employees with information that lets them identify clients with a history of violence.
- Show staff how to anticipate factors that might make violence more likely.

The environment

Provide better seating, decor and lighting in public waiting rooms. Give more regular information about delays. Consider physical security measures such as:

- video cameras or alarm systems;
- coded security locks on doors to keep the public out of staff areas;
- wider counters and raised floors on the staff side of the counter to give staff more protection;
- glass panels that separate staff from the public.

(continued)

(continued)

Change procedures to reduce vulnerability

- Bank money more frequently. Vary the route taken to reduce the risk of robbery.
- Limit the amount of cash on hand.
- Have visible security staff on hand.
- For meetings away from the workforce (for care workers or estate agents), check the credentials of clients and identify what arrangements are in place.
- Arrange for staff to be accompanied by a colleague if they have to meet a suspected aggressor at their home or in a remote location.
- Require employees who work away from their base to keep in touch.
- Avoid lone working by maintaining sufficient numbers of staff at your workplace.

The rise of extortion

Commercial extortion (a demand for money backed up by a threat of violence or damage) used to be associated with product tampering or demands made by organised crime on retailers and logistics companies. Similarly, blackmailers used to threaten individuals, especially celebrities, with the release of embarrassing information unless they were paid.

But as we saw in Chapter 12, extortion is used in cyber attacks where the perpetrators steal information, commit a denial of service attack or take control of a network. In these cases, the extortionist demands money, often in the form of bitcoin. The US Federal Financial Institutions Examination Council (FFIEC) says financial institutions are suffering increasing levels of cyber attacks involving extortion.

Sony Pictures received a demand that it should not release the movie *The Interview*, which satirised the assassination of North Korean leader Kim Jong-Un. When Sony refused, the hackers, thought to be the government of North Korea, released data stolen from the company's servers. This included unreleased movies, embarrassing emails and sensitive employee data. They also used malware to cripple many of Sony's systems. Sony then cancelled the film's release, but the event is thought to have cost it $100m, as well as causing reputational damage.

Mitigating Measures: dealing with extortion

Conduct a cyber security risk assessment.

Harden your internet systems.

Put a continuity plan in place to respond to a cyber attack.

How to fight fraud

Fraud is theft involving deception. Just about anyone can carry out fraud, whether inside the business or outside it.

Blue collar employees may steal goods. A driver can acquire stock from his van by writing some products off as damaged, or by delivering only some of the consignment to unobservant customers. Warehouse staff can under-record incoming goods.

Clerical employees: Despite their lowly status, many clerical staff have access to cheque books and online payment systems. They can 'lose' paperwork or falsify it.

Managers have a big opportunity for fraud. People in finance can create fake invoices and pay them. Purchasing managers can have goods delivered elsewhere.

Suppliers: A supplier can give a purchasing manager a kickback in return for orders. Suppliers can collude to fix prices, or nominate which of them will win specific contracts (known as cover pricing).

Customers make fraudulent insurance claims or return stolen goods for a refund.

Criminals buy goods online using stolen credit cards. They can get goods on credit with no intention of paying. They may also imitate a legitimate business online (such as a bank or software business) to steal money from that company's customers. Some public sector organisations receive fake requests to change a supplier's bank account details. This happens because the organisation is required to publish the names of successful contractors after a tender has been completed.

Why people commit fraud

Those who commit fraud do so for five main reasons.

1 *Disassociation*. Sociopaths and people with a criminal mentality don't believe they have to obey society's norms.
2 *Feeling entitled*. The fraudster may feel justified if the company seems to operate in an unfair manner. This can include 'not getting promotion', or 'not being paid enough'.
3 *Rationalisation*. Fraudsters rationalise their behaviour or trivialise it by telling themselves that 'everyone does it', or 'it's not a big amount'.
4 *Debt*. Employees who are in debt or live beyond their needs may engage in fraud to reduce their financial problems.
5 *Keeping up with the Joneses*. An employee may need to impress neighbours or a loved one by having an expensive car or taking glamorous holidays.

Preconditions of fraud

For fraud to take place, four A's must be present:

* *Avarice*. The person must have a need, a motive or a justification.
* *Assets*. The organisation must possess things worth stealing. This could be money or goods.
* *Access*. The fraudster must be in a position to transfer funds between accounts, take goods from a stock room or have access to a program.
* *Absence of control*. The individual must be free from supervision or audit, and perhaps be working on their own. This causes them to believe they won't be caught.

While the organisation can't do much about Avarice, Assets and Access, it can institute more controls and thereby reduce the incidence of fraud.

Signs of fraud

Be alert to the following indicators of fraud among employees. Several behaviours might indicate fraud.

- *Frequently working late.* This allows the employee to undertake fraud when no one is around. It can also let them remove assets from the premises more easily.
- *Reluctant to take leave.* The fraudster may avoid taking holidays. This prevents management from assigning someone else to temporarily do that job, where they might notice anomalies.
- *Refuses promotion.* This is to prevent their replacement from discovering their fraud.
- *Has unexplained wealth.* Most of us spend up to our limit, and that includes fraudsters. They find it hard to keep the cash quietly in the bank.
- *Undergoes a change in behaviour.* The employee may seem distant, agitated, stressed or vague. Be aware that quite legitimate circumstances (whether workload or family life) can also cause these symptoms.
- *Resigns suddenly.* Fraudsters do this if they know they are about to be found out.
- *Has a close relationship with a supplier or contractor.* This can indicate collusion.
- *A supplier or contractor insists on dealing with one specific member of staff.* The contractor may be giving the employee a kickback.

Mitigating Measures: winning against fraud

Undertake a fraud risk assessment.

Instigate and publicise an anti-fraud policy.

Establish a fraud code of conduct.

Provide a well-trained and resourced internal audit department. Have it undertake surprise audits.

Establish an independent audit committee.

Have a dedicated fraud department, function or team.

Keep internal audit separate from operational pressures. Avoid them being captured by operating managers' business needs.

Ensure auditors use scepticism and a questioning mind. Ensure they always ask for evidence, rather than relying on trust and others' assertions.

Separate people's responsibilities. Whoever raises orders must not authorise payment.

Introduce anti-fraud training for employees and managers. Explain that fraud hurts all stakeholders.

Have support mechanisms in place for employees who face difficulties (such as debt). This can prevent crime from taking place. You might provide a confidential telephone line and employee support services.

Measure employee engagement as a way of determining the probability of fraud and where in the business it might occur. It may also identify areas of perceived injustice and rancour.

Be seen to operate in a fair and ethical manner. This will avoid resentment, and will prevent employees from seeing theft as a reasonable response to a guilty employer.

Arrange for an external audit of your internal financial controls.

Make staff take their holidays.

Rotate fraud-risk jobs so that no employee stays in one role permanently.

Instigate a hotline when improprieties can be reported anonymously. Ensure that whistleblowers are protected and even rewarded.

Don't let managers override financial or operational controls.

On the take: procurement fraud

Fraud is a big temptation for procurement staff. A purchasing department offers many opportunities for fraud: managers have access to the means of fraud (order forms) and they lack close supervision. Procurement fraud takes place at four moments in time:

1   When projects are put out to tender or the business asks for quotes. A tender document can be skewed to favour a specific bidder. Suppliers can conspire to let one of them win.
2   The moment when management chooses a winner. A supplier can bribe the purchasing officer.
3   When the work is carried out, with sub-standard goods or services being supplied.
4   When invoices are submitted. This can include fake invoices from non-existent suppliers.

Mitigating Measures: preventing procurement fraud

Make the risk of procurement fraud visible in the organisation. Ensure it is on the risk register. Give it a risk owner.

Train buying and financial staff to recognise procurement fraud.

Ensure there is a three-way match of the details shown on the requisition, purchase order and invoice. Check delivery notes.

Document the procurement process, and ensure it is followed. Shortcuts should not be permitted.

Segregate the duties of raising orders and paying invoices.

Have two people approve the addition or removal of a supplier from the approved supplier list. The same applies to changing a supplier's bank account number.

Ensure that sub-contractors are known and approved before the work is agreed.

Set procurement thresholds. Ensure that orders are not split to circumvent this.

Kidnap and ransom

Some countries have a high risk of kidnap and ransom (K&R), including Mexico, India and Pakistan. Reported cases have risen in Nigeria, in part due to the prominence of the Boko Haram militant group. But the frequency and severity of kidnap varies from year to year.

Seventy per cent of kidnappings result in a ransom being paid, and 90% of victims survive. Deaths typically result from a medical condition, shock or a failed rescue or escape attempt. So it's reasonable to assume that paying the money will resolve the problem.

Kidnappings by country

1	Mexico	10	Iraq
2	India	11	Syria
3	Nigeria	12	Guatemala
4	Pakistan	13	Yemen
5	Venezuela	14	Libya
6	Lebanon	15	Egypt
7	Philippines	16	Brazil, Kenya (tied)
8	Afghanistan	18	Nepal
9	Colombia	19	Malaysia, South Africa (tied).

Source: Control Risks

Control Risks says that the number of kidnappings in the top ten countries is in the 'many thousands', but is much lower elsewhere. It is only in the 'high hundreds' below the top ten.

Mitigating Measures: the risk of kidnap and ransom

Have a K&R policy.

Set out procedures for managing the event, the media and a negotiation strategy.

Take out kidnap and ransom insurance. This means that a K&R expert will conduct negotiations for you, relieving you of much pressure.

Provide security training for at-risk employees. Educate overseas workers about the typical threats, what to do if a kidnapping takes place and how to work with captors.

Plan the employee's movements in advance.

If an employee is kidnapped, contact a K&R specialist immediately.

Accept that payment is likely to resolve the kidnap.

Strategies for the at-risk employee

- Avoid drawing attention to yourself.
- Don't go into high-risk areas unnecessarily. At night stay in well-lit areas. Kidnappers are more likely to take action if they see you're vulnerable.
- Watch out for suspicious behaviour. This includes being watched or followed, or someone making overtures of friendship, or making enquiries about your business.
- Do not adopt routines. Vary your travel to work plans and routes.
- Be aware of exit routes.
- Avoid the risk of becoming incapacitated by drink or drugs.
- Identify callers before opening the door. Don't open the door if you're in doubt.
- Keep windows locked.
- Use solid doors and good deadlocks.
- At night, close curtains before turning on lights.
- Keep rear boundaries high to maximise your security and privacy.
- Keep front boundary hedges and fences low to maximise your view.
- Keep young children in sight or, if leaving them with someone, ensure that this person is aware that they may be at risk of kidnapping.
- Conduct a risk assessment before travelling.
- Only use vehicles provided by a trusted transport provider and an English-speaking driver.
- Take cash so you don't need to visit an ATM, a hotspot for crime.
- Arrive and depart from dangerous airports during daylight hours. This reduces the risk of opportunistic crime.
- Stay alert, especially when leaving or entering your home or work premises.
- Travel with others where possible.
- Be suspicious of anyone trying to get you to stop or leave your vehicle.
- Avoid parking in places that may be dark or isolated on your return.
- Take a defensive driving course.
- In very high-risk areas, travel only in a vehicle convoy escorted by contracted armed guards. Live in on-site accommodation that's under constant armed guard.

Sabotaging the business

Sabotage is an act designed to weaken an organisation or country through 'subversion, obstruction, disruption or destruction'. There are two types of sabotage: IT and non-IT sabotage, each of which we examine separately.

Perpetrators are either employees (current or past), governments or competitors. The impact of sabotage varies from ephemeral to the devastating. Let's look first at non-IT sabotage caused by employees.

Employees who commit non-IT sabotage

Businesses with bad industrial relations, layoffs or who are the subjects of a takeover can suffer sabotage from employees. Staff with a grudge can also cause sabotage. In these cases the employee is seeking revenge, or wants to vent rage or frustration.

When asked to adopt new ways of working, employees can often sabotage a project by finding fault with it, deliberately misusing it or sticking to the old ways of doing things.

Sometimes this sabotage is wilful, but it may be a simple preference for the old familiar ways, a belief that the change will lead to job losses, reluctance to deal with the stress of the new or even management's failure to get buy-in. Actions can include the following:

- tampering with the company's product or services. Production line employees might put cockroaches into food;
- working slowly, taking extended breaks;
- making negative comments about the project to other members of staff. This can delay a project or even cause it to fail;
- committing arson.

Mitigating Measures: non-IT sabotage by employees

Train managers to recognise signs of employee disaffection, especially at times of change. Make time to identify discontented employees and speak with them one-on-one.

Provide easily accessible information about change projects, and present them as up for discussion. Managers must be receptive to criticism and suggestions. They should also be trained to recognise the pain and distress suffered by people who are used to the old system, may have lived with it for years and won't see any advantage in change. Moving from manual to computer-based work activity will be especially challenging for people with weak IT skills.

Foster a team culture. Encourage staff to see that they can improve the new system.

Humanise project teams and senior executives to make them seem more approachable. Ensure the senior team's faces are known. Empower staff to voice their concerns and make contributions, so they feel engaged with the project.

Place CCTV where sabotage could take place, such as the factory floor or warehouse.

Non-IT sabotage by competitors

Serial entrepreneur Mark Cuban says 'Business is the ultimate sport', and many players adopt dubious tactics to help their team win. Competitors can attack a business in the following ways:

- Poach key team members, especially salespeople.
- Damage competitor launches. An *Inc Magazine* reader said,

  We flooded the market with a bunch of clone products, each with slightly different features (some were pretty much the same). This scared off most of the people trying to break into the market, and we ended up killing off all the sites that weren't driving any value. After about 18 months, we consolidated all properties into one site.

- Buy and then cancel products. According to ride-sharing service Lyft, 177 Uber employees booked and cancelled over 5,000 trips. Uber is also accused of doing the same thing to Gett, another competitor, by booking cars and then cancelling them shortly before arrival, which was tantamount to a DDoS attack in that customers were unable to hire Gett cars.

IT sabotage by staff, competitors or governments

Some senior people see IT as too difficult to understand, or too specialist to be concerned with. This is a risky mindset. IT people are the organisation's most dangerous employees, while the IT system itself is vulnerable to attack from inside and out.

Cybotage, as it is sometime known, a fusing of 'cyber' and 'sabotage', involves criminal acts designed to sabotage an organisation's IT system or internet presence. Staff and competitors can do any of the following:

- launch a DDoS attack: taking down a website by overwhelming it with requests for pages;
- introduce a virus into the organisation's network;
- delete files from the network;
- post negative comments about your product or services on review sites;
- post scurrilous or damaging comments on sites using your competitor's name. On one occasion, a competitor posted information on credit card cloning sites, in the name of the company's CEO ('Hey, this works, try it!');
- sign up for the organisation's emails, then report them as spam;
- damage the company's IT system, such as by deleting a database.

In a survey of 400 IT administrators by Cyber-Ark, one-third of respondents said they had encountered cases of insider sabotage in their workplace. Ex-employees were the leading culprits.

If fired tomorrow, two-thirds of IT employees in the United States said they'd take nothing. But 17% of respondents said they'd take a database, and 2% said they'd take the CEO's email password or the server administrator's password.

Businesses in strategically important industries such as IT or defence are also at risk from foreign government sabotage. The Stuxnet computer worm is thought to have been jointly built by the USA and Israeli governments as a cyber weapon. Stuxnet is reported to have ruined one-fifth of Iran's nuclear centrifuges.

The company that lost everything in twenty minutes

The US division of Japanese drug company Shionogi lost everything – its emails, order tracking and financial data - after a former employee, Jason Cornish, logged in to the network using a hidden virtual server he'd previously created, and erased the data on the company's servers. He did this while drinking coffee at a McDonald's.

Cornish previously had a dispute with one of the company's managers and had resigned. His supervisor, a close friend, then persuaded the business to take Cornish on as a consultant, because he was familiar with the company's network.

The damage froze the company's operations for days and cost Shionogi more than $800,000. Cornish's former supervisor refused to hand over network passwords and was eventually fired. Cornish was sentenced to 41 months in jail, and was required to pay $812,000 to the company in restitution.

Mitigating Measures: IT sabotage

Identify your mission-critical networks and resources. Understand who has access to them and could damage them. Ensure senior management knows mission-critical passwords. Server passwords are often known only to selected IT people.

Control who has access to sensitive servers and their passwords.

Set 'super administrator' access so you can maintain control over your systems and lock others out. Give this access only to a few senior people in the organisation.

Ensure you can change passwords fast. Remove an individual's access to the system within 20 minutes of them leaving the business. This is especially true for those whose employment is terminated. Sensible organisations start to remove access privileges before the person has even gone. If someone is to be sacked on arrival at work first thing in the morning, you can withdraw their privileges the previous evening.

Use monitoring tools to set thresholds and alerts when there are unusual or anomalous activities inside the network. This should send a notification and close down access to those areas. Examples include a remote connection into the server rather than from a user's PC; the arrival of an executable file that, although conventional, is not used by the business or a destructive command line instruction.

Don't rehire any IT person who has a known grudge or personal problem. Shionogi brought Cornish back as a contractor so he could finish a project for them.

Be alert to fake negative reviews by people who you can identify as hostile. Ask the review site to delete them. If this is not possible, reply to the comment in a measured way

---

Injecting fear: the risk of tampering

Tampering with a product is usually carried out by disgruntled staff, extortionists or activists. It's a rare event, but there are occasional outbreaks. In 1982 seven people died in Chicago after consuming capsules of the pain reliever Tylenol that had been laced with cyanide. The tampering abruptly stopped and no one was ever tried or convicted for the crime.

Extortionists sometimes claim to have tampered with a product, even though they haven't, in order to extort money from the manufacturer or because they seek attention. Fears of tampering can alarm consumers and lead to a massive loss of sales. Sometimes manufacturing errors cause objects to be found in food. This gets confused with tampering, and this can cause a scare.

Political groups can tamper with products to reduce sales. In 1978 a Palestinian group told the Dutch government it had injected mercury into Israeli citrus fruits. These fruits were found in several European countries including The Netherlands, the UK and Germany. The adulteration seems to have been carried out at the ports of Rotterdam or Antwerp, where the fruit had been landed. No one died, but 12 people were affected by mercury poisoning and Israeli orange exports to Europe fell by 40%. Many of the reported findings of contaminated fruit turned out to be false or hoaxes. Some believe that the real target was the Syrian foreign minister, Abdel Halim Khaddam, who was unhurt. Others assert that it was a plot to discredit the Palestine Liberation Organisation (PLO).

Although you can use tamper-evident packaging to defeat such efforts, some tampering is hard to detect, for example in fresh or lightly packaged food.

Mitigating Measures: tampering

Make all packaging tamper-evident. Lid safety buttons reveal whether a jar has been opened.

Have a tampering contingency plan.

---

16 Getting alarmed

Mitigating security risks

Security used to focus on the routine risks relating to company buildings, such as burglary and theft. These days there's greater awareness of additional security risks, including the loss of goods in transit, terrorism and extremists.

In this chapter we review the risks that affect the organisation's buildings and the people in them. We also look at security risks beyond those buildings, both at home and abroad.

Not every risk to a building comes from security threats. Other concerns include fire and flood. These can be caused by extreme weather, by careless staff, by maintenance failure and by criminal behaviour. We cover these non-security risks in Chapters 10, 15 and 17. In this chapter we categorise security risk as follows:

Theft, whether by criminals or employees. Criminals tend to commit burglary and holdups, while employees may walk out with goods. Check out Chapter 15 for more considered, longer-term types of theft.

Attack. This can be delivered through the mail, in a vehicle or by an individual. We cover kidnap and ransom in Chapter 15, and IT attacks in Chapter 12.

Conducting a security review

Managing security risks starts with a security review. The main topics are listed below.

Security review topics

The following notes will help to pinpoint vulnerabilities and targets.

History

Past incidents: is there a history of break-ins or losses?

Motivations for possible security problems

Theft of valuable or convertible goods
Extreme politics, religion
Extortion
Commercial espionage.

Context

The building's location, type of perimeter, type of premises (retail, office or warehouse), vulnerabilities, attractiveness to criminals and likely method of theft or attack

Assets

What assets could be stolen or damaged?

Controls

Access control for employees, visitors and unauthorised people; parking.
Guards, radio contact and internal communications
Alarms, closed circuit TV.

Systems

Fire and emergency planning
Management systems and procedures.

People

Recruitment processes. (How stringent are they?)
Business partners: suppliers, agents and customers
Company structure and personnel.

Beyond the building

Money in transit
Goods in transit
Executive travel
Executives living abroad.

Mitigating Measures: security

Undertake a security assessment. Identify how the building might be threatened, whether by night-time burglars, smash and grab thieves, terrorists, bomb threats or hostile vehicles. Consider the modus operandi of such threats.

Implement a plan for managing security.

Match your security policy to the level of threat. Businesses providing uncontroversial or less easily saleable products or services can afford a lower level of security.

Vary your security over time, depending on the threat. If your organisation has a high profile, you may need to adopt traffic light levels (red, amber and green), to help staff know when they should be more security conscious.

Building security

Thieves are constantly working out how to steal from your premises, whether that's cash inside staff handbags, laptops from desks or even lead off the roof.

One large organisation was having some windows replaced, and two men wearing overalls simply walked unchallenged into the building and removed a large television. The business never found out whether it was an inside job, carried out by some of the contractors, or whether two opportunist thieves happened to be passing. Where a site has many trades and different sub-contractors, it's hard to know who is legitimate and who isn't. Access control – challenging people who come on to the site – is important.

There are five steps to preventing unauthorised access, especially for deterring theft. These are shown in Figure 16.1.

1   *Deter* people by means of notices, cameras and the presence of security staff. Many criminals will be discouraged by the appearance of good security, and will seek easier targets.
2   *Observe* people with cameras and video recording.
3   *Prevent* access with fences and locks. Use zoning to harden the more valuable parts of the building.
4   *Alert* people to illegal entry by alarms and lights. Emergency exit doors should sound an alarm when opened.
5   *Physically secure* objects that might get stolen.

Perimeter control

Protecting the building from intruders is the most basic and valuable form of security. Where possible have a perimeter fence or wall. It will discourage, delay or prevent intruders. It also protects security guards from surprise attack, and provides a barrier against vehicle entry and explosions.

* The fence or wall can be topped by barbed wire or spikes. You can also coat the wall in slippery anti-climb paint. Alternatively, bushes with spiky leaves will tear the clothes of intruders. An angled overhang (facing outwards at 45 degrees) makes intrusion even harder.
* Light the perimeter in its entirety. This will require any intruder to pass through a well-lit area. Lamp posts should not help an intruder to climb the fence.
* Limit the number of perimeter openings. They should be controllable and be monitored either by cameras or personnel.
* Install a perimeter intruder detection systems, namely alarms, CCTV cameras and intrusion sensors; but stay within the law. Erect 'Keep out' and 'CCTV' signs.

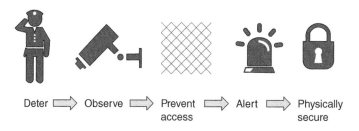

Figure 16.1 Security steps.

Grounds

Have a clear zone around the perimeter so that intruders cannot hide. The same applies to the area near the building. Aim to provide no cover. Low bushes and isolated trees with a narrow form will make the site look less austere.

Area lighting

Evenly illuminate all the area inside the perimeter Avoid dark shadows, for example in corners.

Vehicle access

Seek to control vehicles entering the site. Manage who, how, why and when they enter. In some cases, such as retailers and builders' merchants, this won't be possible and security should start at the building entrance. Where a site is open to the public, non-approved vehicles should be kept away from valuable assets.

- Make it less easy for vehicles to access your property. You can do this by adding security barriers, walls and gates. Ensure emergency access is taken into account.
- Inside the perimeter, instigate traffic calming measures. This has as much to do with safety as with security. These measures can include:

  o Speed humps
  o Passing places
  o Narrowed routes, using bollards, raised kerbs and chicanes
  o Rumble strips
  o Interactive speed limit signs.

- For high-risk sites, add a bund or ditch to stop vehicles getting close to the building.

Control the access

Reduce access points: Minimise the number of doors and other access points to your building.

Institute access management: Prevent unauthorised daytime access by means of guards, swipe cards or proximity cards.

Zoning: Zone the building into public and private access areas. Areas you would want to secure might include design, R&D, finance, IT and the executive suite.

Doors: Doors and locks should be strong enough to withstand or delay forcible entry, while allowing for emergency exit. Doors should be lit at night. Limit the number of doors that can be opened from outside, with the rest changed to exit-only fire doors. Internal doors that lead to secure parts of the holding should be openable only with a keypad or swipe card, and should have alarms, whether ultrasonic movement detectors, photoelectric beams or pressure pads.

Windows: Identify how easy it would be to force the windows. They might be smashed or the hinges or locks forced. Ensure the windows are sufficiently resistant to forcible entry. Alarm the windows where appropriate.

Train staff to be aware of 'tailgating', whereby someone gets into the building by walking closely behind an authorised staff member before the door shuts. Staff must be willing to challenge people who follow them through a secure door.

Conduct penetration testing: Set up a team to see how far they can get into the building. They should go into offices, take photos of what is on desks and screens, and leave a note explaining that the office is insecure. They then provide a report to senior management, detailing areas of weakness.

Security cameras

Maintain and regularly check security cameras. There is nothing worse than finding the cameras have not been recording.

The cameras should cover the entrances and exits to your building, as well as the perimeter. They must cover important areas of the business, such as reception, server room, tills or the cash office. Check for blind spots.

The images must have a resolution sufficient to identify intruders (using a Rotakin test), but surveillance and storage of images must conform to the law.

Exclusion zones

Determine which parts of the building should be available only to selected staff, and possibly only to those with permits. This may include:

- cash office
- server room
- R&D
- executive floor
- warehouse.

In addition:

- Review which staff have permits, and revoke authorisations when staff leave.
- Consider sweeping the executive offices for listening devices.
- Be aware of the security risk of cleaners and maintenance staff. If necessary, get clerical staff to clean commercially sensitive areas.

Obscuration

If there is a risk of attack, espionage or media intrusion, consider obscuring windows into rooms where executives work or critical meetings take place. You might use a window film. Alternatively, you could move the window, block it or fit shutters, though this can make the users feel claustrophobic.

End-of-day routines and night time

The night is a vulnerable time for buildings. International operations, flexible working and complex schedules mean that some staff work into the evening, others arrive early in the morning, and cleaners may arrive as the workforce is going home. So it may not be possible to close the building entirely. Security should be responsible for closing windows, setting alarms, and checking that outside lights are on. They should also ensure that no intruders are in the building.

Foiling burglaries

Burglars of commercial property mostly seek cash or, failing that, items such as video equipment they can sell for cash. Many also find burglary exciting, according to researcher Gavin Butler.

Commercial burglary is less common than other security risks, such as commercial theft or assaults on staff; and the losses are small, averaging only £1,376 per burglary. This may be because the thieves seek items they can easily sell, which is why they often target warehouses or tobacconists.

While security guards and the presence of housing are a deterrent, burglars view conventional protection such as lights and bolts as something to deal with, rather than anything that would pose an insuperable obstacle. A building that takes police longer to arrive at is seen as a good choice by burglars, which puts remote buildings more at risk from burglary.

Mitigating Measures: preventing burglary

Secure your premises with adequate locks on doors and windows, CCTV and intruder alarms connected to a security service.

Use a mobile guarding service for high-value premises.

Vehicle threats

Incoming vehicles are part of the threat to a building and its occupants. The first level of security is to check drivers' and vehicles' credentials, and turn away unplanned deliveries.

You may also choose to conduct a manual search of each vehicle and its contents. After that, you will be checking for smaller items in the owner's bags and their clothing.

Vehicle threats and how to combat them are shown in Table 16.1.

Table 16.1 Managing vehicle threats

Type of device	What they are	How to locate or prevent them
Vehicle-borne explosive devices (VBIEDs)	Large explosive devices necessitating a vehicle for delivery.	Prevent unauthorised vehicles by means of barriers.
Under-vehicle explosive devices (UVIEDs)	These are small explosive devices that target the vehicle's driver or other occupants.	Use hand held under-car mirrors. UVIEDs are often put in place in the street at night, outside the individual's home. At-risk vehicles should not be left in public spaces.
Small, portable improvised explosive devices	They may be hidden in the vehicle (IVIEDs), in deliveries or personal bags.	Check for these in reception.
Guns and ammunition	These are likely to be on the individual's body.	Use scanners at reception.

Buildings: protecting against terrorist attack

Though most organisations are not likely to be the victim of a terrorist attack, that leaves many that could be. They include government buildings and those that represent the Western way of life, whether from marketing lifestyle brands, selling goods to the government or providing controversial services.

There are three main issues to consider when planning for any terrorist attack:

1   Design the building to discourage or hinder an attack, and reduce its impact.
2   Monitor and screen vehicles and people approaching or entering the building.
3   Take steps during and after a terrorist attack.

In this section, we review how to protect against an attack. FEMA, the US government's emergency management agency, recommends the following strategies:

> **Prevent building collapse**: Incorporate measures to resist progressive collapse. Avoid wide column spans.

> **Windows**: Exterior windows should be no stronger than their framing and supports, to minimise the risk of the entire window falling in. There are several ways to minimise the effects of broken glass, including glass curtain walls which can deform substantially without shattering. Anti-shatter film will hold fragmented pieces of glass together, and provides an inexpensive and effective improvement on existing glass.

> **Air intakes**: Place air intakes as far above the ground level as practical.

> **Isolate entries and delivery areas** from the rest of the structure by using floor-to-floor walls in these areas.

> **Harden floors** above unsecured areas of the building such as lobbies, loading docks, garages, mailrooms and retail spaces.

> **Isolate unsecured areas**: Place unsecured areas outside the main structure or in an exterior bay. Don't place critical or heavily occupied areas underneath unsecured areas, since it is difficult to protect against a package bomb placed on the floor.

> **Power and mechanical systems**: Add redundant mechanical and electrical control systems. Separate the systems if possible. This means that smoke protection and power can continue to work in the event of an explosion.

> **For non-structural elements**, use lightweight materials on the building exterior and interior. Materials such as timber or plastic are lighter and therefore less lethal than brick, stone or metal in the event of an explosion.

Screening people

Explosive devices are usually placed in a building by an individual, rather than delivered. You may need people to walk through metal detectors or be checked with a wand, and have their bag inspected.

There are also systems that combine radar and video technology to automatically detect people wearing suicide vests and weapons at a distance. For baggage and parcels, there are scanners that detect the shape of specific kinds of objects such as guns.

Deliveries and mail security

An organisation's mail will be high, medium or low security, depending on the nature of the business and its location. But even low-risk organisations can have former staff who have been laid off and therefore feel resentful. Jilted spouses may want to get their own back on an individual. So it isn't only fanatical terrorists who may deliver a postal attack. Revenge is a common motive.

Train staff to be vigilant. They should be on the look out for letters and parcels containing:

- explosive or incendiary devices
- sharps or blades
- chemical, biological or radiological (CBR) materials or devices.

Seven dead in courier bomb blasts

Eleven people were killed and 51 injured in 17 sites across Guanxi region of China in late 2015. The bombs were hidden in parcels delivered by commercial couriers to various locations across the state. The targets included a local government office, supermarkets, a hospital, a prison and a bus terminal. A five-storey building collapsed.

Police arrested 33-year-old Wei Yin Yong, the manager of a local marble quarry, who was said to have borne grievances against various people and wanted to settle scores against local businesses. The quarry had closed following disputes with residents.

Managing post room risk

Location: Consider receiving mail at a location away from your main offices. This will contain the risk, reduce the amount of security needed and protect your offices. If that isn't possible, place your post room in a location where a device will not damage the rest of the building.

Secure the area. Allow only authorised employees into the working area of your mail centre. Other staff and visitors should be kept at a counter.

Screen. Develop a screening procedure for all incoming letter and package deliveries. Train employees to follow these procedures.

Written procedures. Have a procedure for:

- handling any suspicious looking items;
- confirming what the contents of suspicious letters and packages are;
- isolating suspicious letters and packages.

Audit. Audit your mail centre, security and management staff to assess your letter and package screening programme.

Management standard. Consider adopting standard PAS 97:2015, for mail screening and security.

Parcel delivery

Where possible, only accept planned deliveries. Where employees are allowed to receive personal parcels at work, get staff to collect them from the post room or outside locker.

Depending on the level of threat, implement mail and parcel screening.

Use trusted suppliers, and inspect each delivery. Large deliveries can include apparently innocuous office equipment and catering supplies. Match deliveries against orders, and accept only those that are expected.

Small deliveries and mail

Check for the following risks:

- Anything unusual.
- Hand-delivered items. Just because it comes from a known courier doesn't make it safe.
- Markings that restrict who will open it. They may be marked 'Confidential', 'To be opened only by . . .' or 'Personal'. These will target an individual.
- An unusual quantity of 'Fragile' or 'Urgent' stickers.
- Anything addressed to the organisation or a job title, rather than a specific individual.
- Lopsided or uneven shape. Conventional parcels are evenly shaped.
- Sent from a foreign address.
- Lacking a postmark.
- No return address.
- Oddly or poorly addressed address, possibly with unfamiliar writing or style.
- Unusual array of stamps or excessive value of stamps for the size or weight of the package.
- Oily or greasy stains on or coming from the package. This can include greasy fingerprints left from bomb making.
- Smells coming from package. Some explosives have a plum or almond smell.
- Heavier than expected for its size (bomb material is heavy)
- Excessively sealed with tape all round so nothing can spill out. Ordinary letters have an ungummed gap at the corners.
- Protruding wires.
- Padded or 'jiffy' bag (a common method of packaging explosive parcels). Bomb makers often need to overprotect their package to ensure its safe arrival.
- An additional inner bag, tightly sealed.

The seven signs of a dangerous parcel

Some experts use this list of seven S's. It covers only some of the signs, but may be helpful as a poster in the post room.

- *Smell*. Odd smell
- *Shape*. Unusual shape
- *Stain*. Leaking oil or grease
- *Stamps*. Numerous stamps
- *Sender*. Not recognised, or from an unusual country
- *Size*. Excessive weight for the size
- *Seal*. Excessive quantity of tape.

On finding a suspicious article

In the event of finding a suspicious parcel or letter, take the following steps:

- Stop handling the item.
- Isolate it from the rest of the post room.
- Don't open it or smell it.
- Activate your emergency plan.
- Notify management and security.

Bomb threats

Many organisations never suffer a bomb threat for years, and then get a succession of them. The same is true of industries as a whole.

In Canada, at the time of writing, the West Jet airline received five bomb threats and Air Canada got one, all in less than a week, and all of them hoaxes. In the USA, around the same period bomb threats were made against Delta, United, Korean Air and a Volaris Air flight. They may have been perpetrated by an Isil 'lone wolf' operator. The disruption cost tens of thousands of dollars.

Bomb threats tend to be made against government buildings, law courts, schools, colleges and places of employment. They are usually made for one of the following reasons:

- because of a grudge (for example a disgruntled former employee);
- as a political act;
- to stop proceedings.

Usually their aim is to cause disruption. Sometimes threats can be made against a prominent individual or member of staff because of public comments they made. Most bomb threats are telephoned.

Mitigating Measures: bomb threats

Have a written policy for action to be taken on receiving a bomb threat. Treat all bomb threats as genuine until proven otherwise.

How to take a telephoned bomb threat

1   Listen to what the caller is saying.
2   Be calm and courteous.
3   Do not interrupt the caller or hang up.
4   Obtain as much information as you can. Suggested questions are shown below.
5   Do not put the caller on hold. They may ring off.
6   If possible, get a colleague to phone the emergency services or a supervisor.
7   If you have call display, record the number.

Questions to ask a caller:

1   When will it explode? _____ am/pm.
2   Where is it? Reception, offices, what floor, hallway, stairwell, rubbish bin, other.
3   What does it look like?
4   Where are you calling from? (Check your call display if you have one.)
5   What is your name?
6   Why did you place the bomb?

Date: _____   Time: _____ am/pm

Write down the exact wording of the threat:

_____

Characteristics of the caller: (circle the most appropriate responses)

- Sex: M/F
- Estimated age:
- Accent: English/Irish/French/Asian/Middle Eastern/European/African/Australian/ American/Other
- Diction: Deliberate/Rushed/Clipped/Slurred/Lisp/Nasal/Other
- Manner: Calm/Emotional/Threatening/Vulgar.

Other identifying information:

- Background noise: traffic horns/children's voices/television/animals/other
- Was the caller familiar with the area? Yes/No
- Who took the call?:
- From what department?:

Do not use mobile phones or other electronic equipment in the area of a bomb threat: they can trigger the device. Do not turn the lights off or on, as the same applies.

Evacuation

Have an evacuation plan for any building of any size, especially if it is a possible target. In addition to evacuating due to a bomb threat, you might need to evacuate due to:

- the fire alarm sounding;
- finding a suspicious item, for example a rucksack or suspicious unclaimed package;
- discovery of a suspicious item or vehicle outside the event area or building.

Tell the police as soon as possible what action you are taking.

If the device is outside the building it may be safer to stay inside. If the device is within the building you should consider evacuation. But be aware of the risk that a secondary bomb could be planted along the likely evacuation route. If that is a possibility, consider staying in the building.

Evacuation options

Evacuation may be total or partial. The options are as follows:

- Evacuate everyone outside the event or building.
- Evacuate part of the event area or building. This might happen if the device was small and confined to one location. For example if you find a small bag in an area that you can isolate, you might want to block off only that area for the time being.
- Evacuate all or some people to an internal safe area, such as a protected space.
- Evacuate all staff apart from designated searchers.

Staff must be familiar with the evacuation process and routes. Appoint staff to act as marshals. Exits should be well marked. The assembly point should be at least 500 metres from the incident.

Search procedure

If the threat is not imminent, conduct a search of the area identified by the caller.

Search teams should consist of two people where possible. Employees should be asked to search areas familiar to them. Search rooms as follows:

1 Stand quietly in centre of the room and listen for unusual noises. If there are two searchers, they should go to opposite sides of the room.
2 First scan: Divide the room into two levels. First visually check the floor and all areas up to window sill height (about one metre from the floor).
3 Second scan: Visually check areas from one metre to the top of your head. Move in a circular motion around the room back to the starting point.
4 Third scan: Visually search from top of your head to the ceiling.
5 Fourth scan: Visually check the ceiling, structural supports, window, air conditioning units and light fixtures.

On finishing a room search, if no suspicious item has been found, the person who searched the room should stick a sheet of paper on the exterior of the door or on the outside doorknob marked with a forward slash (/). When police have completed their search of the same room they will add a back slash (\), making an 'X', showing that the room was searched by both teams and is clear.

How to respond to a suspect package

1 Do not touch it.
2 Move everyone away to a safe distance. Communicate with staff, visitors and the public.
3 Don't use portable radios, mobile phones, digital phones or other electronic devices. Keep them away from the vicinity of the item, keep them out of line-of-sight and behind hard cover. They can trigger a device.
4 Do not turn the lights on or off, in case they might trigger the device. Have them remain in the same position (on or off).

6   Notify the police. Report the package's exact location and an accurate description.
7   Ensure that whoever found the item or witnessed the incident remains on hand to brief the police.

Chemical, biological and radioactive devices

Chemical, biological and radioactive (CBR) devices will be attractive to terrorists, being light and hard to detect. They also have the ability to spread panic. Hence we are likely to see CBR attacks in the future.

In recent years there have been few CBR attacks. Those that have taken place have been criminal, or else hoaxes and false alarms. In 1995 a sarin gas attack on the Tokyo underground killed 12 people. It was thought to have been perpetrated by a doomsday cult called Aum Shinrikyo, Six years later in the USA, someone sent anthrax letters to US senators and news media offices, killing five people. Bruce Irvin, a mentally ill defence researcher who later committed suicide, may have been responsible, but nothing was proved.

Al Qaida and other groups have shown an interest in using chemical weapons, but such devices require more technical expertise. So terrorists and criminals usually prefer standard weapons including semi-automatic rifles and suicide belts. Nevertheless the risk of a CBR attack can't be ruled out. Its impact will depend on the type of material used, its toxicity, and the delivery method.

CBR indicators

CBR devices are found in suspicious circumstances, such as in letters, parcels or unexpected containers, and can exhibit the following characteristics:

- granular, crystalline or finely powdered material, with the consistency of coffee, sugar or baking powder. It may be loose or in a container, and may be any colour;
- sticky substances, sprays or vapours;
- pieces of metal or plastic, such as discs, rods, small sheets or spheres;
- strange smells, e.g. garlic, fish, fruit, mothballs or pepper. If you detect a smell, do not go on sniffing it. However some CBR materials are odourless and tasteless;
- stains or dampness on the packaging;
- they may cause sudden illness or irritation of skin, eyes or nose.

Mitigating Measures: protecting against CBR attacks

Adopt standard security methods, including screening of people, vehicles and parcels. Terrorists may attempt to send CBR materials in the post.

Protect access to air intakes for air conditioning.

Upgrade air filters or improve your air-handling systems as necessary.

Restrict access to water tanks.

Review the security of your food and drink supply chain.

What to do if a CBR device is found

When you find a CBR device, you are unlikely to know exactly what it is, or the scale of the danger. Therefore you cannot prescribe specific actions. You do not need to make any special medical arrangements beyond normal first aid. The emergency services will take responsibility for treating casualties.

- **Keep your CBR emergency plan general** and wait for instructions from the emergency services.
- **Be guided by the emergency services** when it happens.
- **Be ready to shut down systems** that could contribute to the movement of air-borne hazards, such as air-conditioning or computer equipment containing fans.
- **Close doors and windows** quickly if required.
- **If you can isolate a hazard by leaving the immediate area, do so quickly**, closing doors and windows as you go.
- **Separate those directly affected by the incident from those not involved**. This will minimise the risk of inadvertent cross-contamination.
- **Move those directly affected by an incident to a safe location** close to the scene of the incident, so as to minimise the spread of contamination.

Major events

Major events are particularly risky activities. Anyone can apply for a ticket to get inside, while large crowds mean there is a risk of panic. Terrorists and hoaxers like public events, because it gives them maximum publicity and disruption.

With thousands of people in a stadium, it is difficult to identify every suspect package or thoroughly check every individual. A big security presence and careful searching can make the event feel oppressive. Nevertheless there are good security procedures to be followed.

Mitigating Measures: major events

Assess the threats. Undertake a risk assessment. This should cover all likely events, such as a bomb hoax, an explosion, fire, violence, stage collapse, illness and death, and crowd panic. Danger can come in the form of an explosion, falling towers, smoke inhalation, stampeding crowds or even a shooter.

Assess who and what needs to be protected. This will include the following:

- People: staff, attendees, concessionaires, contractors, performers, VIPs and the general public in the vicinity.
- Physical assets: buildings, contents, equipment and exits.
- Information: electronic and paper-based data.

(continued)

(continued)

Agree policies and procedures. Determine what security needs to be in place, and what improvements should be made.

Put physical and security controls in place. This may involve:

- CCTV
- perimeter fencing and intrusion detection systems
- lighting
- intruder alarms, fire detection
- computer security.

Adopt good housekeeping practices

- Check bins.
- Check temporary stands such as concessions.
- Keep compactors, storage bins and wheelie bins away from public areas.
- Keep communal areas clean and tidy.
- Use clear bags to allow staff to visually check them.
- Lock cupboards, offices and unused rooms.
- Keep fixtures and fittings to a minimum, to reduce the number of places where devices can be left.

Control people's access

- Direct and control vehicles with good signage, bollards and stewarding; and keep them at least 30 metres from the event.
- Limit vehicle and human access to the performers' area, goods inward zone and catering and bar areas.
- Ensure that the licence plates of contractors' vehicles are known in advance.
- Control human access to the event with ticket inspection and bag searching. Be alert to the risk of fake passes.
- Allocate security staff to physically control access to restricted and back stage areas, based on clear and unambiguous procedures and security passes. Passes must be visible at all times, and staff passes must be returned and checked when the event is over. Change the colour and format of passes regularly.
- Make visitors aware that they may be subject to a search. Legitimate event goers are known to be relaxed about searches in times of heightened security alerts. It increases their confidence about the event.
- Profile visitors if appropriate.
- Security staff must make random patrols.

Communications

- Ensure staff can quickly notify risks to management.
- Install communications that permit a fast and co-ordinated response to threats.

Train staff

- Ensure that all staff have had suitable training, especially those who are involved with security.
- Educate bar, catering and stewarding staff. They play a role in detecting hazards and security risks, and dealing with an incident.
- Staff must know how to report suspicious or dangerous activity.

Risk detection and incident handling procedures

Put procedures in place for detecting risks and handling incidents, especially evacuation and first aid. This will include the following:

- Put CCTV in place and monitor it.
- Get staff to look out for packages, bags or other items in odd places, and items that have been carefully placed, rather than dropped, in rubbish bins.
- Train staff to look out for people being where they should not be, or who show an interest in less accessible places.
- Make emergency power available for lighting and public address.
- Communicate the locations of fire extinguishers. Have the extinguishers regularly checked.
- Ensure all fire precautions are in place.
- Carry out regular fire practices.

Incident handling

Have a detailed plan for handling different types of incident, and test it.
Train staff to do the following:

- Identify and report suspicious behaviour.
- Respond to suspect packages.
- Handle bomb threats, especially a telephoned threat.
- Carry out a search. Staff must be know how to search for devices if requested. Toilets and cleaners' cupboards are commonly used to place bombs.
- Liaise with police.
- Evacuate and invacuate (invacuate is to keep people in one place).
- Secure the building.
- Respond to calls about family and friends.

Post-event activity

- Review security arrangements to allow for continuous improvement.
- Have a continuity plan in place that will enable you to re-start the business as soon as possible after an incident.

Terrorist attacks

Suicide attacks are quite common at the time of writing, almost all inspired by Isis/Daesh. Some are lone wolf attacks, while others have involved a dozen attackers or more.

Attacks focus on crowded areas where they will have the greatest impact. This includes cafes, concerts, buses and underground stations. Terrorists also attack tourist spots in the hopes of either damaging the economy, destabilising the society or killing Westerners. In Istanbul a 26-year-old suicide bomber killed nine German tourists near the Blue Mosque. At the beach resort of Souse in Tunisia a terrorist gunman killed 38 people, mostly tourists.

A suicide bomber walked into a Jakarta Starbucks cafe and blew himself up. He was the only person killed in the blast, though several people were wounded. As people rushed out of the cafe, two waiting gunmen opened fire on them. At the same time, two militants threw hand grenade bombs at a nearby police traffic post.

Suicide attackers may come on foot, motorcycle or car. The attackers may use semi-automatic rifles, together with suicide belts and even hand grenades.

Sometimes a second set of attackers wait to kill crowds coming out of a building that is under attack. While stadiums and concert halls have reasonable security against terrorists on foot and in vehicles, high street premises have no protection.

When working in developing countries, it is unwise to rely on the local police and military, or to assume that an attack could not happen. After the terrorist attack on a gas plant at In Amenas in Algeria in 2013 where 39 foreign hostages and an Algerian security guard died, an investigation by the plant's Norwegian co-owner Statoil found that the plant had relied on a local military that was assumed – wrongly – to be capable of dealing with all security contingencies. Moreover, the organisation had not anticipated an attack by a large number of militants who would be able to successfully enter the production site. It is therefore wise to make stringent additional security arrangements for highly visible targets.

Mitigating Measures: preparations against an attack

Consider good places of refuge or areas that provide cover. Glazing ands wooden fences give no protection, while masonry walls and vehicle engine blocks provide good defence.

Train staff to detect suspicious behaviour and alert authorities.

Train staff to provide first aid.

Be alert to hostile reconnaissance. Terrorists will often visit their target in advance to plan the attack. Reconnaissance visits and rehearsals include the following:

- unusual group behaviour, such as people seeming to plan something;
- an individual investigating places that ordinary visitors have little interest in;
- people taking photographs or videos in a suspicious way;
- people loitering for no apparent reason, and perhaps returning several times to the spot;
- erratic driving;
- delivery vehicles parked in prominent or unusual places;
- unusually probing questions asked of staff, perhaps under the guise of a pretext;
- people apparently separate but actually together, sometimes walking in the same direction.

Share CCTV images of such behaviour with the police.

Mitigating Measures: during a terrorist attack

Notify the police immediately. Give factual details – your exact location, how many attackers, whether they have rifles, hand guns or knives, where they are coming from and where they are headed.

Train staff to 'Run, Hide, Tell'. This is the advice put out by UK police. It means: Run away from the attackers if you can; don't try to negotiate. Hide if you can't run away. When you can, tell the police what is happening. See the video at https://goo.gl/B6vskM

Take customers and staff to safety if possible.

Dealing with protests

Businesses likely to experience protests include the following:

- the defence industries
- animal testing and research
- biotech
- intensive livestock farming or genetically engineered crops
- those with activist stakeholders (universities, for example)
- carbon-based energy (oil, coal and gas)
- extraction industries (minerals and oil)
- financial services.

Legitimate protests include marches and petitions. But the passionate nature of a protest and a sometimes heavy-handed police response can sometimes cause a protest to spiral into violence, or lead to the occupation of buildings.

Mitigating Measures: handling protests

Identify what assets and staff are at risk.

Create policy and procedures. Have contingency plans. Prepare evacuation plans.

Appoint someone to be responsible for protests, where the building is likely to be the target of such action.

Identify points of entry, including unorthodox ones, such as delivery bays. Lock strategically important rooms.

Ensure your CCTV is comprehensive and effective.

Keep staff informed of likely events. Make them aware of the possible impact of disruption to their commute. Allow them to wear civilian clothes if workwear such as suits or uniforms would make them a target.

Consider the use of temporary office space.

Communicate clearly with protesters the reasons for your strategy. Ensure the media hears your side of the argument.

Listen to the protesters. Encourage dialogue. Protesters will be more amenable if they feel you are receptive.

Assess whether your security team is capable of responding adequately. If the staff are more used to dealing with illegally parked cars, they may lack the necessary skills and subtlety. The reverse may also be true: they may be more used to dealing with protesters than outside contractors would be.

Avoid increasing tension. Forcibly removing protesters from your buildings should only be done as a last resort. Students usually go home after they have made their point or when moved by hunger.

Consider undertaking 'professional intrusion', where someone joins a group in order to get advance knowledge of their plans. But be aware that it could backfire if discovered.

(continued)

(continued)

Work with the police.

Consider changing your strategy if its benefits are not substantial. For example, pension fund investment in carbon energy or defence businesses can be inflammatory to some protesters, and other investments may provide a similar return on capital.

Industrial espionage

In today's competitive world, nations and companies would love to know about their competitors' methods and plans. According to Eric Denécé, director of the French Centre on Intelligence Research, China has repeatedly been caught spying.

The USA charged five Chinese military officials with masterminding government-led cyber hacking to steal trade secrets from six major American companies in the energy and metals industries. The targets were the nuclear power station manufacturer Westinghouse Electric, US Steel, Allegheny Technologies and Alcoa, as well as subsidiaries of SolarWorld, the US solar power group. The Chinese hackers also broke into computer networks of the United Steel Workers and other unions.

According to the indictments handed down by a grand jury in Pennsylvania, where most of the alleged victims were based, the five charged were officers in the Chinese People's Liberation Army. The hacking 'appears to have been conducted for no reason other than to advantage state-owned companies and other interests in China, at the expense of businesses here in the United States,' said US attorney general Eric Holder.

Western countries, especially the USA, are equally likely to spy. Bolloré, the investment firm behind Autolib, a electric-car-sharing company, accused BMW of using spies to gain information about its electric cars. The company, which has 34,000 subscribers in Paris, alleged that two employees of a firm employed by BMW were seen several times tampering with charging points and the company's vehicles. Bolloré believed they were trying to get information about its advanced battery and geo-location technology. BMW says it was conducting routine tests to check charging point compatibility on European roads, prior to its launch of its i3 electric model.

Denécé believes that 90% of all corporate intelligence gathering is done in affluent countries by companies using former spies. 'American companies mostly seek sensitive information that will allow them to destabilise rivals or the entire sector to gain strategic advantages in areas like contract bidding,' he says.

> Aircraft makers are notorious for exploiting anything they can learn about rivals to present to clients as proof of dodgy safety levels or inflated pricing. Globally, about half of all corporate espionage involves that kind of activity, the other half involves stealing technology or business strategies.

According to Bloomberg, the US National Security Agency (NSA) hacked into the Petroleo Brasileiro network just as Brazil was preparing to auction off rights to tap into the largest oil fields in the world, located off its Atlantic coast.

Reuters says this isn't the first time the NSA has been accused of spying. Information released by Edward Snowden showed that the NSA spied on Brazil, involving the email and phone calls of Brazil's then president, Dilma Rousseff.

In 2001, Procter & Gamble was caught dumpster diving at Unilever's Chicago offices, seeking shampoo formulae. The company eventually paid Unilever $10m in damages.

Hiring competitors' staff is another way for companies to gain commercial secrets. Mercedes sued Benjamin Hoyle, one of its Formula One engineers, claiming he was planning to take sensitive data to a competitor. Hoyle notified his employers that he did not plan to renew his contract, and when Mercedes found out he was going to work for Ferrari, the company reassigned him to less sensitive duties. He was then allegedly discovered accessing data on the performance of the team's engines.

Mercedes filed a suit against Hoyle, claiming that he 'and potentially Ferrari have gained an unlawful advantage.' At the time of writing, the company was seeking the return of all documents and the payment of its legal fees. It also sought to prevent Hoyle from working for another F1 team throughout the following season.

Information about competitors can come from many sources, including trade fairs and conferences. Staff can unwisely reveal secrets, especially in late night conversations in hotel bars.

Mitigating Measures: preventing industrial espionage

Assess the risk. Identify what information could be of value to competitors. This includes:

- new products and processes
- launch plans
- marketing plans
- customer lists
- methods and recipes
- trade prices and discount structures.

Check in what form this information is held, including printed documents and digital content.

Assess who has access to this information.

Take steps to protect the information, especially as regards staff, physical security and social media.

Staff

Make employees aware of the risk. They should be told that taking confidential information is potentially a criminal act.

Have staff and contractors sign non-disclosure agreements (NDAs).

Hold exit interviews. Remind staff of their obligation not to reveal secrets.

Use monitoring technology. Use data loss prevention software to monitor access and use of IP. Software can notify managers when sensitive information is accessed.

Be especially careful with staff who are dismissed or made redundant. Escort staff from the building. Do not let them use their computer. Remove IT privileges.

(continued)

(continued)

Physical security

Secure access to all or sensitive parts of the building.

Visitors must have an appointment, and should be tagged as guests. Do not allow visitors to walk unescorted through the building. Competitors' spies may sit at an empty desk and access information from the PC.

Shred sensitive printed content. Staff sometimes drop bid information or technical reports into waste paper baskets. Place shredders everywhere.

Dumpsters. Check that commercially valuable information is not going into dumpsters or wheelie bins.

Social media

Train staff not to reveal information on social media sites. They should assume their posts are being monitored by competitors.

Loss of sensitive information

Sensitive information includes content that:

- reveals private information about an individual that could embarrass them or be used against them;
- contains financial information such as credit card details;
- would give an advantage to a competitor;
- would give the media information that the business might want kept secret, such as discussions about future plans;
- could give an advantage to a foreign power, as in the case of government classified documents.

In most countries organisations have privacy laws to protect personal information. We review information security in Chapter 12. But not all information is necessarily held on computer. Sensitive work documents can get left on top of the printer at the end of the day, when they should have been locked away for the night. A member of staff may send confidential information to a supplier, who could in turn pass it on to a competitor.

And sometimes lack of procedures or change of staffing is to blame. Six hundred and ninety-five former employees of the Los Angeles probation department continued to have access privileges which allowed them to track cases including those of juveniles. The department had also lost track of 18 computers.

Mitigating Measures: securing data

Have robust and audited procedures for protecting data.

Train staff in data protection.

Shred sensitive documents. Incinerate discs and other computer media. Overwrite, degauss or re-format hard drives before taking them out of service.

Keep confidential information on servers to which only authorised staff have access.

Require contractors and agencies to sign non-disclosure agreements. They are hard to enforce, because the source of a leak can be impossible to pinpoint. But it reminds people that they have an obligation to protect your information.

Ensure that IT systems are protected with robust passwords and contain no vulnerabilities.

Remove access rights from staff who leave.

Keeping goods safe on the move

With more high-value goods moving around the globe, they represent an attractive target for thieves. Vehicles make good targets, as do consignments in aircraft. A growing international market for luxury goods, plus extended supply chains and dispersed markets, provide vulnerabilities for goods in transit.

While Brazil, Mexico and South Africa experience the most theft, all countries have thieves. Bad weather and other delays can hold up goods, making them even more vulnerable. Sometimes drivers with fake IDs make off with entire containers of goods. Thieves can also jam a lorry's GPS signal, making its location unknown to its owner. They then hijack the vehicle and steal its contents.

Mitigating Measures: transport security

Use GPS to monitor your vehicle movements. Put GPS beacons in the cargo or container.

Minimise dwell time (the time cargo remains in a terminal's in-transit storage area while awaiting shipment or clearance) and touch points (places where the goods change hands).

Consider using an escort vehicle for high-value logistics.

Advise drivers of high-risk areas, enabling them to avoid stopping there.

Paint large, bright numbers of top of vehicles to assist police in tracking them if stolen.

Avoiding shipping during weekends and holidays when staffing is reduced and vehicles may have to lay up.

Educate suppliers about security, including the risk of false partitions, the need to seal lorries, the creation of security zones, how to pack goods so they don't 'fall off in transit', restricting vehicle access in secure areas and protecting seals and paperwork.

Consider implementing ISO 28000, the management standard for supply chain security.

Get properly insured.

Gain certification with the Transported Asset Protection Association (TAPA), the theft prevention group, or use organisations it has certified. It sets minimum security standards, and its certification is an indication of higher security.

17 Stormy weather

Dealing with climate change

Most of us have experienced the effects of extreme weather. Music industry business SFX filed for bankruptcy after bad weather forced the closure of one of its events; the resulting refunds may have contributed to its financial downfall. Marine contractor Cal Dive International went bust after storms halted its work on offshore oil platforms off Mexico and delayed an expected payment of $72.5m for the project.

Extreme events have five main effects:

1   *Violent and unreliable weather events can disrupt your distribution* by causing storms and flooding, and making roads impassable, even in temperate zones. High winds can damage buildings and cause injury, even loss of life.
2   *Cities may be affected by heat*, leading to problems with power failure, increased deaths and a greater demand for medical services. Flooding is another threat for cities located on rivers or a coast.
3   *Low-lying land and the businesses that operate there can be affected by sea level rise.* With 23% of the world's population living by the coast, millions of people will be affected and trade damaged.
4   *Food production can be affected.* Once-fertile areas may decline in productivity; other areas will benefit as they begin to grow new crops.
5   *Earthquakes and tsunamis, part of the natural movement of the earth, will bring death and destruction in their wake.* Many centres of population exist on top of fault lines, including Tokyo (population 35m), Jakarta (30m), Manila (11m), Tehran (12m), Los Angeles (13m) and Istanbul (14m).

Impacts from violent weather include the following:

*   *Loss of power.* This can halt organisations' work. It also means the loss of perishable goods.
*   *Lack of drinking water*, due to flooding, contamination of the water supply and the loss of water treatment plants.
*   *Loss of raw materials* from water damage or physical damage.
*   *Damage to buildings* from storms or flooding.
*   *Impassable roads.*

In the sections that follow we look at the mitigating strategies you can adopt to minimise the effects of severe weather. First though, some general Mitigating Measures.

Mitigating Measures: climate change

Assess your vulnerability to climate change.

Use suppliers who are closer to your operations, or are based in countries less affected by weather events.

Change suppliers if existing ones regularly suffer problems caused by climate change, for example crop failure.

Change from raw materials or products that are affected by harvest failure.

Ensure your premises are located in areas less affected by climate change or sea rise. Select locations that are not subject to flood, storm surge, significant ground shaking from earthquakes or close to hazardous facilities.

Measure your carbon emission intensity. This is a measure of how much carbon is produced per unit of activity, such as the amount of product you produce. In the case of an airline it could be kilometres travelled. This gives you a yardstick to compare future performance, and will provide the basis for targets. It is fairly easy to assess this because you will know how much gas, electricity or oil you consume, and each energy source has a known value for its CO_2 emissions. You can have your emissions verified by the Carbon Trust. Independent verification will build consumer trust.

Flooding

In England and Wales 185,000 business properties are at risk of flooding. Businesses are more likely to be flooded than burnt down. And with extreme weather becoming more common, this risk of flood is increasing all the time. Flooding now accounts for 10% of all business disruptions. The average cost of a flood is £28,000. Even worse is the risk of not being able to communicate with customers, take orders or fulfil them.

Businesses do not always realise whether any of their sites are at risk from flooding. Organisations most at risk are those on a coastal plain, in a river flood plain or in a part of the world affected by heavy rains or storms. However, you don't need to be near a river or the sea to get flooded. When aquifers get overfilled, water can overcome the drains and rising water levels will begin to flood buildings.

A burst water main can cause major damage to the ground floor or basement of company premises. In London's Oxford Street, a 100-year-old water main burst, pouring millions of gallons of water into 14 shops, causing £1m worth of damage.

In the UK, the Flood Line service has a 24-hour number where companies can check their liability to flood. Sitecheck Flood provides a report which assesses the potential flood risk to a commercial site.

Mitigating Measures: before a flood

Draw up a plan to deal with the loss of your building due to flooding. According to the Know Your Flood Risk campaign, it might be months before the building is dried out and usable.

Prevent flood water entering your building. Install barriers that will seal doors, windows, toilets and drains. These can be permanent or removable. They will hold back flood

(continued)

(continued)

water, and give you time to take other measures. Fit bungs in ground floor toilets to stop sewage flowing into the building.

Reduce the impact of flooding

- Turn off all electrical and gas equipment if flooding is occurring. Switch off the electrical and gas main supplies.
- Secure LPG containers so they cannot move. They are buoyant, and their connections can become damaged.
- Store important items high up. Do not put them in basements or on the floor at street level. Keep your servers above the likely flood level.
- Back up your data daily.
- Raise electrical sockets, electrical wiring and heating and ventilation controls.
- Raise equipment and machinery above the likely flood level. Put equipment on plinths. Move equipment to a higher floor or another site.
- Use lime-based plaster instead of gypsum on walls. Lime plaster is unaffected by water and will not soften like gypsum or drywall. Its high pH acts as a fungicide, so mould will not grow on it.
- Store important records such as insurance policies, customer information or supplier contracts safely.
- Ensure the drains in your premises are flowing efficiently and are not clogged.
- Buy sandless sandbags They are lightweight and can absorb up to 20 litres of water.
- Check that your insurance covers flooding. This is not always included, and it is getting increasingly difficult to get flood cover in high-risk areas. Check whether your insurance covers business interruption: you may be unable to use your premises for six months.
- Check whether your lease allows you to suspend payments if you are prevented from using the premises due to flooding. See if there is a break clause if the damage is not repaired within a set time period.

Mitigating Measures: after a flood

Health and safety. Be aware that recently flooded buildings are unsafe in many ways, including the risk of explosion, fire, slips and injuries from sharp objects. The building may be contaminated with sewage and animal remains. You will be liable for any harm that comes to an employee who enters the building.

Do not switch on any equipment, smoke or use naked flames until the building has been checked by qualified gas and electrical contractors.

Risk of electrocution. Switch off all electrical equipment. Don't operate any electrical equipment which is in or near water. Electrical circuits could be live and could electrocute staff. Rats may have been disturbed and may have gnawed cables, making them unsafe. If you have doubts about the mains supply, contact your electricity supplier.

Cleaning up. Contact your insurance company. Check whether it is OK to remove debris from your premises. They may need to visit your premises before you do so. In returning to the premises make sure your employees are safe. Take care with removing debris. It could be contaminated and may contain sharp items.

Rodent infestation. Rats and mice may have occupied the building. Get a rodent control firm to check it.

Gas safety. Gas equipment in a flooded building poses significant risks of fire and explosion from damaged connections.

- Turn off the gas control valve (usually located at the gas meter). Turn off all gas appliances.
- Arrange for a qualified engineer to inspect gas appliances before using the equipment.
- If you smell gas, call your gas supplier and leave the building.

Water supply. Clean any taps that have been submerged in flood water, using a bleach solution. Run the taps for 30 seconds prior to using the water.

Record the event. Take videos of the impact of the flood on your premises. It may support your insurance claim.

Wash and disinfect all surfaces.

Use gentle heat and maximum ventilation. Forced heating can cause floorboards and other elements to warp and may cause additional damage. Open all windows and air vents, even in rooms that were unaffected. Use dehumidifiers to take out moisture.

Get a building contractor to advise you on repairs. Plasterboard and insulation may need to be removed.

Mitigating Measures: mitigating the risk of flood in construction

Planners and developers should adopt the following measures when building on flood plains:

Ensure sockets are placed higher than probable flood levels.

Construct buildings with sacrificial ground floors reserved for utilities, with the middle floor given over to living space, and the second floor used for bedrooms and dry storage.

Build homes on stilts or plinths, which displace less water during flooding.

Use construction materials that withstand the effects of flooding.

Use walls that can be opened to allow for ventilation and cleaning.

Provide sustainable drainage systems such as reed beds and ditches in new housing estates.

Dealing with water damage from rain, storms, plumbing failure and poor maintenance

According to Zurich Insurance, modern residential buildings are often constructed from lightweight materials which do not withstand severe exposure to water. Carpets and curtains are particularly sensitive to water damage. Water ingress is followed by mould or corrosion, which can soon require costly replacement.

High levels of rainfall around the globe are also causing more flooding and water ingress, while stormy weather can damage roofs and allow water in.

Commercial residential buildings are especially at risk with the growing use of water in our lives, from showers, baths, washing machines, sinks and toilets. Dishwashers, water coolers and water dispensers in fridges add to the quantity of water being used in commercial premises. Leaking gutters and old downpipes can cause long-term damage, while burst pipes and unnoticed internal leaks will also cause damage.

Mitigating Measures: water other than flooding

Check that flat roofs are in good condition, without cracks or splits. Bitumen flat roofs need re-covering every decade.

Check that gutters, downpipes and storm drains are sound and can cope with heavy rainfall. Make any necessary alterations to reduce the risk of water damage.

Ensure that pitched roofs are sound, especially after storms. Check the flashing and pointing around chimneys.

Ensure areas with water pipes are kept above freezing point to prevent frost damage. Lag any external pipe work.

Make sure the location of the stopcock is known.

Storms and hurricanes

Forty per cent of natural hazard insurance claims are the result of windstorms. The USA is the top location for losses, accounting for 49% of global claims, followed by Europe (19%), Asia (6%) and Central America (3%).

Storm surge (where sea levels rise due to wind and atmospheric pressure) can often be more damaging than high winds. Storm surge has been a contributing factor in half the top 10 costliest storm losses in US history.

Most of the wind damage will affect the building envelope: roof covering, walls and windows. If your business is likely to be affected by violent weather, take the steps outlined in the Mitigating Measures below.

Mitigating Measures: storms

Inspect your building. Focus on the damage that high winds could inflict. Check that the roof, walls and windows are sound and secure. Check latches and hardware.

Identify and remove any large trees or limbs that could fall and damage your property.

Attach windstorm shutters or plywood. This needs to be prepared in advance.

Install steel bars on the inside of exterior roll-up doors.

Anchor large equipment.

Fill the fuel tanks of generators, fire pumps, and company owned vehicles to make them heavier. Fill above-ground tanks to capacity for the same reason.

Prepare for possible flooding. See the Mitigating Measures listed earlier in this chapter.

Protect and secure your utilities: gas, water and electricity.

Install protective devices, such as surge protectors and grounding devices.

Identify what activity will require power in the event of an outage. This may include:

- lights (interior and exterior)
- computers, printers and other office equipment
- heating, ventilation, and air conditioning systems
- industrial equipment
- major appliances such as refrigerators and freezers
- pumps, such as a sprinkler system
- alarm system

Power supply

- Install a generator to provide emergency power. Identify the minimum of activities that will require power, and how much power they will need.
- Protect the generator and its fuel from winds and flooding.
- Ensure that generator exhaust gases are routed outside the building.
- Make sure you have enough fuel for the predicted outage.
- Decide how power will be switched to the emergency system.

Files and documents. Safely store copies of important documents where they won't be damaged and can be retrieved, in a secure off-site location. This includes electronic files. Take regular backups.

Protect computers and electrical equipment from potential wind driven rain, which may breach the building envelope through windows, doors or the roof.

Move raw materials and inventory to a place of safety. Cover items with waterproof tarpaulins.

Unplug all power, telephone, broadband and antenna connections during a thunderstorm to prevent a strike damaging equipment.

Identify contractors who you can call upon to mend damaged buildings, fittings or equipment.

After a storm

- Secure the site to prevent unauthorised entry.
- Start the recovery process.

When the earth moves

Earthquakes occur along geological fault lines. The following cities are most at risk.

- Islamabad and Rawalpindi, Pakistan
- Jakarta, Indonesia
- Manila, Philippines
- Tehran, Iran

- Istanbul, Turkey
- Quito, Ecuador
- Lima, Peru
- Osaka, Tokyo, Nagoya and Kobe, Japan
- Los Angeles and San Francisco, USA
- Istanbul, Turkey
- Kathmandu, Nepal
- Delhi, India.

The scale of the risk primarily depends on how developed the country is: rich nations have stronger regulations and building codes. Rural areas on fault lines often suffer the most. Mitigating against earthquakes takes two forms:

1   Design buildings capable of withstanding the shock.
2   Manage fixtures, fittings and equipment in a way that minimises damage to them and to people.

Earthquake building design

Building legislation focuses on preventing buildings from collapsing, which is the point at which fatalities occur. Planners therefore aim to prevent collapse in order to get everyone out alive. But the buildings often need to be demolished after the earthquake because their stability has been impaired.

Newer buildings are designed to remain in service after an earthquake. Their design aims to change the way a building vibrates (stiffness and damping) or by applying an opposite force. This takes two forms:

- Active controls use electrical power to oppose the movement of a building. But the amount of power required reduces its ability to withstand large earthquakes.
- Passive systems rely on elastic materials that will reduce the extent of the shaking. Large rubber pads may separate a building from the ground, and these pads will shear during strong shaking, reducing the link between the building and the ground.

Mitigating Measures: earthquakes

Secure objects and fittings to prevent them from moving, getting damaged, and injuring people. Anchor shelving securely.

Store heavy or fragile items on lower shelves, leaving the higher shelves for lighter or less vulnerable items.

Secure equipment that could move or fall during an earthquake.

Index

For Product Safety Concerns and Information please contact our EU
representative GPSR@taylorandfrancis.com Taylor & Francis Verlag GmbH,
Kaufingerstraße 24, 80331 München, Germany

Printed and bound by CPI Group (UK) Ltd, Croydon, CR0 4YY

01/05/2025

01858385-0003